Spoonfeeding Casanova

Dominic Mann-Bertrand

About the Author

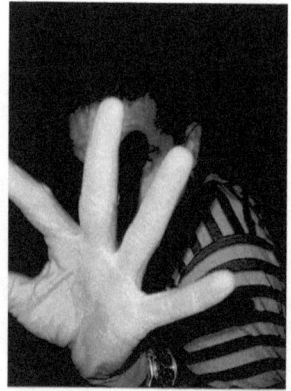

Having (mis)spent his youth in the halls of academia, Mr. Mann-Bertrand eventually abandoned towers of ivory in favor of variegated artistic pursuits, peripatetic adventures, and repeated attempts to be officially recognized as a "Renaissance Man" by all 193 Member States of the United Nations. Obsessed with the fields of theatre, film, and television, the author has devoted considerable energies to deepening his involvement in these interconnected artistic disciplines, all while attempting to fight the forces of evil (well, boredom) by exploring the four corners of our great globe. *Spoonfeeding Casanova* is his novelistic debut, a strong expository effort on behalf of the author to become a serious and upstanding adult; it is possible he may have failed. In unsubstantiated rumors, it is claimed that if writer Mann-Bertrand owned a hat, it would currently be hanging somewhere in British Columbia.

Published by Unsolicited Press
www.unsolicitedpress.com
Copyright © 2017 Dominic Mann-Bertrand
All Rights Reserved.
Unsolicited Press Books are distributed to the trade by Ingram.
ISBN: 978-0-9980872-9-0
Cover Design: In-house UP team

Pour Mams & Pa'a
For, well…. Everything, basically

Contents

Part I	1
The Apparatus of the Game	2
Highway to the Great Divide	22
What a Long, Strange Trip Begins	30
Leading Horse to Waters	42
Part II	67
Res Ipsa Loquitur: Way Over Yonder in the Monarch Key	68
Capital Gains	77
Giddy-Yap	92
Agents of Influence	99
Auntie Mask/Key/Rove/(S)ka {Маскировка}	112
Digestive Divertimento	159
Frenemies, Domestically Foreign	177
Part III	195
Meaningless Rigor Mortis	196
Five Flag Play-by-Play	215
The Tejano Two-Step	224
Ditat Deus	237
Fatmen & Lilbuoy	272
Vintage Valhalla	292

A Camelot Approach	304
Silenus Silenced	326
Near Neorxnawang	341
Consentual Mainland Comeback	365
Home, Turfed	374
Circling the Drain	383
The Alchemist's Opus	401
Doublends Jined	427

"'I grow old... I grow old... I shall wear the bottoms of my trousers rolled.' What does that mean, Mr. Marlowe?"

"Not a bloody thing."

—Raymond Chandler, *The Long Goodbye*

Part I

The Apparatus of the Game

It could have happened to anybody. Who could honestly say he'd never gone to a party, had too much to drink, pawed the married hostess in front of her jackass husband, thrown up mouthfuls of vermouth and duck pâté all over an heiress's evening gown, stumbled backwards into the Champagne fountain of the central foyer, stuck a finger in a cat's rectum, and accidentally slapped a twelve-year-old boy in the face?

Jack, otherwise known as Mitford, couldn't possibly be held accountable for his actions—not with the cocktail of Nembutal and hard liquor he'd ingested. No court in the land would uphold that case. The pentobarbital was prescribed, totally legit, or so the story goes: for a recurring back injury Jack suffered when he fell, from the old stadium stands at Shea, into a soft pool of dugout bats and helmets. The booze, legal as the law had made it, was just a thinly veiled coping mechanism to justify the cirrhosis gene inherited from a crooked bloodline. Of course, thrown together in the right amounts, there was some sort of lethal super buzz known as the "Jesus Christ Superstar," an incantatory combination that drugstore cowboys could only aspire to; but Jack was far from that high, suffering instead, a total bodily breakdown from the ill effects of Sea Island cotton mouth, disorientation, acid reflux, itchy palms, cold sweats, warm fuzzies, temporary colorblindness, permanent (minor) brain damage, ataxia, and momentary Legionnaire's, which led to his peristaltic chain reaction and complete gastric disintegration on the host's front lawn as a Suffolk County police cruiser appeared.

But all these details can be returned to later. Several months earlier was when things had started to get weird. Before becoming awash in conspiracy paranoia, rotgut, and pharmaceuticals, Jack's middling middle-class life had been settled in dust: Nothing over, nothing begun. There was a comfortable continuity to his days, like a perpetual hangover. The floods of resignation had washed over his being.

Jack's social alienation, it should be noted, had been forced. Dumped and divorced, he was denied the natural "in" to the self-satisfied clans of Double-Income No Kids (DINKs), who increasingly gathered in impenetrable suburban scrums and huddled for warmth around burning piles of hundred dollar bills. To cackle like deranged civets at the pointless, magnificent waste of it all had become the odorous call of the urban wild. The quiet desperation of Thoreau's America had turned into a selfish delusion of need: to live was to demand. And in this new world, lonely were the brave.

Merrick had pushed Jack to that edge. Merrick, the inimitable; Merrick, the dominant; Merrick, the ex-wife. She'd stripped away Jack's connubial status and sent him tumbling headlong into the miserably contorted swan dive of a newly singled sap: getting up at the crack of dawn, eating chicken beaks and steamed carrots for breakfast, doing 207 laps down at the Young Men's Christian Association pool (AfrOlympic size), and brushing the neighbor's cats in order to fashion a hair weave for Fritz, the peanut-eating paraplegic downstairs. Jack was also volunteering for sixteen full hours on Saturdays and Sundays as a part-time car wash clown at the Make-A-Wish Foundation in Mechanics Town, reading excerpts of *Finnegans Wake* to a blind group of incontinents at Bellevue (they loved it, go figure!), playing strip-bingo with a gang of war amps over at the Loisaida Legion, sharing Fruit Loop dinners with Bo Schmo, the one-eyed Kosher Nigerian across the hall, and, finally, capping his nights off with a cleansing stroll over burning coals up on the rooftop, accompanied by the yelping whines of none other than Miss Joni Mitchell.

None of this actually happened, of course; they were the disjointed dreams Jack made up for himself, irrevocably tainted with a sorrow of ages that soared through the firmament like Icarus ascending.

Although that past was prologue, and as much as Jack hated himself for it, Merrick was also the reason he was now well into his third Brandy Alexander, fortifying himself. The snug pub, a loose homage to the *Days of Wine and Roses*, was an uptown basement saloon tucked under the Claridge House. The place seemed frequented mostly by Republican windbags in tuxedos, all serviced by a passably attractive waitress who strutted around the floor, protected within the flaunted flirtation of her designer shirt: *I'm not as dumb as you look.*

Jack had only been inside the Claridge House once, in the early aughties, when he was still considered somewhat of a rising young literary star. The boozy evening in the hub of the PLU had been spent doing research on how the multitudinous members of the vast right-wing conspiracy found the time for intricate up-skirt trysts and backbench footsie fondles. Printed in *The Atlantic*, "Sheeeet, Sugar, I Ain't Misbehaving!" was the last piece Jack published under his own name, before he turned ghost and started holding the pen for others. The taste of that choice still lingered, more than a decade later, and no amount of booze would ever wash that away.

But tonight, Jack tried. He guzzled another glass of his cognac and half-and-half, listening as the final touches fell into place up there. The evening's charitable auction was being hosted by the Von Fürstenberg Collective, a recent re-brand of the Westwood Group. Yes, that's right, the same literary luminaries responsible for the Urban Masterpieces initiative on all the City's subways a few years ago. Remember "K'Dee," the Latina Langston Hughes and supposed savior of Latino literacy? No? Well here's a refresher, the best of K'Dee's "Str-eat Poe-eMs" the Westwood Group produced:

Got my peeps on the streets
'Coz my feats in de-feat
When five-oh on the'y beat.
I'm more'an jus' meat.
You see? Me, I mean? For reals?
Thought you wuz lookin' at m'legs, man,
Grabbing at m'titties with yo eyes.
For me, you see,
T'aiint no escape fo' being me.
I could say I'm brave in a country stolen from Braves,
Or swear I was unfree in the land o' the free,
But who g'unn listen t'uh me?
Huh?

    This piece of shit won the hearts of New Yorkers, and for months people talked about K'Dee like a little girl lost: 'Oooooh, wasn't it just so tragic, so unfair, because she was obviously a natural and ex-treeem-ly talented poet, aaahmyGod, and all that without a soupçon of basic education…! What a horrible existence that must be—hmm?—having to make a living on the street like that, with your body—can you just *imagine*? No, I mean, really imagine? It breaks my heart when I hear about people like that, you know? Just awful!'

Ultimately, the swank society set was the one most affected by the news, by the unveiling of K'Dee's hoax, that is. When K'Dee publicly came forward with the truth (or, was "found out," as fans-cum-critics claimed), people—largely women's groups feeling the sting of betrayal—openly called her a "bitch" and a "capitalizing cunt" for doing what she did. "KD" turned out to be Katherine Donnelly, a trained behavioral psychologist, epidemiologist, and professor of "Marginal and Postindustrial Spaces" at Barnard:

"It was an experiment," Donnelly said in a *60 Minutes* interview, filmed mostly in her office or as she strolled casually through Central Park. "I didn't mean any harm."

"And what do you say to the American public? How do you respond to those people who accuse you of being a phony, a *profiteur* only in it for the money?"

"I say: Get your f***ing facts straight, okay? I mean, the majority of the bread I got for those poems went to a battered women's shelter up on 119th Street. They buy soup and clothes with it, for Chrissakes!"

Statements like these (re)gained Donnelly

some supporters, especially in the militant feminist community; but this same support was promptly lost again when it was further reported that the shelter wasn't a shelter at all, and wasn't even for women. The hall was in fact a Portuguese men's club managed by Donnelly's husband, Fernando "Fritata" Raes, where the proceeds were used to purchase Cuban cigars and illegally imported grappa. There was indeed a battered women's shelter next door, but none of those victims could be reached for comment.

In the end, the blatant injustices and classist aspects of the story served to make it a heroic mess, a political time bomb to be avoided at all costs. Meanwhile, as far as the Von Fürstenberg Collective was concerned, the mistakes of the Westwood Group were firmly in the past. And, as they claimed, the re-branding of their organization had nothing to do with pending litigation, corporate tax laws, or nonsensical newspaper assertions like *Eat the 1 Percent!*

The scene in the main room of Claridge House, when Jack finally made his appearance, was a wasteland of self-important nobodies. No wonder Merrick had volunteered him for tonight's auction. Here, he too, could proudly stand up on the dais with any number of the incomparable literary frauds this now humiliated mid-tier organization could wrangle up.

An illegal Mexican penguin walked by with champagne flutes on a tray, and Jack took two. While sipping, he watched Merrick make banal, gregarious conversation. She was a natural at this—always had been.

Beautifully unshattered, Merrick's invincible repugnance towards the love she'd now left behind bordered on the enviable. Hers was a caring drained of care, the privilege of all successful hearts vis-à-vis the lost. She was regal, innocent, and somehow managed to stir souls into her tea.

As she began to move towards Jack, her agate eyes and maple syrup complexion oozed forth in a consuming flow. The room belonged to her. It belonged to her because she believed in herself above all others, sure, but the room also belonged to her, Jack would bitterly concede, because she was a pushy, manipulative virago without a shred of mercy or regret.[1]

"Jack, you made it." She was dressed in a flowing nightgown that matched her highlights. Her pout lips and jimp waist were frozen in a hula-hoop swirl, and she was scentless.

"Did you give me much choice, Mer?"

---

[1] It was insult to injury, or perhaps just cruel providence, that Merrick hadn't inherited her uncle's simoleons or his ancestral flophouse in the Museum Mile until *after* the divorce was finalized. Ah fate, obdurate fate. Luckily, Merrick hadn't let her nouveau riche status go to her head, though, because she'd always been a snob.

"Didn't I?" She hadn't. And if anything, she'd hinted at the fact that her nagging, acrimonious lawyer was still complaining about letting Jack off "so easily," which had meant leaving him with little else than an otherwise empty apartment. Merrick's passive-aggressiveness, along with her sense of style, was also an enviable art.

"So what's this all about anyhow?"

"It's a charity auction, I told you that on the phone."

"Yeah, but—"

"It's usually full of stewed prunes who smell of Oil of Olay, birdseed, and Tommy Dorsey arrangements, but at least you'll get a decent show buffet out of the midden maidens. One other good thing, at least for you, is that some of these bedazzled old wheezebags might actually remember when you had your fifteen minutes."

"When, in disgrace with fortune and men's eyes, I all alone beweep my outcast sta—"

"God, is that Shakespeare again? You really need some new material, Jack. No wonder you ended up where you are."

"You've never understood my choices, have you?"

"No, I haven't."

Jack swallowed what was left of his first champagne. "Fine."

"Look, I really don't think this is an

appropriate time for that discussion."

"You're right about that."

"Good." There was a pause, the faint flint of resentment flickering between them. "Well, like I said, I'm glad you decided to come."

"Sure, Mer, always happy to help. But why the urgency?" Merrick explained that Jack was a last-minute replacement for well-known literary recluse Thomas Pynchon, who'd chickened out after hearing rumors that they would be serving crab cake soufflé (which, as any sane person knew, was *the* CIA food of choice for bugging purposes). "Really? That's too bad."

"Don't worry about it, Jack. I assure you, nobody else here cares."

"And so what're the funds going towards, anyway?

"Beats me. Just think of this auction as being about helping one of those 'good causes' you love so much."

"Such as?"

"Cripples. Mental Defectives. Flood victims. Refugee relief for war criminals—take your pick!" Jack gulped the second champagne to keep from choking on the gurgling, splenetic bile. "Oh, Jesus, is that the time? I really have to get going, I'm already late for—"

"What! You drag me all the way uptown to this pretentious pit and then leave?"

"I have dinner plans, Jack."

"You're unbelievable—"

"What, did you expect me to hold your hand through this?"

He felt like punching her in the face, but bit his lip instead. "Sob softly, my sweet."

"Save it for these impressionable twits, Jack. They may all be rich, but I guarantee you there isn't a single brain in this room. So who knows, maybe all your Elizabethan poetry crap might even get you laid later on." She kissed him on both cheeks, in continental affection. After a few steps, she turned with a noncommittal pause, her shawl draped like medieval armor. "Mn, try not to get too drunk tonight, 'k darling—"

"Screw you, Merrick."

Several local poets were slated for auction before Jack, after which, followed a laundry list of literary agents. In their immaculate suits and madder ties, agents were the undisputed draw of the evening, the only ones with any real jobs left.[2] Yes, agents were the perfect puppets for these pseudo-literary shindigs, the gloss and veneer of respectable economy without any of the wasteful hassle of temperamental *artistes*.

---

[2] For "Agent" here, Jack would easily substitute "Crook," "Cheat," "Charlatan," "Clot," "Clod," "Cajoler," "Creep," "Corndoggler," "Cad," "Cheapskate," or "Cash curmudgeon," and a whole host of other euphemisms that don't all necessarily begin with the letter "C."

Mrs. Kinalty—a frosty heifer of a woman with circumflex eyebrows and saddlebag droops under her vacant eyes—was introduced as the evening's Mistress of Ceremonies and, at once, spoke in a booming baritone from the podium. Her opening, "Ladies and… ladies," got massive applause from both the foreign and domestic trout in attendance, their malapert murmurs stirring a pompous purée throughout the room.

"Yes, yes, settle down now, girls! Before we get to the bidding, I'd first like to thank the Von Fürstenberg Collective, a not-for-profit subsidiary of the Sheridan Society of New York, which is pleased to welcome its most gracious partner, *La Société Michelet-Maisonneuve*, of Paris, in this charitable event. Lawren Christie and Joan Simms you all know, and we salute them for making this event possible. The money we raise tonight will go to a valuable cause, and we thank you for that."

The actual cause was never explicitly unveiled; it was better this way, no doubt, a sort of choose your own adventure for those comfortable enough to afford humanitarian compassion. This chichi charity celebration was the perfect excuse for a midweek chinwag, not that any self-respecting socialite needs excuses—those were for the *hoi polloi*.

Backstage now, Jack paced as roll call began. First up was Kurt Coles, a writer of insipid pentameter who would surely end up Poet

Laureate someday. As Anne Sexton once asserted, in another context, he was *well oiled by his job, his job*. KC was today's true "Ode to the Second Rater," and kudos to Coles for conning the country. A bang-on belletristic bluffer from the Big Muddy River, he'd really figured it out: You could use a system, follow an established scientific method even, and churn out decent, acceptable poetic product wrapped in pretty plastic for mass consumption. Coles, cleverly, used the Anti-System System, which meant that he mostly wrote about meaningful, desperate, and beautiful breakups, even though he'd been happily married for the last decade.

    As Coles dignified the stage with his presence, the women on the other side of the curtain catcalled uncontrollably, unleashing a furious burst of bachelorette-like profanities from the dames-in-waiting. It didn't hurt that KC's looks were more akin to those of Pretty Boy Floyd's than Fatty Arbuckle's. With his appropriate air of nonchalant vacuity, Coles paraded up and down the catwalk with self-conscious exhibitionism, his thinning hair and white sneakers perfectly matched for the unbothered troves. In Jack's mind, a couple of bucks would have been overpaying, even if this was a charity gig.

    A woman in her late fifties began an aggressive come-to-mother bid campaign for comely Coles, the complete cynosure. Her face was pleasant enough, or had probably been pleasant enough about twenty years ago. The wrinkle-sets were deep around her eyes, jutting from the overeager nostrils, and swooping down from her satchel ears. Surgical work had been done to reorder, restore, reposition, reinstate, and realign—that much was clear—and the effort had surely not been cheap. The end result gave the vague impression of well-worked leather.

In the end, Coles went for $6,500, an admirable opening sale.

"Who got him?" Jack overheard one of the organizers say. She was talking to another brassy bint in a sequin purple gown, the favored fashion for women in their frisky forties.

"Looks like Brenda Shrimpton."

"Shitface Shrimpton! Christ on his throne, what a dumbass douchebaguette!"

"What?"

"You think she's getting any play from that poet poofball?"

"Really? He's. . . you know."

"How d'you think the shnook's been married so darn long?"

"I heard he was hung like a horse—"

"Fairies really have all the luck, don't they?"

The following three men to be sold into the mammalian meat market topped out at five grand apiece, but they were unrecognizables. It was a swell, sorry sight to see these elegant fashionistas of the crowd fondle their basest desires. But what was so wrong, you should rightfully ask, about a down-home cattle call of estrogen excitement?

The last to be auctioned before Jack was the reclusive Village poet, Vespasian Bruno. It was a wonder he was here at all. After his public nudity stunts with Ferlinghetti, "Gassy" Ginsberg, and the rest of the Abbadabba Beat bozos in the sixties, Vespasian had been content to haunt a city instead of a nation—the glamorous ghost of the ghetto and venerated Village Virgil. Vespasian's name sounded pretentious and made up but wasn't. His parents had named him after the imposing Roman Emperor, the man we could all thank for the building of the Colosseum in Roma (if he'd used a little more brute force on the workers, some say—like whips, and knives and eye gouging (well, no, not eye gouging)—maybe the damned thing wouldn't be falling apart today. Of Vespasian's most recent poems, Jack's favorite was a 45-part masterwork titled "Back Pedaled," inspired by the infamous peloton pileup at the Tour d'Azur back in '98. The poem traces the anti-Semitic roots of professional cycling back to the Dreyfus affair at the turn of the last century, with *Champagne Antijuif* at the traditional blackheart of corporate sponsorship.

Vespasian had the look of the poet down, too. It was enviable. Now that he was almost seventy, he'd wisely opted for a distinguished virile look by shedding his matted, clumsy, and swollen scraggly signatures. His beard had become sideburns, and the '80s permafro a bare dome. Gone too, were the cotton sweat pants and slippers, traded in for a felt-patch corduroy jacket and suede Wallabies. Vespasian was clean looking, presentable. When he stepped to the stage, a collective awe swallowed the Collective crowd. "Vespy! Vespy! Vespy!" they would have shrieked, given half a chance, revisiting their incarnations as fawning Beatle-ite teenyboppers. Thanks to Vespy's grooming, the poetic prima donna managed to steal the scene and sold for $12,800—a tough act to follow.

    Whisked out to the front of the curtain then, Jack felt nervous. The wanting eyes popped from skulls, wrapped in unsavory ideas. It was a feeling he clearly remembered from the first public readings of his work. What grand disasters! The stuttering, the flubbed lines, the sweaty armpit stains and blistering body odor, the raging bouts of pop-up psoriasis, the ruined underwear, the lack of applause, and the wall of silent receptions:

    Questions in the back? *'What does any of that garbage you wrote even mean? Were you trying to be clever? Did you ever think of having an actual story or plotline? When will you smartaleck, college jerks get over yerselves and just make some damned sense, h'eh?'* And on and on the throng went until the one short, positive review in the *NYRB* that eventually launched Jack's career; what sank it was another matter altogether.

"All right, ladies, all right. Settle! As you've probably guessed, our next literary man-about-town is Jack Mitford. Many of you undoubtedly read his hugely successful breakthrough novel back in the late nineties—*Patagonia Piano*—or maybe his slightly lesser known follow-up, *The Arcades Projectile*. Jack has since been involved in the publishing industry as a freelance editor and ghostwriter at Lincoln Press and enjoys long walks on the—"

"Enough already," a woman bellowed from the back, the paper thin of her lips parting in an echoless gap. She wore a fuchsia cat suit, bodacious Barbi (Benton) sunglasses, and high-heel pleather lace-ups that slinked softly past her knees. The cavernous assertion of her yawp was meant, Jack assumed, as a feral warning to the other bartering bananas poured tight into their cocktail dresses and evening gowns. Who let in the bohemian tart, they whispered, where were club standards? Jack couldn't care less. He just wanted the bidding to be over. "Well, come on! Let's keep this dog-and-pony circus rolling, ladies, while the night is still young!"

"Madam, a modicum of decorum is the usual course in these—"

"Bugger the usual course, missy! The usual course is boring and overrated. In fact, you can shove the *usual* course right up the *usual* hole, got it?"

"Excuse me, Mrs.—?"

"Lippincott. Judith Lippincott, and it's Miss."

"Well, Miss Lip—"

"Look, I'm ready to buy what's-his-nuts up there on the stage right now, and the rest of the swinging dicks you have on display, too. There's a weekend-long party brewing at our little place on the south shore and my driver's sitting on an anthill of toot for me. So what say we speed this puppy up a bit, huh? It's gonna be a gas, and I'm shooting to be out there in the next few hours."

"This is an auction, Miss—"

"No, this is a joke! My sisters and I are hosting a supremo event, the Lippincott Love-In we're calling it, and I don't want to miss a goddamned thing. This is all set, mama, it's our grand homage to that most self-absorbed generation: The Hippies. We're bringing back the bad old days with a pinch of the sultry '70s, too: Be-Ins, Free Love, Acid Tests, and Key Parties, which I know is the closet reason all you moneyed fun bag bit-chez are here right now."

"Would you please—!"

"Fact is my sisters and I need a solid cover for this sex shindig we got going on. This way, my accountants assure me, I can use the shaker as a tax write-off—can y'believe it? God bless "Bubbles" Reagan and the good ole goddamn GOP! My lawyer even says we'll have legitimate protection as a charitable event, under some paragraph subsection of the law, for all the non-legit that's bound to happen. I mean we are talking about a pure Peaches en Regalia event!"

"You and your kind are the reason it's no longer safe to go to the Hamptons," a woman shouted from the back room. Another said: "Shut up, you priss!" but it wasn't clear who she was addressing. The embargo on promiscuity in upper ranks was lifting.

"One catch though," Lippincott continued, undaunted. "The only thing I have to do is make sure I drop at least a quarter of a mil to be protected, tax bracket wise and all, so how's three hundred grand sound for the whole shebang?"

"Um, well, I—I'm not, uh…" Mrs. Kinalty looked like she'd just dropped something unsavory in her drawers.

"This is win-win, lady. You're getting a fair deal and I'm getting my charity men for this party, which I don't want to see go down solely as a dyke out show. Get it? I've got four limos out front raring to go. I'm talking about a step back to those gloriously hedonistic decades here, gals, a chance to travel back in time to the really real, realer than real. We'll have all the necessary goodies too, believe me: Tune-In & Turn-On, that whole deal, ya dig?"

"Does, ah, does anyone have a problem with this—this… deal?" The other women in the room were too overwhelmed to have a problem with anything right now. They stared at each other in shocked silence, the Collective straight showing for the lone-draw freak. Three cheers for Helen Gurley Brown and letting the hurdy-gurdy play. Jack and the dozen or so literary agents behind him had been pissed on, figuratively that is, stained by the unique stench of gracious feminine urine.

Highway to the Great Divide

At first, Jack stood still on the stage, unsure where to go. To the bar was the natural choice; there, he drank two doubles of Sour Mash as a recovery attempt. The daze was dulled by the time Lippincott found him. She was still young enough to have that admirable quality of being full of shit—thirty, maybe not even.

Her incurious eyes were a tint of flashing, white-blue bleach. "Ready to roll, tiger?"

"Uhh, I—?"

"What's your name again?"

"Jack."

"Great. I'm Judith, but call me Jude. The cars are out front."

"Sorry, where are we going?"

"Out to the South Fork."

"The Hamptons? Are you nuts? I can't go way the hell out there, not tonight."

"Why not?"

"'Cause I have a job, that's why not."

"So? Call in sick or something."

"Obviously spoken by someone who's never needed to work."

"Anyway, I thought you were some sort of writer."

"Not really."

"I know, just think of this whole time as

work. Use it as inspiration, maybe, for your next book—"

"There is no next book."

"See? Perfect. I guarantee you'll find something to write about at the Love-In. And if you get bored, there'll be limos doing the yo-yo service back to the City, which sure as shinola beats the jitney. Besides, you and those other guys are my official prizes for the night. You're mine."

"If you think a single one of those agent a-holes is coming, you're crazy."

"You're the crazy one, bub! Literary agents are the most lecherous Lotharios on the face of the planet. Their casting couches are greasier than any Tinseltown producer schmuck I ever met. And you know those jerkweeds jackhammer it like a Messerschmitt on a suicide run down a volcano tube."

"Christ! You're some piece of work, Jude."

"I guess this means you'll come? Not that I was really going to let you refuse anyway. I mean, seriously, what kind of horse's ass says no to an open-bar weekend of this magnitude?"

Outside, the limos were waiting in a row. Each car was colorfully painted in psychedelic peace strands, flashing flowers, and smiley faces. Some crewcut meatheads across the street guffawed in gap-toothed glory and smashed cans of beer on their heads.

Along with three others, Jack hopped in the limousine with Jude. She bounced around like a spun top, bounding from the slim curve of her thighs. Stenciled on the roof was: *Make love and chocolate truffles, not war!* As they began driving through the City, Jude mixed Amaretto and Champagne daiquiris.

Everyone in the car ate vegan chocolate cheesecake, introducing themselves with smears across their cheeks. It was a rolling tub of freaks, absolutely. Martin Belcher (no joke!) admitted that he'd been a crash test dummy for Jaguar, in the mid-eighties, to pay for college (you can learn a lot from a dummy, or so they used to say). Mona something-something expounded on her severe fear of whole vegetables (that's Lachanophobia for all you science geeks out there). Meanwhile, Murray O'Mara (aka the Magnificent Madama Minelli) went into colorful detail about he-she-it escapades singing in the *Loosey in the Sky with Cubic Zirconiums* show, currently playing to rave tourist reviews down at Strawberry Fields.

Once the car left the dense city lights behind, the real fun began. Belcher buzzed open the sunroof. The rotten egg breeze of Long Island poured in with pervasive push, which eventually gave way to a honeyed smell of highway strip malls and open fields. Jude kept mixing drinks and making long rambling speeches about the great freedom of the 1970s, a decade she wasn't even alive for. Before long, there was a light, heavy feeling within the leather-seat confines. Could you feel it? Something was going on.

"Hey, Jude," Mona asked, in a sort of drawl.

"Hmm?"

"How much, umm, alcohol is in these things?"

"Not too much, why?"

"I feel kinda weird, not quite normal—"

"Oh, right, I know." Jude steadied herself in a set of paisley tracers, speaking softly: "Yeah, you know what it is? It's prolly those peyote buttons I put in the fake cheesecake starting to kicking in—"

"What!"

"Relax, precious. They were only halves! A sample tease, you know, just enough to get us going. There'll be plenty more of that and everything else up at the house."

"Aww, Jesus Christ Jude!"

"What is it, Mona? What's the matter?"

"The matter!? The matter! I've—the matter is—I've… I've been 'sober' through NA for, for… fuuhkkkk…"

Mona was leaning her head back, swaying in short shifts. She was the first to reach for the icer, retching heaves into the bucket of gelid Champagne water. Her blurp-blurps were grotesque enough to be almost comical, "Hhhhrghraghgh, aaarrrghf'uh-rrrrraaaaaacck, huuuhgghg, bbbbbbrrrroghghghghwhjemnvvvvvvxdrw!!!!!"

"No worries, Mona, we're all headed there, girl!"

"Huh," Belcher eloquently asked.

"Obvi, dude, this stuff makes you throw Technicolor yawns." Jude took the bucket from Mona, whose eyes were already round as rainbows, and croaked a few convulsions of her own. "See what I mean? Now, expectorate buccal excreta!" She passed the container around, everyone adding a couple mouthfuls of rejected bile.

Jack was last to go, probably because he'd only taken a few bites of his cake. Still, the combination of the earlier excitement, the booze, and the drugs, forced at least a slight spittle trickle down into the dollop drain. Possibility, as Yogi Berra once said, is the greatest natural aphrodisiac (after coitus).

The rush was mild, sharpening contours more than it was distorting them. Jack hadn't tripped out for almost fifteen years, not since he'd worked as a speechwriter on the Florida *Just Say No* revival campaign for Clinton. He'd lost his marbles on four tabs of red ant blotter, sitting on The Magic Kingdom's "It's a Small World, After All" ride for half a day before two security guards in Goofy suits kicked him off the property.

"Mone? Hey, hey, Mona?" Jude's face was sweating, which gave her skin a glossy glint.

"Did you say—before, I mean—did you say that you were kept sober by shooting off guns? That's so mercenary, babe! I think we might have a few old shotguns up at the house if you need to squeeze off a few rounds."

"What?"

"You said you were sober because of the NRA, no?"

"No, no. I said NA, *NA*! Narcotics Anonymous."

"Oh, shit. Sorry. So… I, like, totally ruined your straight buzz…?"

"Mm-hmn. Yup." Mona was bobbing her head to feel its weight. "Hey, my head kinda feels like a lollipop."

"Wait, this is serious, Mona. How long were you—you know—clean for?"

"Six years. But hey, it's worth it. You guys should really try this; it feels pretty amazing." They all started bobbing their heads back and forth for a while. Mona was right; it did feel amazing. "Keee-raassst, I feel grrrrreat!"

It was magic hour from there on in. And by the time the limos got to the Lippincott property—dubbed "Epsilon Indi"—everyone swam the crest of a wave towards a great, unfathomed buzz.

A grand, gated complex of rejected restraint opened wide its arms as the cars began ascending the lane to the main house. Strewn over sprawling acres, several futurist bubble domes, light-plan installations, and glowing air-balloon trampolines grew out from the grass. Glow-in-the-dark dirigibles hovered a hundred feet up, next to flying pigs and blooming sunflowers. Strobe lights glinted and popped from tree house forts, their sinewy paths lit by the floret glow of candlelight. It was an enormous playground for the wealthy stoned; the place to ditch all risk.

"Terrific!" Belcher screamed as he gawked out the window.

"Isn't it boss," Jude said. "One of my sisters is an architect, totally in to that New Mexico bubble barn thing from the mid-sixties. Jacques Couëlle and Antti Lovag rip-offs mostly, *Maison-bulle* type stuff, you know?" No one did.

"Holy smokes, Jude—"

"What?"

Murray Minelli was now wearing a Pluto-blue wig and sniffling loudly between each syllable. "To be honest, doll, I thought you were a little full of it. But this… this is like a freak out festival for the senses."

"Pack your psychotropic raincoats, boys and girls," said Jude, as the car pulled up to the main house. "The sky is raining gumdrops and lollipops!"

An olla podrida of cheerleading go-go girrrrrrrls greeted the crew, bopping in trance outside the house. Their slim-fast fists pumped through the air while their stelliform hips swayed. Bannered over the wide front trellis, hanging between two Doric columns, was a rework of the divine poet's baleful ode: "Abandon Any Hope *Of Sobriety* All Ye Who Enter Here…" The city of woe and eternal pain was the pale paradox to pleasure in this deep den of debauch.

So start the shenanigans of the Southampton *vieux riche*. The roar of bass-driving funk echoed across the grass and through the hills, the sour-sweet breeze of enveloping impetuousness all around. People dispersed in drugged magnetism to the lights, colors, and sounds. They were bewildered little children, lulled into submission. A perfect pagan party and co-ed Matronalia to the gods was begun. The circus was finally in town.

What a Long, Strange Trip Begins

Inside, the Lippincott house design was open and free form. Double-arc stairways led up to the second floor in a tiered cupping of wings. Massive, mosaic sculptures were everywhere. Harmonious hues of green, brown, and orange blended in a buttery burst of warm welcome. Hundreds of shoes were scattered across the terra cotta tiles of the hall.

Barely inside the main door, Jack leaned on a six-foot tall foam cactus coat rack as the trail of people trickled through. A guru group sat on sheared Shetland carpets playing mild tabla music, mixed with zither tones, in the far corner of the front room. From the high clerestory ceilings long, luminous streamers dangled, sausage-like. It was a well lived-in house where you felt unafraid of breaking anything, even though everything was fragile and priceless.

Jude's sisters were in the foyer, greeting guests. Because of all the booze and the minor mescaline munch, it took Jack more than a few seconds to convince himself that he wasn't seeing double—or, more precisely, triple:

"We're triplets," Jude said, hugging both carbon copies from behind. They wore matching black, sleeveless evening dresses. Stunning. "This is Becca, the 'oldest,' and this is baby Miriam.

Girls: this one here's Jack, and those respectable types back there are all agents. They're our official charity cases for the long weekend—I got 'em for a steal at 300K. The rest are just some good time folks we picked up along the way. Come on in everybody!"

One of the agent peddlers slipped past Jack, using the oily residue from his palms to slick back his hair. "So this is like a real seventies Polanski thing," the man said, his face twisting itself into a wax apple as he walked further into the crowd.

Jack needed fresh air, and a smoke. But just as he turned, Jude bounced on him in piggyback style. She smelled vaguely of smoked oysters and graham crackers.

"Jack!"

"Jude."

"Listen," she began petting his forearm into a smooth rough. "Mona and I are going upstairs to get freaky. Wanna join?"

"Nm, not just now. I think I'll go outside for a smoke first."

"Why? Smoke upstairs, smoke in the bathtub, smoke standing on your head. Smoke wherever the fuck you want! This is a '60s party, man, even that dog over there is smoking."

"I know. I just need to grab a bit of air. Go on, I'll catch up to you two later—"

"Fine, suit yourself." Jude hopped off in a huff. She reached at Mona, who was slobbering all over one of the angel-faced agents. Froth bubbled at the corners of her mouth, fang-like.

"Is she going to be all right," Jack asked.

"She'll be just dandy! C'mon, Mone, let's leave these deadbeats and go have some real fun." The way Jude shook her head at him, Jack knew he'd blown a good one.

"Absence makes the heart grow fungus!" Mona belched, while being led up the stairs. Then, in a boom for all the deaf duds in the room, the Pretty Peyote Princess added: "I'm pining away for my fun guy! Aha, get it? Fungi! Fungi!!! Don't you asswipes hear me down there? Huh? I'm handing out jewels of wit here!"

All around, large fictile candles, supplied by the International Society of Approved Krishna-Konsciousness (ISAKKON), burned brightly. Plexiglas and stripes were the décor of choice, while shag carpets and elephant armchairs put the lounge in its salacious mood. On one of the leather sofas in the shape of a hulking catcher's mitt, five girls sat around in bare tops and bikini bottoms. They listened to what sounded like The Fugs and MC5 records played simultaneously, which was almost too much for Jack to bear as he fumbled over limbs. You could play a drive-in movie on all the glazed stares.

In the study, a couple sat nakedly groping at each other under a Mind Expander II. The Battenburg-pink dome, like a massive hair salon hood, buzzed above the two on their PVC beanbag as they slinked and writhed, playing an involved game of *Hide the Candybar* just like Mick "No Nuts" Jagger and Marianne "Un" Faithful used to do.

The punchbowls, fruit baskets, hors-d'oeuvres trays, sideboards, and countertops freely displayed colanders of Ketamine, Fentanyls, Methadols, Methamphetamines, Amidones, LSD, Mescaline, Peyote and Quaaludes (those indelible classics), as well as, all the babe-a-licious bastards of the Barbiturate family. All the colors of the rainbow were present and accounted for in order to ensure that, whatever your chosen vibe, the Lippincott Love-In would be one helluva score to remember… or forget.

It was impossible to make much sense of all these happenings and, decidedly, it was going to take a truckload of something illicit for Jack to feel right in this scene. In the kitchen, he stopped to stare at a woman with long, California-blond straight hair parted down the middle. She jawed with her clone—yet another anorexic anodyne in frill bra and pumps—about someone called Ramona from Pomona, a trailblazing groupie.

Jack stood propped on the granite counter, trying his best not to seem like a blazed-out narc. Next to him was a large auburn pot filled with simmering mushroom caps and stems, the perfect answer to his predicament. He took a quick scoop, dolloped sloppily into his mouth, and made for the freedom of the sliding glass doors.

Outside, Jack stretched forth, poised on the line—that tightrope arc, without a net. He managed to calm his nerves with two cigarettes before the rustling behind the barbecue began. A man was propping himself up, the little bits of sallow hair he had left scooped in a weave to the side of his head, his pants down around his ankles.

"Jesus," Jack said, "are you all right?"

"Sure, sure, just needed to pass out for a while to get m'bearings. I nearly took a deuce in those azaleas earlier to help with the what's it called... composting."

"Uh, okay. Sure you're all right?"

"What, you one of those hophead yutzes who drinks nothing but that wheatgrass piss? Don't be such a namby-pamby, all I need is a shot a' whiskey to be right as rain."

"Suit yourself."

The man then pulled up his pants as he stood, taking out a Zippo to relight his half-smoked cigar. Together they stared out from the terrace for a time, silent. There were faraway giggles in the breeze, the plangent sound of women laughing. The high moon was on a late rise.

"Ah, Christ, looks like I've gone and lost my manners again. Sorry, kid, I've never been much of a morning person. Anyway... the name's

Richter, Clint Richter."

"Jack Mitford."

"Charmed, I'm sure." Richter picked up his glass from the stone ledge, its cubes long drowned in a whiskey sigh. After dropping what looked like Alka-Seltzer pills into the highball, he chugged what was left of the liquid, growling with a purr as he swallowed. The fumes from Richter's cigar enveloped his balloon head in a temporary crown of gossamer smoke. The man wore a life of hard living in the whittled creases of his face. "Jack, something tells me you're a bourbon man—"

"You bet."

"If you look behind ya, there's a bar cut into the stone. Just yank on that jagged marble edge. Should be bottle a' Maker's we can give hell to." Jack ably followed instructions, grabbing the bottle and a glass for himself. He lit another cigarette as Clint poured out two full measures to the brim. They raised their glasses, silently.

"So, Clint, this is your place I take it? You're Jude's dad?" Whiskey jettisoned itself from Richter's nose, followed by a cackle. When he laughed, the man's throat sounded like a rusted pipe scraped with the serrated edge of a crowbar.

Richter gulped half his drink and poured himself back up to the top before speaking. "Sorry, son, just caught me off guard. Nah, I was at Andover with their old man, Lucius, and later, West Point: Duty, Honor, Country, that whole song and dance. Always liked the sonofabitch—bless his soul—but he was koo-koo nuts, and I mean bananas. Batshit crazy. I've known those girls since they were knee-high to a whippoorwill, though. Love 'em like daughters, I truly do."

"Huh," Jack said, thinking about the comfort of the floor in his apartment.

"So, what's your deal, Jack?"

"Deal? Don't have one. I used to be a writer, I guess."

"*Used* to be?"

"A novelist, yeah. But things happened along the way, got tangled up, and I guess I got disillusioned—"

"Ah, Jesus, not another one!"

Jack sipped hard, ignoring the ignorant tone. If there were any justice left in the world tonight, the old creep would keel over soon and Jack could use his head as an ashtray. It was a mean hallucination, sure, but the limousine mescaline was trailing into a drawn whiskey sway. Oh, yeah, and the mushrooms were gearing to kick in, too.

"Anyway, somewhere in there I decided to drop the fiction angle, and now it's ghost stuff, mostly."

"Hot damn, Jack! Am I ever glad I met you!"

"Oh, why's that?"

"I'm gonna have a helluva lot a' fun with

you—"

"What are you, a greedy little hustler?"

"Partly, yeah, but isn't everyone? What kind a' things y'working on these days?"

"Screed."

"Now I really am tickled pink as a weasel's belly! What's the last thing you worked on that had any real meat on it?"

"*The Hainan Harem*—"

"That book about the yella hook 'n' heroin trade slithering from China into Cambodia during the war?"

"You read it?"

"Right up my alley, kid. Though, you obviously weren't filled-in on all the sordid details of the operation."

"Is that so?"

"Let's just say that we had a whole lot more of a stake in the whole enterprise than you were led to believe. They fed you the cover story, the donkey gruel of well-placed information to absolve us of involvement."

"Who, *us*?"

Clint poured more bourbon into both their glasses, relighting his rancid cigar again. It smelled like a burning cow patty dipped in a bucket of puke. "Like Groucho used to say: Politics is the art of looking for trouble, finding it everywhere, diagnosing it incorrectly, and applying the wrong remedies—"

"Look, Clint, I think I'm a little too

buzzed for word puzzles right now. My mind is rushing."

"You too? Good. I just popped a few Dilaudid back there, and it's usually pretty fast-acting. Sorry I didn't offer you any, but I needed all I had left if I want any hope in Hell of getting the pecker up tonight."

"Ever heard of Viagra?"

"That's for pussies. Besides, you don't even get a decent buzz. What's the point of that?" A wave was cresting again, straddling the high-water mark of past and future eventualities. It wouldn't be long now. "Listen, Jack. I'd like to run something by you while we're both only half in the bag."

"An idea for a book?"

"You run a carnival act on the side?"

"Call it a hunch. But sorry to break the news to you, you're too late."

"Whadd'you mean?"

"Hadn't you heard? People don't read anymore."

"They'll read this."

"Why?"

"It's all about the pygmy wizard behind the shiny curtain."

"Even worse. That whole Conspiracy Theory angle is pretty old news, Clint, or don't you use the Interweeb—?"

"Conspiracies are for chemically imbalanced kooks who've never been inside the castle—"

"*'Like, totally question the answers, maaaaan!'* Those people?"

"Exactly. All those idiots ever see are the locked doors. Ever heard of Daniel Paul Schreber?"

"No."

"Check him out. He was a Saxon judge. Freud did a study on him, and the Prussian putz has got all the telltale markers of the paranoiac modern man. He's what the world's Fort/Da game is about—"

"So, what, you're proposing to… expose... some sort of—?"

"I'm not proposing anything. I'm just saying that this jackass exemplifies the roots of the modern—or the postmodern, if you believe in all that kind of crap-oh-la—condition. We're talking massive self-absorption, inflated importance, obsessive obsessions about governmental surveillance, and the immanent destruction/salvation of the world, which, inevitably, depended on his invaluable global role. Schreber is me, he's you, and he's everybody else out there."

"Ever consider becoming a motivational speaker?"

"Wake up, son, this social *dis*-ease has been with us since long before the Cold War. Man, those were the days!"

"*Those were the days*? Gimme a break,

what were you, like 5 when we sent troops to Korea?"

"Nine, actually, but that's not the point—not the point at all."

"Well, sounds… intriguing, Clint, but—"

"You know Sam Starr down there at Random House?"

"Sure. I mean, I've—I've heard of him, of course, but I…"

"That bastard's been angling me to get this done for years now. The eager little prick wants me to get it all down before I croak. He's a good guy. I'll let him know you're onboard, first thing in the morning. He'll set you up with an advance and an expense account."

"Whoa, wait a second. I already have a job—"

"Oh, where?"

"At Lincoln Press—"

"Don't worry, I'll take care of it—"

"Take care of *what*?" Before Jack knew what was going on, Richter had slammed back the rest of his drink, smashed his glass against the side of the house, and swooped the rest of the bottle under his arm in his make for the door.

"Jack, no offense, but m'johnson jus' got hard. I need tension release, pronto!"

"Hang on a second—"

"No can do, Jack-O-Moe, this is a pressing matter. Like I said, don't worry about a thing, it's all under control. Exterminate the brutes!" As he slid the door open, Richter made a fake gun with his finger at Jack before disappearing into the sea of glistening, beveled bodies.

"Holy Christ!" Jack exhaled loudly into the sere, crisp air. His peak was coming up fast, hard on the horizon.

Now that he was alone, Jack began to wonder if he'd even been talking to a real person at all. Had his mind simply conjured the utterly ridiculous character? The idea was, at this very moment, somehow one of the funniest things he'd ever conceived. Jack began cackling into his glass, slurping at the liquid like the propeller of an outboard motor. "Conspiracy Clint!" he finally blurted out, words that echoed, fluttered, crashed, and died, until all that remained was the resonant sound of voices pulsing inside.

Leading Horse to Waters

Jack woke up under the light of a custard sky. His lids, scraping the surface of his eyeballs, were the only part of his body currently functioning. Where was he? Or better yet, *when* was he? Moments crackled with absolute vigor, only to vanish suddenly down sloe-eyed hallways of memory that might never again be revisited.

The room, right now, was configured in such a way that let the thick overhead glass reflect the bright of day in an all-encompassing prism. It was like being bathed in a uterus of sun, which meant that Jack's feng shui hangover was birthed here. His limbs were listless and wrinkled, curbed by the clutch angle of the hard wood on his back. Why was he sleeping on the floor, in a dusting of pillow skin? He could only recall disjointed bits of his East Hampton clambake, shattered flashes of complete synapse. Was it over, or was he still here? He wasn't home, that much was clear.

Little pieces began to materialize, flickering. Jack had managed to lose his clothes on the first night of the Love-In and had ambled around for days accompanied by a soundtrack of Erik Satie preludes, sounds drooping in stringy jellies of elastic slime.

One moment he'd be consciously awake

in a quiet room, surrounded by wooden posts, sweating like a pig in a mess of limbs. Later, he was outside, skinny-dipping with thirty others in one of the property ponds or riding horses down to the beach. He'd spent a few soft hours, perfection dangling, lying stretched in the plush of sand with one of the Lippincott triplets. She'd fed him dried figs—pulpy rounds of flesh dripping with the honey of the gods—while dreaming of a life they would never spend together.

At some later point there'd been another girl—Babette, maybe?—who'd fiddled with the record player, listing off old Buddy Bolden Dixieland tunes in the comfort of a G-string. Time pulsed in flashes, infusing the world with possibility anew. The days were bright and free, a pastel-haze brownout with no discernible future except the afternoon.

The perversions and polite positions signaled an absurd dialectic of the subdominant, sumptuary, and salubrious undercurrents to an orgiastic mess so thoroughly enjoyed, yet now so thoroughly clouded. Depraved uselessness and incoherent accountability made for an intoxicating, schizophrenic cocktail. The dream was ending, and to the collective call so: Indulge, indulge, and again indulge. Oh, yes, you bet yer purdy necks we do, ♫♫♫: "We dooodoodoooooodooodooododooooooooooo!" ♫♫♫…

Keep all of this straight, Jack kept thinking, even though he couldn't think at all. Despite the open window, the air in the room felt staled and wan. He crawled up to the bed, in a scoliosis stoop, the heave of his stomach making him gag up the taste of half-chewed bean burgers and rotted sashimi. Brain-trust confetti cells had been thrown to the wind, firmly following caution out the door.

Lying still on the thick weave of sheets, he stared deeply into the bland blue of the ceiling windows. As the traditional Zuni saying goes: Out of the pan, and in to Zahpan....

The knock at the door, when it came, was loud and decisive.

"Mistah Mitford, s'uh, you awake?"

"Uh... um, yes...?" Jack's throat was cotton dry.

"May I come in, s'uh?"

"Aaah, o—okay...?"

A stout black man stood at the threshold.

"I'm d'manservant," he said, simply.

"Huh?" The man(servant) was ugly as a newborn and wore a flashing mauve tuxedo with frills. His polished shoes were immobile on the tanned marble. An elaborate rosette weighed elegantly on the fold of his lapel, complementing the dignified salt-pepper miscegenation of his miniature curls. There, on the doorsill, the man's gloved hand held up a silver tray in a pose reserved only for outdated mannerists and freakystylie bumboys waiting to score.

"Mistah Richter want me t'bring you dis—"

"Mr. Richter?"

"Yes, s'uh."

"Who the fuck's Mr. Richter?"

"He suggest you drink it, A-Ez-A-Pee, s'uh."

"Wh—what is it?" He handed Jack the glass of russet liqui-pus. Next to the glass was a note:

Tastes like an old man's shriveled ballsack and kicks like a mule's fifth hoof, but I guarantee it'll make you feel halfway human again. Take your time with it, then come on down and we'll pop some profiteroles and shut the hell up together!—Clint.

"Conspiracy Clint!" Jack exclaimed, but the manservant had already left the room.

The beverage went down like sewer water, its liquid shooting past his intestines faster than Dengue fever through a pallid, lanky Swede. For forty-five minutes, Jack sat atop the en-suite throne making a symphony. After a warm bidet wash and a cold shower, he dressed in a set of clothes that had been laid out on the nightstand. The shirts were an absurd assortment of argyle and plaid, matched with knee-high socks, and plus fours.

The mood in the hallway was a hushed quiet. Hanging opposite the doorway were two equally matched, equally dull Jasper Johns pieces.[3] Down the stairs, a different serving-man stood at the newel. This one, a light-skinned black gent, wore a powdered wig and renaissance hosiery. His shoes were buckled in pilgrim fashion, his prim face bearing the chiseled features of an ant.

"Is…? Is Mr. Richt—"

"Jackie-O! Get the hell in here!" The loud voice came from an open doorway down the hall. The dusky Louis Quatorze courtier ushered Jack over to the study with a stern nod. Desiccated game heads, bonito fish, and taxidermy snakes cluttered the walls of the hallway. Clint was sitting behind a large desk smoking a cigar and polishing a shotgun.

"Come on in, Jack. Jeezuhz! You look like a links lunatic teeing for a 19-hole straight jacket. Fore!"

"They're your clothes, man." Clint got up to shake Jack's hand and pat him on the back. His face was wider and much older than Jack remembered.

"Interest you in a spot of lunch?"

"No, thanks. Not after that criminal concoction you sent up."

---

[3] That's right, you guess it! An American flag and a target bullseye, what else?

"The dumpster dirt? Worked, didn't it? That snake juice is a home remedy hallowed by time. Trust me, the best thing for you right now is to eat."

"Ahhhh, I really don't think that's—"

"Pappy!" Clint screamed, bringing the footman instantly to the doorway. "Have Panayotis reheat some of his *Volos varenikis* as a nibbler plate."

"Yez'uh."

"And tell that Greek fattub not to smother it in so much fuckin' sauce this time. Tasted like a goddamn pile of steaming dog shit last time."

"All right, s'uh."

Clint blew his cigar smoke out towards Pappy. "Well, wha'chou waiting for, a Holy Writ? Get going!"

"Yez'uh."

"Unbelievable," Clint said, turning back towards Jack. "I'm employing a house full of halfwits."

"White man's privilege, that sort of thing?"

"Hey I'm olive-skinned, pal, not white. And don't misunderstand, I may be 1/128th spade on my mother's side, but I'm also a full-blooded human being. Ask anybody, I give back to the lesser blessed every old day of the week."

"'*Pity the aristocrats and kings for they bear the world's heaviest burden.*'"

"Blake?"

"Soupy Sales."

"Genius." They sat. Clint's lips pulled on his cigar, its tip-ash blazing coal. He pointed to a molded, ivory cigar box on his desk. "Feel free to have one, Jack."

"No thanks. Don't think I could handle it now."

"Pamatelas and cigarettes in there, too."

"No, really. Thank you. My throat feels wrecked." More precisely, it felt like it had been force-stuffed with the wrong end of a cat in heat suffering from a violent bout of the Mexican Two-step.

"Not feeling well, I imagine."

"Nope."

"You'll be all right in a jiff, don't worry."

"This, uh, this is a little delicate, Clint… but, if you don't mind me asking, how is it I ended up here, exactly?"

"You drank the punch."

"Punch?"

"Yeah, it's an old trip-out broth we used to brew at Peter Beard's house up the road, in the '70s. Miriam, one of the Lippincott girls, got a hold of the recipe and made a batch. Not for the faint of heart—"

"You drink some?"

"Christ, no! I think most of us fogies stopped drinking the stuff after Nancy's re-election party at the White House in '84—man, talk about Morning in America! Ronnie went swinging from the rafters in the West Wing, stripped down to his BVDs, all while making godawful Tchernenko impersonations wearing a lampshade on his head."

"Reagan?"

"Are you gonna answer all my answers with questions?"

"Sorry… I, I was just trying to remember a little more of what happened. H—how long have I been asleep here?"

"Thirty-six hours."

"Thirty-six hours!"

"Mmm-hm. And sleeping like a brain-damaged baby, too, ever since the girls called me wanting to know what they should do with your sorry ass after the epic Bacchanalian sex swap and pharmaceutical phree-phor-all ended. Apparently you were howling out at the top of your lungs, still running wild with some pamba-freak named Bitzy or Bambi or—"

"Babette."

"You remember?"

"No."

"Well, apparently you two were wandering around the acreage, spreading dirt and god knows what else on each other's genitals, making a real scene for the neighbors around the fences. Normally that kind of stuff is totally kosher around these parts, but with the compound reverting back to ashram status this week, the girls didn't want to ruffle any feathers down at

49

the IRS. Loose liens, those are common capitalist facts, but morally questionable morals? Forget it."

"Ashram status? I don't follow."

"How else d'you expect the girls to keep up with the property taxes on that country mansion? It's all a game, boy-o, just like the Love-In was an excuse to write-off expenses under Uncle Sam's top hat."

"I think I'm in the completely wrong tax bracket to have the slightest clue about what it is you're talking about."

"It's not important. The point is, Jude called over here in a panic and asked me to step in when you started freaking out—"

"That was sweet of her—"

"Don't flatter yourself, chief, it was just as much for your benefit as hers. Take it from me: You do not want to mess with the local 5-0 around here if you don't own a shack in the area. *Po*-lice here are a brutal band of cornpone bastards—dickless fascists, really."

"Thirty-six hours! I still can't believe that. What day is it?"

"Tuesday."

"Fucker! I'm supposed to be at work."

"Don't worry about that."

"Don't—? Hey, I've got a deadline this week."

"It's not a problem."

"What? Look, can I use your phone?"

"If you think you need to." Jack called his boss, who was more mad than worried.

"No, I promise…" Clint listened to Jack say into the receiver: "And it wasn't really a bender, more an extended camping trip with friends, with no cell service to speak of… no, I understand that… yeah, a few too many rum & cokes… absolutely… first thing tomorrow, yes, you bet… don't worry, Flor, I'll be back as soon as I can." Jack put down the phone and stared at Clint. "Thanks."

"No sweat. Was that Florian Edwards?"

"Yeah. You know him?"

"A little, through Starr at Random House. He's pissed?"

"Not as much as I thought. But I have to get back to the City, like, immediately. What's the nearest station? I'll call a cab—"

"Nonsense. I'll have my driver run you in to the City, after we eat."

"Really? Thanks."

"One condition, though."

"What's that?"

"You listen to my book proposal while we chew."

"Oh right, your conspiracy-theory treatise—that part I *do* remember."

"I prefer to call it an exxxposé memoir."

"A tell-all about how Clint Richter came into his blue-blood fortune, that it?"

"Nah, that's boring. I know the bestseller

dopes gobble that kind of shit up, but it's a con, just like all this ornamental garbage is a con. Everything around us is built on the sweat of invisibles and the misplaced longing of inbreds, psychopaths, and rapists."

"Gee, that's quite the ancestral pride you've got." Jack's head suddenly stopped pounding. The headache evaporated and a grumble hit his stomach. He was hungry, and he did feel decidedly decent, just as Clint had predicted. "You know what, Clint? I'm not feeling half-bad right now."

"Good, the Crotch Cocktail's kicked in. Told ya, peach as pie."

The bewigged servant came in to the room, on cue, with the appetizers. Clint looked over the plate. A long sigh bubbled from his mouth when he saw the sauce on the food. "Shit, I knew it. I goddamned knew it! Can't trust that nitwit to do anything right!"

"S'uh?"

"Never mind, Pappy, never mind."

"Very good, Mistah Richter."

"Oh, Pappy, wait. Seeing as this is drenched in yo-yo sauce, I suppose I wouldn't disagree with a biscuit to sop it all up—"

"S'uh?"

"A biscuit, damnit! You deaf? Get that Greek idiot to send out some of those cheesy, raisin-filled ones from last night. There has to be some of those still kicking around, unless that fucken hippo ate them all himself—"

"Iz guessing we've plum run att-a do'se, s'uh."

"Well don't just stand there guessing, go check for fuck sakes!" The black Ganymede ran out of the room as if a starter pistol had been fired. "See what I have to deal with? Utterly ridiculous! And to think of all the bread I pay these donkeys."

"Guess the domestic life just ain't what it used to be, hmn?"

"You've got a point there, Jack. But still, I pay that gap-tooth yahoo over 150Gs a year, plus benefits! You'd think he'd have a lil' hop-to ya know, some stinkin' initiative."

"Wait, his salary is a hundred-and-fifty thousand? ... Dollars!?"

"Just a bit of forethought, that's all I'm saying—is it really too much to ask? Now his sister, that's a whole different kettle a' fish. Would you believe she actually had the inventiveness to change her name, legally, to Domesti-Kate? Clever, huh?"

"Original."

"Absolutely. Talk about wearing your heart on your sleeve. But oh no, not Ol' Pappy, he's better than the rest of us!" Clint went to the cabinet behind him, uncapped a bottle of gin, and started swigging for a good fifteen, twenty seconds.

Jack didn't speak until the bottleneck

tipped back off the lips. "You okay?"

"Sure. I'm calm now. That'll bring my blood pressure back to normal." Clint sat down again, his palms smoothing the surface of his desk. The young, brown servant came into the room with another tray of treats, acquiescent. It was a revolving door of derangement. Not even for a brief instant did Jack consider switching places with the kid, not if it meant serving this delusional nutjob. "So, Jack, where were we?"

"You were talking about your—"

"Ah, you know what? Screw it. Doesn't matter. My mind's still too pissed right now to think straight. Let's talk about anything else."

All Jack wanted to do was get the hell out of here, back to the City and his empty apartment, before he got suckered into this eccentric madness, which was way out of his league; but polite social etiquette, not to mention the promise of a rejuvenating hair of the dog tumbler, got the better of him: "Y'know, I think I will take one of those cigarettes, after all. If you don't mind?"

"Go right ahead, Jack-O. Here, join me." Clint poured himself a huge glass of gin, mixed with three drops of tonic, and did the same for Jack before speaking again: "How was the food, by the way? A little smothered, am I right?"

"Hmn, maybe a little."

"I knew it! Son of a bitch!" Clint pounded on the desk with his fist as he sat down. Jack smoked in silence during the tantrum, eventually prompting Clint to relight his cigar, calmly. A cloud began dominating the room, quite a feat to witness.

"You were in the Program," Jack asked then, noticing a small silver and diamond globe on Clint's desk. It was a service memento only given to former astronauts. He'd seen one in John Glenn's office, when doing research for his first novel.

"Yep, I took the big ride. Drank buckets of Tang & Tanqueray with Randall Avers and Jo Kemp."

"Really, when?"

"During the early Apollo missions. I'm second-string, don't get me wrong, but at least I've been up there. Shepard, Glenn, Wally Schirra, and the rest of those Mercury 7 dickwads can all kiss my ass. They may have been up there first, but I've seen it too."

"Wow, that's privileged company."

"Forget those schmucks. You know what the biggest disappointment was?"

"No. What?"

"Seeing the earth."

"What d'you mean?"

"I mean, *actually* seeing it from orbit. It's a total and complete letdown. Bullshit hype! Not even the Grand Canyon is as bad."

"I don't think I've ever heard anyone say that before."

"Another round?"

"Uh, sure."

Clint starting mixing two more drinks. "And don't believe conspiracy cranks like Billy K. Singsung who say that we all ended-up as high-powered execs—only the smart ones did. As for the rest, you have no idea how many times, at an old galaxy fly-boy reunion, you'll hear: 'All my wives left me, I haven't seen my daughters in twelve years, I'm working part-time as a mini-mall security guard to supplement my NASA pension…' Boo-hoo-hoo. They can really be a bunch of crybabies when you get right down to it. The Ancients had it right, *Sic transit Gloria mundi*—"

"'So too passes away the glory of the world?' That's a bit grim, isn't it?

"The problem today is that the Program's become a joke to people. At least in the old days the joke was on everybody else, perpetrated by the Agency—"

"How d'you mean?"

"You know, things like the moon walk—"

"Oh, I get it, this is the part where you tell me how the whole moon landing was a 30-billion dollar swindle, right?"

"Don't be a complete dumbass! Of course we made it to the moon, just not the way everybody saw it in black 'n' white."

"And how's that?"

Richter sighed loudly, adjusted his seat, and then took a long gulp from his glass. He was digging in to spin a yarn, full thrusters: "Dollars to doughnuts you can name the first man to walk on the moon, right?"

"Who can't? Neil Armstrong."

"Well, they're wrong."

"Oh, really?"

"Don't sound so incredulous." Jack took an apologetic gulp. "No, the actual mission did, in fact, happen pretty much like everybody saw it on the idiot box, but with one key difference. Aldrin was the one who stepped out first, not Armstrong. Poor Buzz."

"Uh-huh."

"See, the problem was this: although Apollo 11 did shoot the original landing on the lunar surface, none of the footage they got up there was any good. It had to do with the camera speed or something; you get part of that answered by the missing slow-scan tapes. Anyway, NASA couldn't rightly justify all the dough it was burning up for fuel without showing results, especially not after what Johnny "Playboy" Kennedy had been dumb enough to blurt out nine years earlier. By 1969, sure as shit our government wasn't waiting for the change of decade to watch two Soviet *apparatchik* faggots twirl each other around like a couple of Baryshnikovs through the moon dust, I guarantee you that. We'd already been up there; we just needed the visual proof. So, what to do? The whole moon mission team had been back on

Earth an entire week before the pencil-necks got them into the Northern Studio for the moon shots."

"Northern Studio?"

"It's a place we used up there in Canuckland—you know Ottaw'ah?—when dealing with sensitive issues, national security business, that type of stuff."

"Okay."

"Anyway, they mobilized Aldrin and Armstrong, even got Collins up there too for the window dressing, and serious kudos to those northern boys for hitting the ground running on that project. They even rigged a specially modified Hasselblad camera that could be operated with the fat hands of the spacesuits, it was genius—everything about it was. The basic plan, in a nutshell, was to shoot everything in a couple of hours, have Armstrong and Aldrin interact 'live' with mission control for the whole world to see and hear, then get all three boys back into the tin can, blast it up into the ionosphere from one of our Project HARP (High-Altitude Research Program) bases in Vermont, and have them splash back into the ocean as proven heroes. Simple, right? Easy."

"Sounds plausible enough."

"Only problem was, the night before everything was supposed to go down, a poker game fueled by vodka gimlets and bad tempers broke out in the Hangar."

"What's the Hangar?"

"That's what we used to call the studio up there—loose code. Anyway, I say 'bad tempers' because Aldrin and Armstrong hated each other's guts—not many people know that—and to tell you the truth, even I have no idea what it was all about. At any rate, everybody playing that night gets blasted, and late in the game Buzz is down in the stakes, and I mean way down in the hole. In a sort of Hail Mary, he bets quadruple-or-nothing on a hand there was no way in hell he could bluff, and lost. The pot was so outrageous that Aldrin was staring down the barrel of a lifelong debt. That's when Armstrong gave him the easy out—"

"'I want to be the first to walk on the moon.'"

"*I want to be the first to walk on the moon*, that's right."

"So let me get this straight, you're saying that Armstrong got fame and credit, all these years, and it was because of some lousy poker hand?"

"That's what happened."

"Right. But not really, because all this went down on a sound stage, somewhere up in Canada."

"Like I said, the moon walk is real—just not the way people think it is."

"And this is the kind of nonsense that you'd want me to get involved with in this memoir of yours?"

Clint took another run at his cigar, which had once again gone out. While Richter fiddled with the disgusting, soggy mess, Jack cooled his throat with a splash of gin and lit another cigarette before things resumed:

"Look, now is the time for a proper witch hunt, Jack-O, wouldn't you say? Why are people so down on those nowadays? Where are the Rosenbergs when you really need them? It's about time we pulled out our pitchforks and shovels again. Let's burrow deep down into the underbelly. Let's bring back a real badass Babayaga, that's what the people really want, a true eater of children."

"You might find that you're a little out of touch in that kind of thinking, Clint."

"Are you kidding me? *Operation Just Cause* in Panama, political plot involvements in Paraguay, Ron and Ollie's Iran-Contra debacle with the Sandinistas, Ho Chi Minh City, the October Surprise, Khomeini's return, the Madrid putsch, Arafat in his bunker—the list goes on, and it's too good to be true. This is all about the Lazarus soul of a nation. So why not go out on a limb? That's where the best fruit is, as Will Rogers well knew."

"Right, well... How should I put this? It may not be important to you, Clint, but publishers, and certainly financially precarious ones like, say, Lincoln Press, aren't really used to taking those types of chances. Publishers aren't risk takers, even in the best economic climates. No way any of them would ever go out on a limb."

"Well, if the times are getting' tighter then we might as well get tight, right? So fuck the publishers, I say. I've got no heirs and plenty of money to burn, and I honestly don't really care what they think. I'm starting you off on a retainer of 250 large, plus expenses a' course. There'll be a bunch of traveling involved, no doubt, but just keep your receipts. You know the drill."

"You're crazy, bub!"

"No, I'm serious."

"What's the difference?"

"A whack load of capital, usually."

"Look, Clint… I—I've gotta admit, I'm not really sure what to say."

"Simple, say you'll do it."

"But I'm not even clear on what it is you're asking me to do exactly. If, in fact, you do have this money and all these ideas, as well as what you call 'proof' about things that happened in the past, why d'you even need me?"

"Well, for starters, I'm not a writer."

"Any joker can write, that's *our* big inside secret."

"Horseshit."

"Look, I'll edit the chapters for you, if that's what you're afraid of. It'll be my pleasure. Honestly, why not just write it yourself?"

"I'm not a young man anymore."

"So? Neither am I."

"And, like I said, this job is gonna require a whole lot of running around—"

"Who cares?"

"I'm agoraphobic, Jack. You wanted the truth, there's the long and short of it."

"Agoraphobic? Give me a break! I met you at the Lippincott's party. Obviously you can leave your house."

"That place *is* like my house. Besides, not all agoraphobes suffer in the same way. Don't think just because you know something about a word that you know precisely what it means. I hate that kind of Ivy League arrogance, and I'm a Yalie."

"Okay. Sorry."

"I mean, I can wander around the area here, drive to nearby towns in my golf cart or walk down to the beach, but hop a ride into the City? Forget that! I can't do it anymore. 'Sides, I paid my dues with the likes of Meow-Meow Hawks, Franny Tufo, 'Lee' Harvey Vanderbilt, Dick 'Ain't-youse-happy-ta-see-me?' Feigen, Kenny 'G' Lane, and the rest of the Park Ave A-holes. I'm done."

"Wow, I can't believe it."

"Well, do."

"But a man like you? From what little you've told me, it's clear that you're worldly, well-traveled. How's this possible?"

"Happens to the best of us, like

Alzheimer's."

Jack pulled hard on the filter end of his cigarette, which now tasted like the ass end of a wet wire-haired terrier. He butted out in the tray, sighing long before speaking again. "Shit… I don't know. Can't you do all this from here, Clint? I mean, you could make phone calls, surf the web, investigate that way—"

"Not really, no."

"Why not?"

"Because a lot of what's needed now is to see what's happening in these places today. I can give you intel on certain things that went on back when, and I even have some old diary entries and notes I've collected that can help you out. But you'll have to do the legwork, track down the modern embodiment of these places."

"For what logical reason? To see that some old base or military command post is now a falafel stand or a burger joint?"

"Hey, that's a great idea—"

"What is?"

"Never mind. Listen, if nothing else, it'll be a record of the changing state of affairs—a collective conscious memory of the Great Society! C'mon, that kind of hooey is hip these days, right? And on top of everything else, it'll be like those time capsules everybody used to be so fucken fond of. Look at it as a legacy for future generations."

"It'll be a huge joke is what it'll be. A

very expensive, pointless, inside joke."

"You let me worry about that part, all right? Besides, I love pointless jokes. I'm positive I'll have fun with you. Did I say that already?" Ol' Pappy came to the door, in balletic swirls, motioning to Clint for the food being served in the next room. "What, you making a habit of standing at doorways now?"

"The late lunch is served, s'uh."

"Well just say so, don't stand there like some big-eared asshole eavesdropping on other people's conversations!"

"I wasn't, s'uh."

"Like hell!"

"But—!"

"No 'buts,' Pappy! Now get outta of my sight before you ruin our appetites." The man stomped his heels and executed a perfect military about-face. "Oh, Pappy, wait!"

"S'uh?"

"I done changed my mind, as usual. Hold off on the grub for a few shakes and bring us a pair of brandy balloons first, would ya. Pretty please, with cherries on top?"

"Very good, s'uh."

"All right, I said I'm sorry, now what are you waiting for, get!" As soon as the servant was gone, Clint burst into a laugh that was more akin to a hyena's cackle. "Man, it's just too easy with him sometimes, he's so damned earnest. C'mon, let me show you 'round the flop a bit before chow. You a fan of Hanafuda?"

"I'm a fan of almost anything accompanied by a tall, stiff drink."

"Attaboy." Richter wheezed loudly as he stood, his throat convulsing in a rage of coughs that bellowed like a Gatling gun discharging. Once the fit ended, he patted Jack on the back amicably and began leading the way out of the study. "You're a good man, Jack, I could see that the second we met. And don't worry, I can't foresee any problems whatsoever on this gig."

"At least that makes one of us."

Part II

Res Ipsa Loquitur: Way Over Yonder in the Monarch Key

The weeks that followed the Lippincott Love-In toppled under boredom of the unchanged. Merrick called a few times—always at some inconsiderate hour of morning—usually to keep Jack abreast of her social calendar. These calls inevitably consisted of, but were not limited to, name dropping the various multinational magnates she'd been having dinner with that week (all millionaire mopes with too much money and no hair); then, before hanging up abruptly, she'd casually gloat about the latest useless tchotchkes she'd bought with Jack's settlement cash.[4]

Jack tried not to think too much about Clint's ridiculous offer or the swinger party at Jude's, but something about the experience had changed him. This world of lush possibility had exposed the phoniness of his previous existence,

---

[4] Merrick's lawyer, Mack Mutzger, had successfully shystered all of Jack's minimal savings ($64,000) and pettifogged 72.5% of his hebdomadal paychecks for the next two years. You got a Y-chromosome, yo? Miranda Rights ain't for you, man, and better believe in two strikes (XX), you're out!

his cowardice. Yet rather than confront those realities, he tried instead to sink deeper into drowning routine as a means of forgetting what he'd seen behind the curtain.

At work, Jack kept his head down, practicing his usual avoidance tactics in the hallways and the men's room stalls. This way, he never got trapped into meaningless water cooler conversations or bothered having to ask whatever office shithead about "the wife."

Publishing was a miserable, thankless business. And while ghosting paid for Jack's habits, it provided no spark. Mostly, he fell into a pattern of pretending to work while drinking hourly measures of whiskey and stepping out for innumerable smoke breaks. Time was slow. He could hardly stand himself or where he lived, which in its vast furniture emptiness had all but turned into a receptacle for old *Glamour* magazines, empty bottles, and fruit flies. To avoid going home, he usually ate dinner at one of the cut-rate ethnic joints near his place, and then sat alone in a dive called *The Meet Market* swilling cheap hooch until last call.

Days were a fog; so when his telephone rang, Jack had no idea what time it was—his head hurt, he knew that much. A breeze from the window wafted up the smell of wet garbage juice from the street. The phone rang at least two dozen times before he answered, a curdled bone stuck down his throat:

"Hel… grrhh… hello?"

"Jack-O? You need a cell phone, or at least a voice machine."

"Who's this?"

"Clint." The line was quiet. The arc of an entire life rounded itself in that miserable slice of silence. "Richter. You remember, from last month?"

"I thought you'd forgotten about me."

"How you been?"

"Busy."

"Is that what you call sitting up in an office with nothing to do all goddamn day? That's quite an avocation."

"What d'you mean?"

"Those books you were working on, they're done. Edwards, your editor, says they're not planning to publish anything else until at least the New Year at the earliest. Not in this economic climate. Personally, I blame the 99%—"

"You've been talking to my boss?"

"Some. I was gonna go through Sam Starr at Random House, like I mentioned previously, but he was hit by a bus last week—"

"Jesus! Really?"

"So with that possibility down the pooper, I decided to lease out Lincoln Press and scoop you out of your miserable existence."

"What's your problem, man?"

"What's yours? Out getting shitfaced every night in that pathetic booze can around the corner really doing it for you?"

"Christ, you're following me around now, too?"

"No."

"No?"

"No. All I've got to do is pay other people to follow you, which isn't very hard when you more or less just stumble around. Anyway, none of that matters right now."

"Oh, no? And why's that?"

"I've got you booked on a flight to Canada—"

"Isn't that an Ishmael Reed book?"

"You leave tonight."

"Thanks, but my boss might have something to say about that."

"*Bon voyage*, I think, were his exact words."

"Bullshit."

"You were cheap, too."

"Look, Lincoln won't touch your stupid fucking idea, Clint, I guarantee it."

"Why not? Publishing's a bitch, and the proposition's win-win for Edwards: he has no concrete work for you and I'm perfectly willing to finance you to play the part of the Wandering Jew—say, you're a writer, was it C.S. Lewis or that Lord of the Rings guy who said that not all who wander are lost?"

"Look, if what you're saying's true, then I'd rather simply do nothing at all."

"No doubt, but your bank account says differently. Your ex-wife's raped that treasure chest pretty clean, son."

"What is your deal, buddy?"

"Don't worry, that two hundred and fifty large I offered you as retainer is still on the table, but let's just make it 3 even; and trust me, I'll hide the funds so deep even that mangy Mutzger and his legal beagles won't whittle out the scent."

"Why d'you even want me, Clint? Seriously?"

"I guess I'm old school. I like the personal touch. Plus, I know you."

"No you don't, not really."

"Maybe you're right, but I know your type and that's even better. You see, I used to be just as out of control as you are. There's a strange sort of comfort in that."

"You are so full of shit, man." Jack fumbled through his pockets for his cigarettes. The pants were crumpled in a ball next on the floor and smelled of coriander. He lit a cigarette and found his watch. It was 2:30 p.m.

"Jack? You there?"

"Yeah. What?"

"I've FedExed a package to your place—should be outside your door now. It's got all the flight and hotel booking info, and some traveling cash. I've also included some directions and notes on people and places to see up there. I still have a friend at the 'Hangar'—son of a friend, actually—so you'll be able to get an idea of the public dream machine."

"Am I supposed to know what you're talking about?"

"You should probably hurry, too. Your flight leaves in less than four hours, and y'know how our Homeland Security boys are these days. I don't recommend dilly-dallying."

"Wait. Where am I going?"

"Canada's Shadow Capital, a real pisswater burgh called Ottawa. You'll love it. Oh, and Jack?"

"Yeah—"

"Think of all this as a heuristic hunt."

"A what?"

"Trust me, you'll figure it out."

It was a close shave, but Jack made it to LaGuardia in time for a top-to-bottom, zip-a-dee-doo-dah body+cavity+junk search. One brushcut halfwit supervised (peeped), while his uniformed twin took a flashlight deep between Jack's hairy cheeks. Once satisfied that every last orifice was clean as a mudwhistle, the good people of the airport border control then followed up the physical manhandling with a verbal one. The beloved, time-honored process lasted for what could have been days.

Afterwards, Jack picked up a carton of duty-free cigarettes and made for the bar. In the lounge, he drank three triples before boarding the flight. Richter's so-called traveling money was a fat wad of hundred-dollar bills, which would surely translate into a phenomenal amount of Cana'jun funny munny.

Who knew why the paranoid old man was tossing around this kind of cash, but if the stupid son of a bitch wanted to burn his fortune on senseless errands, so be it. Jack, now that he gave it some proper thought, had been more than a little slow on the angles. Why had he resisted the chance at a paid vacation? All he'd have to do was look at a few crumbling buildings, talk to a couple aging peckerwoods, and take some spotty notes. He wouldn't even need to be sober for that.

The flight across the border was uneventful, except for the fawning male stewards who kept bounding up and down the aisle with their denture-tight grins. The airy airport on the other end was a neat freak's dream, decorated with bland Inuit art and totem poles. The space smelled like candy and felt almost like the real thing.

On the lower level, people were funneled through what was called *Les douanes,* which sounded like "Lady Wan." There, pleasant exchanges were conducted with plump men and women in beige fatigues. They smiled diffidently, did a lot of nodding, and seemed to play double-duty roles as customs officers and official greeters for the struggling tourism board.

Down at the baggage carousel, meanwhile, it was a purgatory of the plain. All

Jack wanted to do was hop a cab to the hotel, rip the mini-bar to shreds, and plow through the pay-per-view. If he was going to be diligent, though, he should probably at least skim through some of Clint's notes—but who could be bothered?

A firm, lanky woman struggled to heave a large suitcase off the rubber conveyor. She was a slightly younger version of Merrick, minus the crow's feet. Jack immediately stepped in to help, pinching his sciatica for a shot at the big time.

Her recognition came in the form of these words: "And who says chivalry is dead, eh? Name's Colleen." She held out her hand, that most manly of gestures. Her nutmeg skin was naturally soft.

"I'm Jack."

"Where you headed, Jack?"

"Uh," he fiddled with the papers in his pocket. "Some place called the *Château Laurier* in the… Marketplace?"

"It's just called the 'Market.'"

"You know it?"

"Sure. I'm headed close to there. Wanna share a cab?"

"All right." It was about then that Jack noticed the bald limo driver holding a misspelled sign: Jacques Meetford. "Would you hang on," he said to Colleen, walking over to the man. "Hey, pal, that isn't for Jack Mitford, is it?"

"You are heem?"

"I'm Mitford, yeah. M-I-T-F-O-R-D."

"Ah, oui. *C'est ça*. My stupid Franco-Ontarian mistake, non?"

"So, you're here to drive me to the hotel?"

"Shat-Toe Lauree-EH?"

"That's the one." Jack looked back at Colleen. She was a real giraffe's triumph. Her legs were endless, with only minimal water retention in the ankles. "Uh, hold up a sec, would you? What's your name, bud?"

"My name is Marc."

"Give me two minutes, okay, Marc-O?" The carousel was already stopped, and Jack's scuffed leather bag was leaned lonely against the streaked rubber. Colleen was pretending to check her phone messages.

"So," she said, "we ready to go?"

"Listen, seems like that guy over there is here to pick me up."

"Well, well, well, look at chu: high roller, h'eh?"

"Believe me, no. But I'll give you a lift to wherever you want to go. Better than splitting a cab, right?"

"You bet." As it happened, Colleen wanted to go straight back to the hotel with Jack. "And if you're a really good boy," she said to him in the elevator, "I'll let you make panty soup." Canadian hospitality was looking up.

The two trashed the mini-bar and danced the horizontal boogie until sun-up.

Capital Gains

The phone rang several times throughout the morning, but Jack ignored it. When he finally did pick up the buzzer, he was alone in the room.

"Where in the hell you been, boy? You said you'd call when you landed!"

"Clint? What, are you my mother now?"

"You're still sleeping?"

"Um… no, I'm up."

"Hey, get your shit together, buster, it's almost noon! I'm not paying for the privilege of being your alarm clock."

"I know. I apologize. It's just jetlag, you understand."

"Jetlag! It's the same goddamn time zone."

"Yeah. It probably only feels different because of all the clean air."

"How the hell would you know? You haven't even left the fuckin' hotel!" Richter slammed down the phone.

Jack bumbled his way into the bathroom to take an aching piss. Used condoms, like landmines, littered the floor, walls, philodendrons, and overturned chairs. The place looked like a Vegas party pad soaked in grume, with bunched sheets marinating in the bathtub.

A knock was at the door. "No

housekeeping," Jack hollered back. But the knocking continued, persistent with a thumping fist. He stormed to the door, "Christ! I said, no hous—"

"This ain't housekeeping, shitbird!"

"Holy fuck! What's this?" One plainclothes man and three uniformed policemen burst in on the scene. The three skulked, weapons drawn, until they secured the room.

"All clear," each one said, before the man in the suit spoke:

"Where is she?"

"Who?"

"Don't jerk my chain, asshole!" The man stooped, picked the floppy end of a condom up with his pen, and wiggled it for effect. "Where's the chicka?"

"I—I don't know. I mean, we went at it all night, and when I got up she was already gone."

"Gone?" He snapped his fingers, "Just like that?"

"Yeah. Gone."

"You officers can wait outside." The man waited until he was alone with Jack. He was a slouching, middle-management type in a downy soft mustache. Basking in his off-the-rack brief authority, he first flicked the soiled latex snake at the trash (but hit a lampshade instead) and then turned one of the chairs right side up. Jack, meanwhile, quietly lowered himself to the edge of the bed.

"Look, uh...?"

"Inspector Griggs."

"What's this all about?"

"Put a bloody shirt on at least, would ya? I don't wanna have to look at your sicko chest hairs while we chew the fat." Griggs waited for Jack to find his shirt, mentally decocting the clambering mess of the room, before speaking again. "You're in some very serious trouble, Mitford."

"Why? Was there a noise complaint or something? Is it illegal to have sex in hotel rooms in this country?"

"With prostitutes, yes."

"Prost—! Gaah, are you kidding me? Colleen wasn't a prostitute."

"Oh no? You didn't pay her?"

"Of course not! I've never paid for sex in my life!"

"As a matter of fact—and just to clarify—I misspoke a second ago: it is not, in point of fact, *illegal* to pay for intercourse or *coitus in os* in this great country of ours. It is, however, illegal to solicit sexual favors in a public emplacement."

"Great. I'll keep that in mind next time I'm looking for a Canadian hooker down at the local hockey rink."

"This is no joke, Mitford. We have several eye witnesses who are prepared to testify that you propositioned the young woman by the airport baggage claim and offered her fiduciary compensation—"

"The only thing I offered her was a lift. You can ask the driver, uh, what's his nuts. . . that Marco Polo bozo, from the limo company. I have no idea what his real last name is. You'd have to ask them. The perv kept his eyes in the rearview more than on the road, though, I can tell you that much."

"The man's name is Marc Moussier, and he's already corroborated the prostitution claim."

"That no good snake!"

"Calm down, Mr. Mitford."

"No! This is ridiculous!"

"Lower your voice, or I'll be forced to take you downtown."

"Look, I don't know what kind of inbred, back-asswards sort of town you people are running here, but I haven't done one goddamned thing wrong, okay? I met a woman at the airport, we hit it off, and I offered to give her a ride into town. One thing led to another, that's it. I mean we are adults, after all."

"Does this sort of thing happen to you often?"

"What the hell's that supposed to mean?"

"And was this woman with you on the plane?"

"How the fuck should I know? I assume she was, seeing as her luggage was coming off the stinking carousel!"

"Shouting won't help matters, I'm afraid. We're only trying to do what's right."

"Right! Well, you people sure have a screwed up way of showing it."

"You see, the woman in question has been seen, repeatedly, at this hotel escorting both men and women. There is a case pending on a sleazy local madam, Pauline Kale—a real nickel-and-dime gutter slut with delusions of grandeur—and it's believed that your spirochete sexpot from last night is part of the ring. You called her 'Colleen,' but she's used countless aliases, particularly when she moonlights as a stripper and escort at the old folks home. The front desk staff downstairs recognized her immediately when she left the hotel. They called it in."

"*Left* the hotel? So, you knew damn well she wasn't even here when you came barging in? Why bother going through all that breaking down the door shit show, then?"

"Protocol."

"Aw, this is too much!"

"Will you be willing to help us?"

"No. Absolutely not! Like I said: there were no propositions, no money transactions, none of that bullshit, all right? End of story. Now, if there's nothing else, Inspector…" Jack stood up, his bearings gathered, and stepped towards the door. Griggs sighed as he stood, surveying the room one last time.

"That's your wallet?"

"Yeah."

"May I see it?"

"Sure. Be my guest." Griggs began leafing through the billfold with the chewed tips of his fingernails.

"And how much was in here, would you say, approximately?"

"Not that it's really any of your business, but a couple dimes, U$."

"Two grand? Hah, seems you've come up a little short then, Mr. Mitford."

"What? How? Let me see." Griggs handed the wallet to Jack. "This can't be."

"Well, look at it this way: at least she's honest."

"Honest? Honest! How d'you figure?"

"A thief would have taken it all!" Griggs opened the door in a rush. Startled, two of the three officers in the hall took their fingers out of their noses. "And how long will you be staying in our fair capital, Mr. Mitford?"

"Ahm," Jack was still dazed, mentally slowed by having been taken for a sap. "Not sure, yet. No more than a week, maybe?"

"Be advised, we've started a file on you. CSIS—that's our version of the CIA, eh—is now tracking your movements. Additionally, you are also now known by the Royal Canadian Mounted Police—"

"Those are the guys with the shiny red uniforms and pretty horsies, right?"

"We won't hesitate to detain you if you get involved in any further suspicious behavior—

Canadian capias or not, *comprende*? So don't get any fancy ideas. I run faster than your mascara, cupcake—"

"I'll keep that in mind, thanks."

"And if you'll permit a friendly local suggestion?"

"Shoot."

"If you get the chance while you're up here, you should take a drive out to Gatineau Park. T'really is quite splendid this time of year."

"Yeah, I've seen pictures before."

"Oh, so you know—"

"I know it's a dump."

"You Americans are all alike." Griggs twirled his finger and the four flatfoot baboons began to move. "You're absolute filth, Mitford."

As soon as the door closed, Jack grabbed the nearest lamp and threw it against the wall. It shattered in several shards across the bed. He found his cigarettes, sat by the window, and smoked. The puddles of water in the lock system below were a wintry black. Jack just sat there, shaking his head, smoking.

After a while, the smell of perfume on his skin made him ill. He showered, put on some of his wrinkled clothes from a bag, and tidied up a little for the maids. There was a violent need in him to flee the scene, to vomit, and to torch his clothes from last night. As he left, Jack screamed at the empty room: "un-fucking believable!"

Downstairs, all the desk clerks seemed to

be sniggering, but it was probably just Jack's imagination. A fat-lipped bellhop with toothy gums pointed Jack to a pub across the street. The coppertop spires of the provincial parliament buildings and their limp-flag salutes cast the appropriately long shadow of the old British biddy's tiara.

The Cock 'n' Balls, a brummagem drinking hole, was full of ex-pats never actually expatriated from England. The place was a crumbling cenotaph impeccably maintained for the apparatchiks—rabid dogs on a jimmy leg. Jack sat behind two regal rubes discussing reruns of *Masterpiece Theatre*. Both men looked like perfect hang-a-bouts for bus terminal lavatories, especially in their twirled pencil moustaches, the sort well known for quietly gathering bits of boiled sausage and mash.

Jack was too hung over and ego-wounded to do much else than recharge. In the end, he choked down some fries and beer while sifting through Clint's notes; they were written in aphoristic style and didn't make much sense, as expected. But as near as Jack could figure, the documents detailed an elaborate plan on behalf of the US government to fabricate a national Canadian identity through something called "Disidentity." Via various bullying methods—including border intimidation and name-calling tactics that dated back to their humiliating defeat of 1812—America had been psychologically wearing Canadians down into a collective inferiority complex, abraded by centuries of blatant brow-beating.

Clint's intricate apothegmatic analysis of tribe migration, commodity exchange, railway expansion, maple syrup empires, and ski resort destination spots was one colossal, cross-societal monster of data and deductive reasoning. The bottom line seemed to be that Canadians weren't Canadians at all, but were really just clever Americans masquerading as Canadians. The "Canadian" designation was, therefore, to be understood figuratively; or, if you will, more a socio-economic determining factor than a nationalistic one. Thus, on a crudely drawn Stanford-Binet ziggurat scale, the goofy Canuckleheads ranked somewhere between Californian Republicans and the top echelon of the eastern liberal Ivy League intelligentsia.

Clint was well and truly coo-coo, Jack was coming to believe, and completely clueless about the neoteric, twenty-first century world. All the aging jagoff seemed interested in were pieces of a broken, fifty-year-old puzzle. No one really cared about Oswald and Kennedy any more, right? The Internet geeks and WikiLeaks losers had long moved on to Klinton konspiracies, secret Saudi sects, the HAARP (High-frequency Active Auroral Research Project) death ray, TWA Flight 800, inimitable W and his daddy's Middle-East Tea Party Clan, Hollow Earth theories, fluorinated mind control Kool-Aid powder, Pop Tarts, Cheese Whiz, and not to mention the big daddy of them all, namely the Co-World Domination plans set forth by the dastardly duo of Oprah Winfrey & Céline Dion. Who cared if the majority of illegal American activities of the past centuries had been systematically filtered through the Canadians? Big deal.

Richter, besides his extremely helpful deconstruction of North American society, had also provided two local contact names and numbers. Jack found a payphone near the washrooms. He dug around his pockets for change, which Colleen had had the decency to leave him. The telephonic doodad gobbled the quarters without demanding an exchange rate.

"Yeah?" The voice on the other end said, gruff and distant.

"Is, uh, is this Michel Giddioneh?"

"Who's askin'?"

"My name's Mitford. Jack Mitford."

"Is that supposed to mean something?"

"Clint, uh, Richter told me to call."

"He's here?"

"No."

"You in town?"

"Yep."

"So, what, you're making the deals for him now?"

"Look, he just told me to call. Didn't say much else. Are you Giddioneh or not?"

"You free this afternoon?"

"It's why I'm here."

"Be down at Dock 36, four o'clock. You know where that is?"

"No."

"You'll figure it out. Unless you're one of Clint's usual morons."

"Listen, what's all this about? I'm supposed to be doing background research for his book—" The line went dead with a buzz.

Jack tried not to take things personally and dialed the second number. The answering machine belonged to "Louis Riel Provisional Party Supplies." He stammered through a message:

"Uh, hi, yeah. I was looking for an Ernie? Ernie Roberts? Maybe I've got the wrong number? Anyway, if there *is* an Ernie around, could you have him call Jack Mitford back at the Shat-Toe Lauree-EH, it's a hotel. I don't have the number offhand, but my room is 568. Thanks."

Jack finished what was left of his beer, riveted by a hotly contested game of PLR (Professional League of Ringette) blaring on the flat screens. When he paid the waiter, the oily-faced kid said: "Ain't ya got no real money, Mister?"

"What's the matter? Those are legal tender, American greenbacks."

"And? This is Canada."

"I know."

"So, ain't ya got no real money or what?"
"Yeah, *that*."
"All right. Whatever. You Americans are all the same."
"What's that supposed to mean?"
"Never mind. Just bring it up ta the bar, they'll do the con-verg-a-ma-jiggying."

Finding the exact location for the meet with Giddioneh proved especially problematic. Apparently, there were no docks to speak of in this town. The idea of a waterfront city with no dockyards seemed utterly ridiculous, but there it was.

After several cold shoulders and a few one-finger salutes, Jack was finally pointed to the beloved province across the river: Qwee-Beck. He hoped the place would be as quaint and delightful as the nearby tourist traps of the Market, where most stores traded in wooly goods and a northern variant of fudge.

Halfway across the bridge, Jack stopped to read a plaque dedicated to the suicides who'd done the Dutch act in a tall, watery tumble. Next to it, some rancid bum was busily puking his beery guts out over the side. Mercilessly cross-eyed, the man's alco-bile drifted down, swept up in a squall and scattered to the winds before hitting the water. With beer in hand, the charming hobo then belched a few times for punctuation and bummed a couple smokes before Jack trudged on to this undiscovered, distinct country.⁵

The Québécois quadrangle was, quite purely and simply, replete with barrel-sucking lowlife scum for the asking. In the park across from the docks, pedophiles and pederasts shotgunned dragon pipes, while single-mother crack-whores watched their tobacco-chewing pimps pushing illegitimate infant bastards on a swing. These shitsacks were cowards, quislings, and addicts, all.

Down on the docks, the mood was no better. At the end of this penny-ante pier, clinging desperately to the subsidence of the land, a sign was painted with the number thirty-six. Moored next to yachts and pleasure crafts, raggedy ropes reined-in tin rowboats, crumbling launches, and deflated dinghies. All manner of unemployed mariners were here rigged too, fore and aft. No sympathetic soul could fail but be touched by the sorry sight of a sailor stripped of his ship.

Jack let the bull-necked humblebees yammer and yar awhile, then approached. "Ahoy

---

⁵ Arrived in this Brave New *Monde* qalled Québec, the providence and province of poutine, qould you perhaps qomment on the quaint qontext of the surroundings? Why yes, gladly! Although, Mama(n) did used to say "Iff'n you ain't gots nuting good to say then shut yo' big ole mouth"… but she was always too opinionated for her own good. So, back to it:

there," he said, waving a grin.

"You needin' some help there, Kemosabe?" The six or seven sloop soldiers were on Jack before he had the time to move, wafting of ambergris. This floating end of the line looked like the gathering point for all the rust-bucket bruisers and drunken swabs of the area. It wasn't a place to be at night, or now.

"I'm just looking for someone."

"Rephrasing: What the hell d'you want, arsehole?"

"Like I said, I'm looking for a guy—"

"Faggots are back across the water, mac."

"A guy by the name of Giddioneh? Not sure if I'm saying it right."

"How's about this: Fuck off! Is that saying it right?"

"Look, guys, I'm not out for trouble here. I'm just supposed to meet this Giddioneh down at Dock 36."

"That so?"

"Is there another one besides this one?"

"Nope."

"So, I'm in the right place."

"Pal, you're pretty fucking far from being in the right place, understand you foul-mouthed fuck? So why don't you take your preppie little ass and abandon ship before we tie your shrouds and stays with a halyard and make you float."

"Preppie? I've never been called a preppie in my entire life. Listen, don't you guys have anything better to do, some poop decks to spit polish?"

"Either do an about-face this instant, landlubber, or lose the face."

"Take the tough sailor act to Broadway, all right girls?"

Thanks to St. Elmo's fire of fists, Jack took the beating of his life. First, two men held on to him from behind as the crocodile of crusties pounded his stomach and chest in alternating sequence. Once Jack was down on the wooded slats, the group swooped in and laid the chains to his back, ribs, and groin.

Jack coughed blood in his throat, horking it back up into his mouth. The last semi-conscious thing he remembered, before being smashed across the ear with a beer bottle and slammed in the sternum with the bottom of a bat, was spitting a championship glob of bloody saliva into the pugnacious crowd of weathered faces. When Jack finally deliquesced into the drink, floating face down, the men all laughed: one more no-good, city slicker punk slung out to dry as fish bait.

Giddy-Yap

Jack woke up in a dark room. Redolent incense, musk, and birdseed pervaded the air in a fusty effluvium. A glass of water, with dentures soaking, was on the nightstand. Next to the glass was a black and white picture of three midgets in military uniform, purple hearts pinned to their chests. Behind the frame were scented massage oils and a thick, black rubber vibrator. Had he ended up in some geriatric weirdo's sex dungeon? Part of his perineum surely hoped so.

Jack tried to turn over to his side, his other side, but his ribs hurt too much. He tugged at the macramé blankets covering him. Pressure was tight. Running his hands down his sides, he could feel the rough of bandages from his chest to his waist. His family jewels were intact (praise Jesus!), though he seemed to be wearing another man's underwear.

When he looked back around, a red-cheeked woman was standing in the doorway. "You're awake," she said, her other facial features indistinct in the shadows.

"Who the fuck are you?"

"At least you're polite. Oh, shit," she added, rushing to the bedside table to stuff the oils and dildo inside the drawer. "Sorry about those. This is my grandmammy's bedroom and I didn't think you'd be awake yet."

"What?"

"You're probably feeling a little woozy. Don't worry, that's the Demerol talking. It'll see you through this."

"Through what?"

"You kidding? The beating those testosterone monkeys gave you."

"The sailors… right."

"Wet Welfare Warriors is more like it—"

"Who are you?"

"I'm Michèle Giddioneh."

"Giddioneh? I was supposed to meet your father down at the docks."

"I hope not. He drowned trying to swim the Northwest Passage back in 1982."

"Your grandfather, then?"

"Not unless you were meeting him in Davy Jones's locker. His fishing boat went down by the Flemish Cap, way passed the Grand Banks, almost forty years ago. You ever see that piece of shit movie *The Perfect Storm*? They pinched a lot of that from my Grampy's life. Our family has better luck on dry land." Michèle sat on the side of the bed, inches from Jack's elbow. She felt his forehead with the back of her hand. "You were running a bit of a fever, but it's gone now. The sinciput's simmered, as the quacks might say."

"Huh?"

"Never mind. Oh, just so you know, I also

spread some tree salve, Echinacea, and Turtle wax on your johnson and testes t'a ease the swelling. You ain't exactly hung like a donkey so that shit should really work wonders."

"You—you mean, you were the one who, who changed my underwear…?"

"You'd barfed all over your pants and boxers when we fished you out a' the 'Twa River there, it's got that emetic effect on most folks. Anyway, I found a couple old pairs a' tighty-whiteys lying around in my grammie's closet, so I slapped 'em on you. Not like I ain't never seen a man's pisser before."

"Well… thanks, I guess. What about the doctor, did he say anything?"

"Doctor? Buddy, have you ever been to see one a' them retards salaried under universal health care? They can't even take a pulse. A sexist like you would be well advised to stay away from those medicinal ding-a-langs."

"*Sexist?*"

"Hey pal, you were the one who assumed the doctor would be a 'he.' Better learn to use your personal pronouns correctly around here, that's all I'm saying."

"You're right, I'm sorry."

"Nah, I'm really the one who should be sorry. Sorry I was so aggressively late in meeting you. In a way, it's kinda my fault you got yourself whopped."

"Wait, you? But I was meeting a Michel

Giddioneh."

"Yup, that's me: Michèle."

"Michèle?"

"See, you're doing it again. Sexism is a natural instinct in you, huh?"

"Oh, shit, it was Michèle, not Michel! You're a woman, not a man."

"You noticed."

"I got the Giddioneh part right. Right?"

"No one calls me that."

"No?"

"No. Sounds too much like this Frenchie Quebecer expression, *Géguille au nez*."

"What's that mean?"

"Snot nose. Fucken Qweebs."

"Well, sorry."

"Stop saying that, there's a Canadian copyright on it. 'Sides, you're the one got your ass beat, buster. You should have been told to call me Gabby, everybody else does."

"But I could have sworn I talked to a man when I made the meet over the phone."

"Nah, that's Grams for ya, she sounds like a Mack truck. 4-pack a day habit'll do that to you, go figure." Gabby lifted the sheets to look at Jack's bandages and then touched his cheek, lightly. "Man, I don't know what you looked like before, but you sure do look like shit now. Let me go get you some milk."

"Milk?"

"Yeah. We keep a cow in the ungulate

shed. You ain't one of them lactose intolerant motherfuckers, are you?"

"No."

"Good. Cause milk is d'bomb for you." Gabby stood up, and Jack almost bounced off the other side of the bed. "I'll throw a little castor oil and anchovy juice in there to spruce it up and you'll be right as rain."

Jack's body was sending him mixed signals. Did he want to eat or throw up? Piss or shit? Sleep or stay awake? "Um, Gabby…"

"Yeah?"

She paused at the door, enveloped in a Florence Nightingale glow. She was sweet, kind, gentle, caring, and compassionate, Jack could tell. These were inner traits you couldn't fake, which had nothing to do with how pretty Gabby was because, actually, she wasn't that pretty at all: her hair was one tangled, stringy beige mat; her eyes were beady and a bit too close together; she hunched when she stood, clomping around the floor like a clumsy ogre; also, through the thin shirt she was wearing, Jack could make out the droopy-sag silhouette of banana Bs. Shallow, much?

"Well, anyway, thanks a lot for patching me up, Gabby."

"No problemo. But, uh, Jack…?"

"Mn-hm?"

"Now that you're awake and all, you feel well enough to get a move on?"

"A move on, to where?"

"Outta here, for a start. I'll call the cab while I'm up. You see, my Grams is busy watching her night soaps right now, but she won't last forever you know?" Gabby tipped back an imaginary bottle with her hands. "You understand?"

"Mmn, I... yeah. I mean, if you need me to go, I can... I can go."

"You do have a place to stay, right?"

"Um, yeah. The... the Westin, downtown." Jack wasn't sure why he lied to her about the hotel. Thoughts?

"Holy smokes, that swank joint is ten times better'n this shithole. Clint don't skimp, does he?"

"Yeah. Speaking of which, why was it he wanted us to meet in the first place—?"

"Don't worry about that right now. You need to get better. We can talk about it some other time—"

"Well, I really wouldn't mind talking about it now—"

"And I'd really like to go call that cab instead. Is ten minutes enough time for you to get your shit together?"

"Fine."

"Oh and—before I forget—those sailors lifted all the do-re-mi from your wallet while you were floating face down in the waves."

"What, that was almost a grand!"

"Don't worry, I wormed a honeybone of Canuck coinage out of the old boot to see you through this dark pass. Hope it'll do."

"Okay. Thanks, again."

"I'll be right back with that moo juice. Hope Homo 3% is okay?"

"Ah…?"

"South a' the border you guys call it whole milk—on account of your rampant silent-majority homophobia, I'd guess. When, I'd say, skim's really the drink of queers."

"Are we still talking about milk?"

"Ontologically? No…"

Agents of Influence

Back at the hotel, Jack barely made it from the cab to the lobby to the elevator without passing out. Gabby's milk concoction and pastille prescription were all that were keeping Jack afloat. Luckily, he survived the trip up to his room, which was once again immaculate. Everything was in its place, as before. Even the lamp had been glued back together. Except for a change of towels and sheets, the only new addition to the suite was a love note from management slipped under his door:

Lamp Labour[6]	*$ 1,136*
De-smokefying of linens[7]	*$ 4,350*
Full Mini-Bar Re-stock[8]	*$ 429*

Total Charges:
$ 5,915

---

[6] Notice the arrogant Commonwealth "u"
[7] ?
[8] Fair enough.

Jack grabbed his lighter and set the itemized invoice ablaze. Off the flame, he tremblingly lit a cigarette. He was hoping to play it cool, to make it to the bathroom in time to drop the flaming sheet into the tub, but he was way too beaten and buzzed for that. So, of course, the thing burned too fast and nipped at his fingers. The paper immediately scorched the carpet before Jack managed to stomp it out in one crisp, bubbled mess of black fibers. The burnt blob looked like the skin of his face, already going purple.

Turning to the only true remedy of all lost souls, Jack washed away part of his pain with whiskey. He slammed back half a dozen mini bottles along with a minor handful of horse pills. Despite her arrant inhospitality, Gabby had at least been kind enough to give up her vial of Demerol—as if those fifty or so Category C capsules could justify the beating he'd taken for her lack of punctuality. Why were they even meeting in the first place?

Once safely in bed, Jack slept for the next twenty-six hours straight. When he finally awoke with a start, drool crusted the sides of his mouth. The message light was blinking on the phone. Thanks to an almost superhuman effort, he hobbled to the toilet. There, he stripped down in a grotesque pantomime, slowly. His once piercing cobalt eyes were going a dulled gray. Examining the worst of his exposed wounds, he turtled his face back and forth at the mirror. He was a mess.

He was a visual disaster. He was a puffed, spotted owl.

Jack eased himself carefully to the throne. There was a significant amount of blood in his urine, which turned the bowl a watery pink. He pulled off the tape that had been wrapped around his body, exposing several more blueberry blotches across his chest and abdomen. He crept into the tub, turned on the faucet and showered under a lukewarm spray, crouched in the fetal position. After re-taping his chest with a roll of hockey tape Gabby had also been kind enough (though reluctant) to give him, Jack sat naked by the window and smoked two cigarettes, one off the other, staring at the bleak night outside.

He was weak, and utterly defeated. Although he wanted to eat something, the very thought made him dry heave in esurient gasps. So instead, he crawled back to bed and checked the messages on the phone. There were six or seven hang-ups (probably from Clint), though the last was a callback to Jack's message from a few nights before. The instructions were to meet this Ernie character for lunch the following day at a clinic not far from the Parliament buildings. He wrote down the information, took a few more Demo-lozenges, and promptly passed out again.

In the morning, Jack felt better but looked worse. There was only a trickle of blood in his piss and stool, and at least his energy to hobble around had returned. He called room service and had them send up the hotel's signature Deluxe Breakfast for one ($CAN 216). It looked like a mash of green, orange, and straw-colored hog vomit, but he choked the victuals down anyway.

On his way outside, Jack stopped in to the lobby gift shop to see a man about a cane. The store only had a few models, predictable souvenir jobs littered in cutesy beaver cartoons and maple-leaf designs. The canes and crutches were all supposedly made from some space-aged material and, consequently, cost just shy of a thousand apiece—that's dollars. Jack settled on a moose motif, which he had billed to his room, leaning heavily on the carbon-graphite stick as he shambled through the late-morning air.

The lunchtime meeting spot was in the cafeteria of the Brookings Institute, a long-term pet-care facility and insane asylum for human borderline schizophrenics and manic-depressives—or so said the ground floor sign. One thing's for sure, its lunchroom prices were a steal, and Jack finished a pint of porter before the scheduled chinwag. The beer almost managed to help him forget about the excruciating pain pulsing through his veins.

"Excuse me, are you Jack Mitford?" The man stood straight as a stalk, the stiff weed that grows through a crack of pavement.

"Yeah, I'm Mitford. You're Ernie Roberts?"

"Ernesto Robertson, DVM, at your

service." Robertson was a leggy, toothy, bald-headed hippo, with remnant ginger tufts of 'fro creeping out at the side of his ears. Perspiration stained rings around his collar. "But most people juz' call me Ern-Dawg."

"I'm sorry, for some reason I thought your name was Roberts. Clint must have abbreviated."

"Either or, doesn't matter."

"Here, have a seat." Jack didn't even attempt to stand as he motioned to the high stool in front of him. They ordered from the waiter, who clearly recognized Ernesto and took his "usual" in stride.

"Don't take this the wrong way, Jack, but you look like a real pile of shinola."

"I know."

"What happened?"

"I had a little run-in down by the docks the other day."

"In Hull? Stay away from there, man. It's hard to keep up with identity politics at the best of times, but those French pukes are bad news."

"You mean you're not…?"

"A Canook? Hell no, bro. La Jolla, born and raised! I'm a California kid through and through. My old man was Dean of Arts at UC San Diego in the sixties."

"You're a long way from home."

"Not by choice, believe me."

"What does that make you then?"

"Another casualty of the Conscientious

Objector Movement Exodus, COME. Who knew the acronym would get us in so much trouble? I missed Woodstock, man." The waiter arrived with their drinks. Robertson's "usual" was a Pink Lady in a pint glass, with double egg whites.

"So, Ernesto…"

"Hmm?"

It suddenly occurred to Jack, at that very moment, he really had no clue what he wanted to say. Clint's notes hadn't prepared him in the least. So, Jack's mouth just made words: "You, ah, you say you work for the DMV?"

"No, man. I'm a DVM, means Doctor of Veterinary Medicine."

"Oh, a vet?"

"I specialize in canine surgeries."

"But the phone number I called was for party supplies, wasn't it?"

"It's a cover, just in case."

"In case? In case of *what*?"

"Believe me, Jack, you can't be too careful with these INS and Homeland Security moles nowadays; they're everywhere. Some rogue operatives are still punishing people for missing out on the last few wars and so-called police actions."

Such territory seemed like quicksand, best avoided. "I, um… I heard that veterinary college is twice as hard to get into as med. school. Is that true?"

"Yeah, but I was pretty lucky, got

recruited under the Continuum Program out of Drama City—"

"*Continuum Program*? Never heard of it."

"Why would you? It isn't the type of shit that makes the six o'clock news. Landslide Lyndon and his goons first funded the development project, building on the CIA's MKULTRA babystep experiments in the '50s and the Army's piggyback mind-control efforts with *Operation 3rd Chance*. Later, the tricky Dickwad administration took over the various 'politically correct' projects to test the resiliency of inner-city minorities—spics, spooks, and chinks, mostly. They just kept upping the ante on the poor bastards, from coke to heroin to speedballs, crystal meth, and God knows what else."

"Jeezus," Jack said, taking a swig of his cocktail as he studied Robertson's face.

"But it was a whole other ballgame when I was there. That's actually where I first met Clint, at the Program. He was one of the administrators, before he started testing himself. In those early days, we were paid $4500 for two years."

"For what?"

"For being continuously locked-up in a room, staring at a light. We're talking holed up with a mega-stash of LSD-25a, legal lysergic—stronger than any of that blotter Bear was making for the Muir Beach and Watts Acid Tests or the shit the rest of those SanFranFeaks like Kesey were munching down on at Stanford. First, you climb high that marijuana mountain, then pop! Down the rabbit hole to see juz' how far it flows."

"Sounds awful."

"Awful? You kidding? It was great! We'd just sit around all day: food, booze, and dope pumped into us, intravenous style. We got to skip out on the whole Vietnam thing, which I heard was a total drag."

"That was it, you all just sat around stoned immaculate?"

"Pretty much, yup. I mean there were the occasional shock treatments, but we were usually too out of it to care. My two years turned into ten, almost a solid decade in the wind. I didn't really come down from that mega-trip—fully, I mean—much before Christmas of '75."

"That long!"

"Scared me shitless, let me tell ya, especially when I realized I wasn't even living in the States any more. Someone at the border burned my passport. I was exiled up here—a defenseless, demented defector—just like they did to that perverted apostate, Benedict 'Huevos' Arnold."

"Why'd they do that to you?"

"Beats me. Didn't want me talking, I guess. Craziest part was waking up like that, all of a sudden, realizing you've been working, eating, breathing, and defecating but(t) you've got no real memory of anything, you know?"

"I'm sorry, what are you saying?"

"I'm saying, like, I had a wife, two cars, a house—the full deal. Turns out I'd even pioneered surgical procedures, was a regular keynote speaker at international conferences, had an honorary doctorate from Pembroke College, Cambridge. Heck, I'd even been knighted by the Queen."

"No shit?"

"No shit! By the mid '80s I already had more money than I could spend in about three lifetimes, mostly thanks to the cross border tax-break initiatives of the Reagan-Mulroney junta. Far out, huh? The only thing I can say for sure, and what I'd tell my own kids if I had any, is: If you're willing to give up a part of yourself, drugs can have a really positive effect. I say go for it!"

"Oh that reminds me," Jack said, reaching slowly into his pocket. The beer was doing an adequate job of dulling his extremities, but the numbing notch could stand some tweaking. He popped one of the pills from Gabby's vial.

"Hey, lemme see those. What's that, Demerol? That shit's weak, Jack, *passé*."

"It's all I got."

"Here, let me." Ernesto grabbed a prescription pad from his inside jacket pocket. It was a lab coat of sorts, though it looked like it also doubled as a straightjacket. "Being a vet should have some human benefits, too, right?"

"You're allowed to prescribe medication?"

"Not entirely, no. But don't worry." The good (doggie) doctor scribbled on five sets of sheets. "Here, this should keep you going for a while. Sorry, I wish I could prescribe something useful, like Desbutal, but the stupid bureaucratic bastards won't let the boluses be produced anymore—"

"Ern-Dawg this is for like, 1,500 pills—!"

"Yeah, is that enough? Whatever you do, Jack, don't cash them in all at once. Idiot pharmacists get jumpy when you do that, sets their tiny brains a reeling, so I've postdated them to last."

"What are. . . Nembutal and Sagatal?"

"They're both good all-arounders as far as tranquilizers go—pentobarbital. You know, yellow submarines to spirit you away to the Valley of the Dolls. We mostly use the stuff to knockout the pets for surgery and shit like that. But the buzz is actually pretty decent. Think of it as sleepwalking through a lucent fog."

"Will these prescriptions work back home?"

"You betcha. That's courtesy of a dandy little loophole in the FDA's GRASE policy, which, of course, is: Generally Regarded As Safe and Effective…"

"Huh, thanks."

"No sweat. And what the hay, I'll write

you out some scrip for Adderall, too, which is one a' the best psychostimulants around. Beats coke and meth hands down, and it's a good change from the tranks and downers. But if anyone should ask, just tell 'em it's for—oh, I don't know—some recurring back injury, narcolepsy, or foot cramps."

"I took a tumble into the dugout at Shea Stadium, after catching a foul ball, back in the day."

"Perfect, use that." Ernesto thought about ordering another round and then changed his mind. "Look, Jack, I should probably be getting back to the office. I have a triple bypass on a Lhasa Apso this afternoon."

"I understand."

"But listen, I guess we ought'a get to the reason Clint brought us together."

"Well I hope you've got a better idea than I do, 'cause I have absolutely no clue."

"As is often the way with our Mr. Richter, it seems. Here," Ernesto slid over an ID badge with Jack's picture digitally scanned above the word VISITOR. The name underneath was Stanford Marwicke. "That'll get you into the building. Don't bring any other identification, just that. This is the address here. It's a US Consulate Auxiliary warehouse, across from the Embassy coat-check building. Low-level clearance."

"But I'll still be needing a fake badge?"

"You'll be meeting a man by the name of

Montell Rabinowitz, codename: *Bojangles*. He's a real song-and-dance man, this kid. They're grooming him to be Head of Counter Intelligence someday, so be on your toes. They have him on the nightshift tonight and he's expecting you. Rabinowitz is good shit. He's New School but with Old School values, a real down-home, well-connected, jovial mensch—one righteous dude, you might say. He'll show you around to whatever you want to see: the sets, the production estimates, and all the rest a' that sort of business. And don't forget to ask him about the cartoons, that was always my favorite part of the scene."

"I'm not sure I'm really following you here."

"Don't worry, Monty'll take care of you. You should probably show about nine o'clock. I know he starts his shift at eight, but he's useless before six or seven cups of coffee. So, I'd wait until then, if I were you."

"Look, I'm—"

"You'll be fine, Jack, don't worry. Nobody cares about this kind a' jazz nowadays, not even the military. We're just doing this thing for show, okay? Covert Ops for the clowns—call it a fun furlough for the freaks. Just have a look around, take a few notes, and humor Richter on this scheme to publish his memoirs. We both know it's a poor excuse to expose some governmental dirty laundry that doesn't even need to be washed anymore. So who cares?"

"Yeah. I guess." Robertson excused himself, saying he was going to take care of the bill, and never came back. It seemed like the natural way to part.

Auntie Mask/Key/Rove/(S)ka
{Маскировка}

  Jack took a six-hour nap before his meet with Rabinowitz. The slight booze rush was gone after his afternoon snooze, the lingering effects of the Demerol still barely twinkling. Constipated and cranky, Jack popped two more pain pills as he struggled to leave. The last thing he wanted was to go out. He wanted to be at home, in his empty, filthy New York apartment, sleeping for a week.

  Instead, he preemptively ditched his moose-meat cane and everything in his pockets—just as Robertson had advised—and was out the door in a halting dodder. The evening air was fresh, and alive. Pharmabuzz regained, Jack hobbled along the sidewalk to the nearby Consulate Auxiliary with a moronic grin and club-footed lurch.

  Inside the unassuming building, Jack underwent the usual security manhandling. Three green lasers crisscrossed his torso, while he was conveyored through the full-body metal detector of the lobby atrium. Eventually, he was spit out at the far edge of the reception area where—behind the oblong, large, and metallic surveillance desk—beamed an intricate mural.[9] For the first

---

[9] A truly magnificent work of art: two bald

time in days, Jack felt calm.

A polished turd sat behind the desk, stains of mustard blotched along the front of his rent-a-cop uniform. He had a shiny badge on his chest, reflecting the fast food jowls of his microcephalic face. The man was absolute sheriff of his domain.

"Whassup," Jack started, in a pleasing tone.

"What can I do for you?"

"I wouldn't say no to a backrub—"

"What?"

"Or a mineral water, come to that. You guys got any Ramlösa?"

"Is that some kind a' foreign joke?"

"No, not exactly—"

The man's menacing meathook inched toward his taser. "State yer been-uz!"

"Uh, well, sir. I'm—I'm actually meeting Montell Rabinowitz."

"He's expecting you?"

"That's right."

---

eagles, wings fully spread, held up Ole Glory in their beaks as they soared high above the plains of the Allegheny Mountains (you knew they were the Alleghenies because the fresco said so in unique uncial forms, inserting the additional cursives of West Virginia, Maryland, Virginia, and Pennsylvania underneath, just in case the visual clues hadn't been enough for the pictorial illiterates).

"You sure?"

"As sure as that quantum kraut Heisenberg was uncertain, yeah."

"Say what?"

"Yes, he's expecting me."

"No one told me about this! Hang on." The lard got on the phone, patting his blond crewtop back in short, soft strokes. His voice was the croak of a warty toad: "Uh-huh, this is Dookowski down at the desk. There's a, umm…" He snapped his fingers to see Jack's ID badge. "A… Mr. Marwicke here to see you, sir. Says you're expecting him? ... A huh… okay … will do. Absolutely! Yes, sir." The guard hung up, changing tones: "If you'll be kind enough to have a seat, sir, Mr. Rabinowitz will be out shortly."

The waiting area table was littered with *Body Builder, Eschatology Today!* and *Good Housekeeping* magazines. Jack began absentmindedly leafing, eventually catching his eye on an intriguing article—"Flower Power"—about the benefits of Azalea spores on the skin. The wait was interminably short.

"Mr. Marwicke?" The man was black, African American if you will, which Jack hadn't expected.

"Uh, yeah?"

"My name's Rabinowitz." Here he was, codename *Bojangles*, in the flesh. He wore one of those beige turtlenecks once so popular with suave and sexy college campus agitators, and smelled vaguely hypoallergenic; he was synecdochic of the environs. Rabinowitz smiled a wide set of crooked, ochre teeth, and politely added: "If you'll please be kind enough to follow me."

"Sure." Jack stood, the two shook hands, and together they walked down the marble hallway. Along the way, Rabinowitz pulled an antiseptic flask from his breast pocket, slobbered some of the clear liquid into his palms, and rubbed them furiously with a pink chiffon handkerchief.

"Please, Mr. Marwicke, you mustn't take my hygiene habits personally. I'm afraid I suffer from Mysophobia—"

"Sorry to hear that. What is it?"

"In my case, a fear of germs from shaking hands."

"That's a bummer, especially in your profession."

"Not at all, we get so few visitors here. As a matter of fact, it's an especial treat to have you here tonight."

"Gee, thanks."

"To tell you the truth, my phobia is a lot more common than most people know. Abraham Lincoln had it, for example, as did Gertrude Stein, Josephine Baker, 'Sloba' Milosevic, King James, Rimbaud, Keats, Wittgenstein, Ceausescu, André the Giant, Errol Flynn, Amelia Earhart, and Shakespeare." Bojangles stopped in front of an open elevator shaft, protected only by a waist-level wooden barricade and a silver screen. "Are you pressed for time, Mr. Marwicke?"

"Nope."

"Good. We'll go to the break room first. You like coffee?"

"Who doesn't?"

"Idiots and Commies." The elevator arrived. It was an old service style model, the open-air kind. According to the panel, there were eight levels: two stories above ground, the rest below. Rabinowitz pressed a button for the top floor. It hardly seemed worth the effort. "I'm sorry, Mr. Marwicke. I know it hardly seems worth the effort for a measly two flights, but I didn't want to exacerbate your injury. You seem to be limping and your face… a recent accident?"

"I bumped into a lamppost."

"It happens."

"Then I fell down five flights of stairs."

"Ouch."

The break room had a small microwave, a kettle, a mini fridge, a four-slice toaster, a coffee maker, and some shelves for cups, bowls, plates, and cutlery. Over the sink, a ruffled wall hanging beamed a grotesque reordering of the Uncle Sam brand. The demonic, 1970s blaxploitation Bozo clown cartoon was frozen in a fiddle with his hair: 'Yez, Y'all, I Sho iz PairNOID, but U be pa-ra-noid eeeenuffff?'

Below the poster, condiments and bread

were strewn across the compact counter. It was thoroughly unexciting. The window, however, overlooked the street and had a good view of the Parliament buildings.

"Good view," Jack said, looking out.

"Yes. Have you been in there to visit yet?"

"No, I'm not much for government."

"Then you've come to the right place. We try to keep a low profile here, which I'm sure you can appreciate, but we can't help but have some contact with the RedTape Gang. MI5, 6, 7, and 8 have buildings a few blocks away—the Brits still pretty much run the show in this candy-ass burg." Rabinowitz poured two cups out. "Milk and sugar?"

"Do you have any cream?"

"No, sorry. Against federal administration policy—"

"Excuse me?"

"A recent bill passed by the dirty Demos in the House and Senate, don't you follow C-SPAN? Anyway, we're no longer allowed—legally—to contribute to on-site weight gain, diabetes, or early onset morbid obesity. As a matter of fact, I don't even have *real* milk to offer you. It's something call 'SimuMoo.' Totally fat free, it says."

"Thanks, I'll pass."

"Wise choice." Rabinowitz gave Jack his mug, stenciled with *I'm kind'uv a BIG deal*

Around Here on its side.

They both sat at the small, round baize table, drinking coffee. They watched the cars going by and the night tourists wandering. Jack wasn't sure if he should initiate the conversation or not. It took him a few minutes to decide. After half a cup, he started.

"So, Bo… uh, I mean Mr. Rabinowitz—"

"Please, call me Monty."

"Sorry. *Monty*…" Jack took another quick sip and laced his hands together on the tabletop. "I'll be completely upfront with you, Monty: I have absolutely no idea what I'm doing here."

"Oh! I was under the impression that you wanted a tour?"

"A tour of what… exactly?"

"Of the 'Store.' Though some of the diehards—like Clint—still call this place the 'Hangar.' Force of habit, I suppose."

"You know Clint, then?"

"Of course. He and my father first met here, back in the late '60s. That was the time of the last hurrah of our magnificent *männerbund*—or band of brothers, if you will. Pappah was one of the first 'Negroes' to be let in on the Top Secret scoop, way before anyone in the oligarchy knew what Afro-Americans were. 'Prolly goes all the way back to our family ties to Henry O. Flipper, and West Point. Pops is one of the Joint Chiefs now. It's kind of a muscled narcissus, but his contacts helped me get the posting."

"So, what, this is a military installation?"

"No, no, no. That's way too linear in thinking. This here is a multi-plane, multi-task, multi-purpose facility, really."

"Sounds like a whole lot of multi going on."

"Nothing like it once was. Just imagine: at one time, especially under Ike, this entire building was buzzing top to bottom: secretaries, assistants, secretaries' secretaries, assistant-assistants to the secretaries, deputies, acting assistants, adjutants, acting-adjutants'-assistants, file clerks, and sanctioned sanitary engineers; and that was only the non-commissioned staff. Then, you had all those power domes pounding out the prop. It's kind of a trip when you stop to think about it. Hell, back then, sixteen floors fired on all cylinders: a ruinous ken of glyphs, disasters, and misinterpreted kerflooey."

"Wait, I thought I only saw buttons for eight floors in the elevator."

"You did."

"I don't get it. How many actual levels are there?"

"Who's to say? That's part of the charm of this place, its versioning of the truth. You say 'po-ta-to,' I say Fourth of July."

"So, the 'Store' here is a kind of covert propaganda plant?"

"*Was*. Yeah, you could say. This dates back to when the compound was under the aegis of the DOSS, Department of Secret Stuff. Things really started moving on a massive scale when Igor Gouzenko defected from the Soviet embassy here in September '45. You remember those histrionics?"

"Hey, man, I may be older than you, but that was waaay before my time."

"Sure, sure. Obviously. I was speaking in colorful historicist fashion. We're not generally recognized for our mordant wit here. Anyway, no, that kind of slip-up—which, of course, led to the Klaus Fuchs debacle in Scotland and the Ethel and Julius Rosenberg trial—enabled this place to come into its own with gusto. We became *the* prop-a-gaga place after that, the do-it-yourself studio extraordinaire for the catachresis cats and spin doctors of the governmental subversive set: manufactured product, with easily manufactured consent as result. Refill?"

"Sure, thanks." Bojangles took the pitcher of java and filled both cups back to the brim. "Listen, Monty, am I all right to speak freely in here?"

"What do you mean?"

"You know, what with all that security equip downstairs, laser scans, and the—"

"Ah right, the lightshow? Don't sweat that, it's all just smoke and mirrors. We got that thing on super-discount from Pink Floyd after the *Momentary Lapse of Reason* tour in 1987, it's been here forever. And that other gizmo, the one that looks like a metal detector, is just a fancy change counting machine. We have those to wow the bigwigs, if any ever stop in—which they don't."

"What about the guard?"

"Dookie? Forget about that twit. First of all, he's got Asperger's and has absolutely no clue what it is we do here, actually. At best he thinks this is a top-secret lab for military-grade inflatable underpants and the like, which we've dubbed The Anathematic Anti-Doomsday Cult HQ for the World Police."

"Oh—kay, but what about the…" Jack shifted his eyes from side to side, rounding them with intent. "You know…?"

"What, bugs?" Rabinowitz burst out laughing. "Are you kidding? This department is so low on the totem pole now that it can't even afford eco-watt light bulbs. You're way too paranoid, man."

"D'you blame me?"

"Not at all. Like I said, that's part of the charm of this place, Jack."

"Sh—should you be calling me that?"

"It is your name, isn't it?"

"Yeah, but, what about my Marwicke cover? The ID badge?"

"They're a dime a dozen those things. I even make 'em for my puggle, *Miss Charlotte Gainsbourg*, when I'm bored. You just need a home scanner and crayons."

"Why all the cloak and dagger then, if it's such a big joke?"

"Because the surface shit is what tickles everybody's nut. That's the American wet dream right there. Relax, Jack, you take things too seriously. You'll grow old fast doing that."

"To tell you the truth—"

"Oh, don't do that—"

"A ciggy would really calm me down. Don't suppose I can smoke in here?"

"Now, sadly, those are about the only thing in this whole damn compound that do still work: smoke detectors. They're ultra-sensitive, top-of-the-line, EK-570 alarm models linked straight in to a Black Ops kill-unit on 24-hr stand-by. The second one of those babies is triggered, the team is deployed throughout this building in under three minutes flat. They're ordered to drop any smoking target on site, by any means necessary. It's quite impressive, as a matter of fact. I've seen them perform drills."

"Is that right?"

"At least you can be comforted by the knowledge that half the taxes collected from sold cigarettes in the US are going to the right place. Namely, the military militating or preventing, if you prefer, people from actually smoking the cancer sticks—disgusting habit anyway."

"You said *half* the taxes, where's the other fifty percent going?"

"The Reservations. The government's

funding the contraband trade of US smokes across the line into Canada—BC and the Alberta Tar Sands mostly. It's quite an ingenious scheme, in its way. Another gout of coffee?"

"No thanks."

"Suit yourself." Rabinowitz poured out the rest of the coffee into his mug.

"Well, Monty, this place isn't at all what I expected. Neither are you."

"How so?"

"Your name for one."

"You were expecting a pale, pencil-pushing Semite?"

"Something like that."

"Sammy Davis doesn't have exclusive rights on being a moolie Jew, you know? He *did* have that whole Cyclops thing going for him, though."

"Mm, yeah." Jack took a long sip of his coffee, hoping to climb into the cup.

"Lighten up, Jack. That was a joke! Race and religion are ripe for a roast, man, it's our very *raison d'être* here."

"Sure. Absolutely."

"All right, you about ready for that tour of the compound now?"

"Yeah." Jack propped himself up using the back of an empty chair. He hobbled over to the counter and rinsed his cup out with water. He wondered about leaving traces of DNA on the rim.

"You're sure your legs'll hold up?"

"I didn't think it was a good idea to bring my cane along—because of metal detectors and everything—but I popped two Demerol earlier, so I should be fine."

"Serious? Share the wealth, brother."

"You want?"

"Hells yeah." Jack reached into his breast pocket and handed over a pair of pills. They were warm and sticky wet.

Rabinowitz crushed the pills on the back of his hand, making two small mounds of powder. Snorting one into each nose hole, his face came up lit. A crust of white crested the edge of his nostrils. "I suffer from mild Unipolar Dysphoria, and when I forget my Parnate plus lithium kicker, 'drines really do the trick."

"You, ah, you have a little bit of—" Jack motioned his fingers under his nose.

"Mn, right." Rabinowitz rubbed off the white, smearing the excess across his front teeth. "Man, I really dig the way these things interact with caffeine. Don't you? C'mon, let's roll."

They stood, side by side again, waiting for the elevator. Jack still couldn't decide what kind of situation he'd been roped into. Clint had specifically advised him *not* to bring a pen and paper, a Dictaphone, or any other kind of recording device. Let's face it, nothing had made much sense since Jude's party, but Jack didn't want to look a gift horse in the mouth, which was his usual M.O. Still, now was as good a time as any to find out what might, in fact, be going on:

"So, Monty, I'm not sure if this is totally germane to the present context or not, but: what is it that goes on here, then… primarily?"

"Nothing really, like I said. Our building stands like a brick-and-mortar threnody to triumphant might; it's sad, but our heyday's done. The Web destroyed everything tactile, everything real that needed to be built to make a fake, investing instead in the interstitial intersections and anti-aliquots—meaning, in other words, nothing fits any more. The fucking geeks made the Credibility Gap obsolescent, man, they ruined the true Misdirection."

"You think?"

"Oh, I *know*…" Rabinowitz abruptly grabbed hold of the protective wood barrier and started shaking the cage furiously. His pupils exploded and his face was popping out to burst. "Whhhooooa, holy moley!!"

"What! What is it?"

"These Demmys are really kicking in, Jack! Whooo-hooo! I feel amazing. Thank the Lord for the FDfuckin'A! Pharmies, man, nothing like 'em!" The elevator appeared and they got in. Monty pressed the bottom button. The low whir of the movement seemed to calm him to store-bought normalcy again, his pupils readjusting. "Let's start in the first basement and work our way up."

"Okay."

"What were you saying before, Jack? Sorry, I totally zoned out there for a sec."

"Well, I was wondering about the whole Misdirection angle you were suggesting; or, 'Disinformation' as I know some people call it. I mean to me—and maybe you can explain this—I don't understand why the US would've bothered to base any of its operations, TOP SECRET or otherwise, out of Canada."

"Why? Boredom, I think, was the main reason. Have you seen how much farmland these fartknockers have up here? It's a jawstomping good time for the know-nothings in the know, you know? Not to mention the fact that it's been impossible to contain our obstreperous spread ever since we became world class Imperialists, during the SpAm War. Those Baroque backyard shenanigans and maneuvered monkeyshines set a precedent, you see, for us and the whole of the twentieth century."

"What's that?"

"Arrogating ourselves worldwide—when it suits us, of course—and rewriting the fastidious folderol we don't like. That sorta gravid stuff takes time, effort, and commitment, *compadre*, and it's a way of life. For example, did you know that the slavery trade was ended because of a bet?"

"What?"

"Sure, Sir Ogden Carls and Lord Philips-

Taylor, two inbred English yutzes with too much money and influence. Check it out in places like *The New Yorker* and the *Utne Reader*, it's right there between the lines. But, that's beside the point I'm making. Fact is: we didn't come up with the game, that's been around since the salad days of Moses and that Roman dude, Tacitus. We only perfected the playing field, sandwiched in the middle of poor *pobrecito* Juan Montezuma and Jean-Guy Crybaby. That's what North American power politics are about. It's one super-size Neapolitan ice cream ball of self-perpetuating outrage feeding on itself, fueled by invisible disgust. She's as American as rhubarb pie."

"But it doesn't really make much sense."

"*It don't make sense*? It makes perfect sense, man! Who's looking to Key-Yan-A-D'uh for the pulse of the world, huh? *Dis*-information, as all those conspiracy cowards are so fond of calling it, is right up their noses but those dipseedoodles are too busy looking in the wrong places, you dig? The blockheads are knee-deep in dust and cowshit down in Roswell and Area 51 looking for flying saucers and MJ-12 documented proof. Well, good for them! Meanwhile, in the last two years, there's been something like 17 Foo Fighter landings in Grass River Provincial Park alone. Know where that is?"

"No."

"Exactly. You think these alien dingbats

are dumb enough to land in Midtown Manhattan, calling attention to themselves like that? Central Park! C'mon, they're supposed to be smarter than us, ain't they?"

"Guess I never really thought of it that way."

"You an' every other braying jackass in the conterminous 48."

"So this is the kind of stuff you monitor?"

"Are you out of your mind? Hell no. UFOs? That's MIB, Men in Black territory. It's FBI, CIA, NSA type stuff, and a couple other acronym departments I'm not supposed to talk about—security matter filed under X in the pages of Project Bluebook."

"Oh, like the show."

"Yes. No. Kind of. Anyway, me, I'm more like a janitor, a Ganymede to the gods of the executive branch, keeping the dust off the really important silverware." The elevator sputtered to a stop, slamming down on the lower floor. Everything was dark, and more than a little dank. "Welcome to our museum, mind the gap…"

Rabinowitz lifted up the protective barricade and walked out into the black. He flicked a series of switches, and with low-level whooshing buzz light corridors came on one by one by one across the vast ceiling. It was a cold, concrete slab of wide-open nothingness that went on for miles.

"What is this place?"

"It's a bunker-style cryogenic lab for every President since Lincoln, and for all the Secretaries of State since the Harding era. They keep the Vice Prez gang in a shack down the street, along with the diplomatic spittoons of piss. How's that for wrinkled flesh? On top of that, this place here also sort a' doubles as a Fallout Shelter. Nifty, huh?"

"Gee-sus."

"It used to be an autopsy lab for outer-space foreigners and a testing ground for adaptive autonomic technology, too, but that unit was moved out to Prince Edward Island—into the Anne of Green Gables House—once the kooks calmed down. That is one thing the Internet helped a lot with, actually, I'll give the techno-nerds that much. The eggheads have disseminated the facts into such a dense intertextual weave that no one knows what to believe any more, everybody's become wickedly inured. That's good for us. This is the true Golden Age for the quidnuncs and acute paranoids."

"Shit, Monty, is all this true?"

"'Course not, none of it is. Not a word." He sort of bellow laughed, inwardly. It was an endearing turn. "'Ask stupid, paranoiac questions and ye shall be repaid in kind'—as the good book says."

"The Bible?"

"No, the Operations Training Facility Manual, Five-Four-Seven Dash 8. Required reading by the Strata before getting the posting up here."

They stood dwarfed by the void. The capacious room could easily have fit seven football fields, Canadian size. Jack felt like yelling out, or farting, if only to hear the deep reverb of echo. Instead, he said: "So, if you've just been jerking my chain this whole time, what is this place really about?"

"Like I told you, Jack, not that much nowadays: vacuum cleaner sucks up budgie! Quiddity, that's what you're after right? But, not to split hairs, the essence of a thing is near impossible to define. What d'you think cats like Hegel, Kant, Feuerbach, Husserl, Gadamer, Heidegger, Schopenhauer, and—what the heck, let's go crazy and throw a Frenchie in there—J.P. Sartre have been up to all this time? True truth ain't for the faint of heart, man."

"I get that, sure. How 'bout a dumbed down overview then?"

"Well, the next three floors up are all identical: Epic, empty spaces. We've become a charnel house, declassified. The goods are being dismantled, down to the last tangible object—no use for the practical in the military now, too much evidence. So, anything left with any value or significance is being crammed into the two floors directly below street level. Those other eight floors I mentioned earlier never really existed here, and certainly not officially."

"Wait a second. You're saying this—everything—is just what it looks like? A humongous empty room?"

"Uh-huh. Gotta appreciate the simple elegance of that, right?"

In fact, Jack couldn't; at least, not inherently. He too wanted more, or wanted to know that at the very least there *was* more, even if he would never know what that more was. He could sense, as if emotively, the huge, chaotic, and convolved whilom threads of the conspiratorial ball of twine—humungoid in scope; not surprisingly, what he wanted most was to tug at its dangling, disorderly filaments to witness its balletic unraveling. But there was no way to vocalize this ingrained desire adequately, so instead Jack just pointed to some symbols painted on one of the far walls. They resembled scrawled, runic hieroglyphs: "What's that over there?"

"Oh, those. One of the old timers left that. They're words to an ancient Alaskan Yupik folksong. I heard it once. Sounded like an off-key rendition of *Volare*. I think it's something they used to make everyone memorize as a kind of hazing ritual."

"What's it mean?"

The shrug of Monty's shoulders was a silent, bodily equivalent of *I dunn'kno*. After a moment or two, Rabinowitz turned the lights off again, muting the static shutters to a halted hiss.

Show's over, kids. And with the duo climbed safely aboard, the elevator started moving up.

"I don't understand," Jack said, "why even bother to keep this place going?"

"Honestly? It's mainly for the benefit of the senile set. A lot of the 60, 70, and 80-year-old asshats who've become State Senators, Governors, or Presidential golf buddies don't want to see it die. They've got clout now, and all those wrinklebags did stints through here at some stage of the game. The Store used to be a big deal, the limbic system of the nation, and a real breeding ground for *les enfants terribles* of the ruling class—I'm talking the Andover, Skull 'n' Bones crowd. This was one of *the* last major stops before going on to something high profile, something with real responsibility. Guess it gives the geezers a sense of order to know we're still open for business. To them it's like an important part of our cultural heritage, even though no one knows about it."

"Hmm, totally weird." If they were to share a moment, this was it. A lot can transpire, unsaid, between two men in a tight spot.

"This is it." The elevator stopped in a shake, bouncing slightly as Monty opened the gate to the floor. It, too, was dark. When the lights came on, there was barely enough room to see a passageway through the accumulated debris. What a shitshow. It was a back-lot nightmare, pack-rat heaven, and a chronicle of history gathering dust. This was a Storage War$ sloppy, wet dream.

"You guys ever consider a garage sale?" Jack hobbled forth into the mothball abyss, his guide close behind.

"Worse part of it, of course, is that those same geriatric garglebags have no idea that this place is being systematically shutdown, piece by piece. We haven't done anything worthwhile out of this field office since the Net sepsis really took off. Persian Gulf and Oklahoma City shit was about the last of it. And that's twenty years ago, man! They don't want to hear it—people like Clint, I mean—but this place is disappearing and can't last for much longer."

"How come?"

"Fiscal downturn and military budget cutbacks. New kids in charge have plans in the works to clear this entire building out, tip to tail."

"Aren't *you* one of these new kids?"

"Yeah, technically. But I'm talking about the twerps who grew up after ColecoVision, Atari, and the Commodore 64. I'm talking about the dweebs who go to wine tastings to argue the finer points of concepts like 'cognitive maps,' 'inside and outside,' and 'Historical Marxism'— things nobody should be discussing with a straight face. Anything with worldly mass is antiquated to these New Management jokers, which is why they've packed everything in here tighter'n sardine shit in a can."

"What are they going to do with all this stuff, for real?"

"Burn it, I guess. The sets and props we still have, as you can tell, are wood, canvas, and plastic for the most part. Probably have an Independence Day bonfire on the Promenade out there, complete with smokies and s'mores. Some of the really sentimental schmucks, the retired ones who aren't blind to the coming end, have already put in requests for bits and pieces. Souvenir, that's what we're good for these days. Moon landing crap is pretty popular, so is HUAC stuff and sets from the Reagan and Carter assassination attempts, as is anything from the Kitchen Debates or the endless tickertape reels for the yahooism of the Great White Hopes like "Add 'em UP" Adlai Stevenson, Spiro "Show me the Money" Agnew, and Barry AuH_2O—the true Conscience of a Conservative crook, responsible for the Rotten Ronny Revolution."

Jack motioned dumbly. Then, "Um... so they're just gonna incinerate everything?"

"Yep, that's the plan. Kerosene and a match—pretty cost effective. It's one sure way to get rid of the past. Phase I focuses on the bottom levels, like the one I just showed you, which are all being converted into paying parking garages."

"Parking?"

"In a way it does make sense, from a civil engineering and fiscal conservative perspective. You wouldn't believe how much traffic has increased in this city in the last couple of years. People up here couldn't care less about their carbon footprint, it's all statistical horseshit to them."

They stopped in front of several stacked billboards, the top plate being a one-of-a-kind Gary Trudeau cartoon endorsing Nixon's CREEP {Committee to Re-Elect el Presidente} campaign, lauding the brilliant Yippie slogan: "Don't vote, vomit!"

Jack leaned against the massive, abraded posters to rest. His ribs ached and his face pulsed. The Demerol was beginning to wear off. He'd need to recharge soon if he wanted any hope of finishing the tour in only mild discomfort versus agonizing pain. Once he caught his breath, Jack started again: "I'm really not sure why Clint wanted me to see all this, to be honest."

"To know it was here, I'd say, to know it existed. Sometimes, that's enough." Monty started walking again, and Jack tried to keep up. As impressive as the collection of signs, memorabilia, and Truman-era trinkets were, the oppressiveness and grandeur of the accumulation led to a nauseating familiarity. The relics of a Great Nation, build on a Great Notion, rotting in discard and insignificance.

"So, what about these other floors—the ones with actual *stuff* in them—what's the plan for them?"

"Coffee shops and designer boutiques,

mainly. They're planning to build a tunnel-link to the Embassy and the Consulate holdings in the downtown core here—a sort of funnel for the lunchtime and after-work crowd. Contracts are being finalized, as we speak, with almost all the heavy-hitting conglomerates and big brand chains. The disappearing act will only be complete once the Military Industrial Complex gets its make-over into a Shopping-Plaza Complex, probably in less than eight months—it's the natural modern evolution of something into nothing."

"That's kind of sad."

"Maybe. But this dusty conspiracy shit, it's old hat, man. You think anybody really cares about the Space Race anymore? People just want to check their email accounts in peace, update their social network pages, get drunk on weekends, and have some pension security saved away for the geriatric grind. What happened, happened. End of fuckin' story."

Rabinowitz and Jack passed a cage of rotary telephones—hundreds, maybe thousands—piled up against a massive wall of mahogany operator switchboards. Next to that were costumes, military uniforms, and soiled terrorist garb of wide variety, along with stacked prop handguns and rifles. The floor was nothing more than a storehouse of antiques, a collection that could have been absolutely anything and therefore, nothing.

Jack had found an old wooden crutch and was using it to hobble around, through the labyrinth, towards what Monty called *The Toon Room*—last stop of the whistling Dixie tour. The more he spoke, the more Jack's shadow guide beamed excitement:

"If you ask me, the real brilliance of this place was the Toon Offensive. The Hangar's real power wasn't the high profile, balls-out bravura of the political coups initiated by advance men wizardry here, but rather the underhanded cartoon tech-no-goods that imprinted decentralist doctrines into our psyches from the tenderest ages. I mean think about it: total fragmentation achieved by embedding subliminal advertising and prop 'n' dissem, all of it hard-coded yet thinly submerged under the flash veneer of kiddie cartoons—that kind of out-of-the-box thinking was... well, totally boss; we're talking about millions of tiny twits getting a constant eyeful of politics, class barriers, rainbow discrimination, and broad-range xenophobia. Medium is da message, member?"

"That makes sense, sure."

"Ever read Spengler's *The Decline of the West*?"

"No."

"Pick it up, man! It's prophetic, precursor shit for the crumbling of the western hegemony. But, credit where it's due, the Frogs and those Belgian toads were the real sedulous pioneers of this world caliphate and bailiwick, brain-scrambling, spies-without-borders type a' baloney, especially when politics became so gray in the '70s."

"I—I guess I'd never put that much thought into it."

They'd stopped in front of a large metallic door, which Monty used a multi-ring set of keys to unlock.

"It's all fifth and sixth column stuff, Jack, which took us a little longer to get the hang of. Even Herr Doktor Seuss had to learn a thing of two about politically correct diplomacy from Double-U Double-U TWO. Before that, he'd been a full-blown, loudmouthed supporter of cracking down on our homegrown ZipZapanese by hucking 'em all into one big yellow slammer."

"Wait, isn't that's a whole other issue—"

"Is it? Try telling that to Tommy Tatomi, my best friend growing up. Both his grandparents and parents were interned at Manzanar. You think they stayed up late at night in the barracks reciting Seuss's propagandist rhymes for shits and gigs? And I quote: 'When the Japs are planting their hatchets in our skulls, it seems like a hell of a time for us to smile… If we want to win, we've got to kill Japs… We can get palsy-walsy afterward with those that are left.' And as we know, Seuss *said what he meant and he meant what he said.*"

"Oh, come on, that's a context thing—"

"Yeah? I'm sure all those we interned would love to hear it, fat compassionate smile beaming off your face. If you think I'd be letting my nippy, moon-faced babes read some Green Eggs and Ham after that you'd better think again. I'd sooner shove that shit down their little Tiddly Wink throats than take it in the steatopygous derrière like that. But hey, that's just me."

"You got kids?"

"No. My point is, it took our cartoon gang a whole lot a' back-pedaling, backhanding, back-bending, and back-in-the-day speeches to make it all right again. Like I said before, people forget and time passes. For the Gerrys, it was from Adolf to Adenauer, but we went the opposite route from Kennedy to Nixon—that's why we needed the cartoonists so badly, because nothing that was going on along the top layer seemed to make any sense. The real movement, the real story, was going on way below the surface. All you can do in that case is go subversive, mainstream style."

"Well, that's one theory."

"It's not a theory, that's what happened. The cartoon books and newspapers did their thing, but kudos really go to the moving form. It's a stellar, rabbit out of the hat lineup, too. Just look at gnomic shows like *Quick Draw McGraw*, *Colonel Bleep*, *Clutch Cargo*, *Peter Potamus*, *The Magilla Gorilla Show*, *Courageous Cat & Minute Mouse*, *The Banana Splits Adventure Hour*, *Here*

Comes the Grump, The Perils of Penelope Pitstop, Tennessee Tuxedo & His Tales, Groovie Goolies, Help!...It's the Hair Bear Bunch!, Hoppity Hooper, Underdog, The Amazing Chan & the Chan Clan, Hong Kong Phooey, Jabberjaw, Inch High, Private Eye, Goober & the Ghost Chasers, and *The Great Ape Show*..."

"Yeah, I remember some of them!"

"Those shows defined an era, and every single good idea and plummeted propaganda pitch originated from here, in this very building, in this very room!" Monty's arms were outstretched, as he twirled in wonder, pirouetting proudly in what was yet another empty space, stretching as far as the eye could see.

As he caught his breath, almost crushed by the disappearance of what once was palpable here, Monty's voice regained a composed steadiness. "Things slowed down in the '80s as you know because 'Dutch' Reagan seemed like entertainment enough; though secretly, of course, he was just a well-orchestrated, somnific puppet used to lull everyone into a calm decade sleep—chalk one up for the Gipper! After that, the dust slowly started gathering, and the geeks won the war. Computers really started taking off and this place has slowly withered away ever since. Automation eats itself: no need for an actual machine when the virtual contraption will do—and at half the price, too. Welcome to the COSTCOefficient of the double-blind, if you know what I means…"

"I think you lost me somewhere around *Quick Draw McGraw*—"

"Yep, that seems about right. Look, put it this way: It serves a man to have the apropos information, at the appropriate time. Still, it's real hard to have a career without a job, so they say. And even though people everywhere recognize the bluff of both the avant- and the après-garde, they pay into those things, invest in them, and ultimately expect to collect compound interest on the whole schmegegge until the lines don't need blurring anymore."

"That sounds like Huelsenbeck's pamphlet, *En avant dada*—"

"You've read it?"

"Research for a book, long ago. What you're suggesting here, all this, sounds like *folie à deux*—a willed delusion by both parties…"

"More like folly à millions. Don't you see, Jack, it's a safety mechanism. Like DJ Tricky Dix said, it isn't illegal if the President—or, in our particular case here, the entire military government machine—does it. That's what democratic elections are all about. Go ahead and be a Nazi in your spare time if you want, just don't use the "N-word" in public, you know? Hope & Change is still just horseshit and dream jam, the '08 election proved that much. Ideology's a bitch, especially the counter-culture kind. Am I right?"

"Sounds to me like you're a lil' jaded—"

"Did anyone blame the Wizard of Oz for suffering from the very same ailment?"

"Point taken."

"Now, Jack, let's get back to the really important stuff: my coffee break."

"Another one? But we just had—?"

"You can never have too much coffee, I say, or too many breaks for that matter. Ain't that part of the American Dream, too?" Rabinowitz smiled in a way meant to appease slow, mongoloid children. "Feel like you've seen enough?"

"I haven't seen anything."

"Then I'd say you'd seen it all."

The lights went off on the past as the elevator rose into the bright, even flash of the lobby. There was an unsettling breeze in the shaft. The fluorescents sparkled in white predictability. It felt like being snapped from a warm, uterine dream.

With so much said, there was almost an embarrassment to the silence. It was the awkward lead up to the door after a great first date. Should you shake hands? Do the French poodle? Grab tit? What do you do when words fail?

"Jack, would you mind waiting here for a second? There's something I'd like to give you before you go."

"Yeah, sure." Rabinowitz slipped out a small side door, cat-like.

Deputy Dookie was at his desk, streaming what sounded like a Bicentennial World Series' game. Next to the computer was a salami, sausage, smoked meat, and sauerkraut super-sub, smothered in mayonnaise and syrup.

Monty came back out into the hall, through a different door completely on the opposite side. He was sheltering something from sight, cupping it in his hands, until he presented Jack the souvenir key chain with a flourish: "Ta-daaaa!" Attached to its brass ring was a 6.5 mm Carcano ammunition round, with *I ♥ Constipation Theories* scrawled along its side. They both chuckled, nervously.

"The boyz had 'em made up sometime after Dallas," Rabinowitz said. "Bad taste, I guess, but this is the last one of its kind around here. Who knows where they all went? Anyway, it's a piece of history; thought it was appropriate somehow."

"Thanks, Monty." They shook hands, firm yet warm in intent. Something of friendship, or communion, connected them.

"As someone once wrote," Monty said, leading Jack towards the exit: "We keep hearing the faint echoes of the Song of Solomon, but even that rolling thunder machine fades away in time. Nostalgia versus the clout. We can hold on to the records, the pictures, the song and dance, but never the song. Inevitably, motivational belief disappears and everybody's left holding the bag."

"Huh, not bad. Who said it?"

"Good question. Beats me."

ΩΩΩΩΩ

Jack sipped at his champagne flute, the fourth so far. It was a well-deserved come down after his tour with Monty, but mostly it was a recovery aid from his recent surprise, which Clint had orchestrated. Here's the skinny on how the stunt went horribly pear-shaped:

Richter, you see, had arranged for a chilled bottle of *Crystal* to be sent up to Jack's room—a gesture quite considerate in itself, though the accompanying note was creepy and more than a little familiar (*I know what's g'wine on*).

The hotel lackey in charge of the conveyance, however, had taken his delivery duties way over the top, to a whole other level in fact. How, you ask? Well, instead of bringing the gift to the door—like any normal human being would do—the boy had insistently broken into Jack's room and proceeded to hide in the closet. Patiently waiting for his victim's return, while twiddling his thumbs or god knows what else, the kid bided his time. He waited precisely eleven seconds after hearing Jack come through until he finally burst out, yelling at high decibel:

"Aaaaahhhh-haaaaaaaaa!"

"Cccchhhhhrist! What the effing fuck, man!" Jack had stammered, pass key still in hand and with half-soiled Poughkeepsie shorts dangling in the wind.

"Sorry, sir," the little cockalorum said, sniggering, as he re-latched the closet door. He was one uptight bugger, that's for sure. "Mr. Richter hoped your meeting went well and insisted we do the surprise this way, assured us it would amuse you. Was he right?"

"Richter's never wrong, I'm starting to think."

The stunted, displeasing ninny wheeled over the cart and Champagne. "Glad to know it. Here we are, sir."

Jack first steadied himself against the wall, regaining some slight composure, then felt the bottle with the back of his hand. "This shit's warm, jackass."

"I *have* been waiting for several hours, sir."

"Hours? Man, you must be a real hit at the stalker's convention."

"Huh?"

"Nothing. Thanks for the bubbly. Now take a hike, Barbara."

"My pleasure. And I will, sir, but…" The bellhop stood still, waiting patiently. He was either after a tip or a smack in the mouth.

"But what?" They both stood motionless,

dumb, breathing. "Well?"

"Well, Mr. Mitford, sir… you see it is customary to—?" He rubbed his greasy thumb to his forefingers, soiled with a thin film of glaucous gratuity goop. "Cough up a little Canadian bacon, as it were. If you catch my drift."

"Hang on a second here, cause I'd like to get this straight. First off you scare the living beejezus out of me, and now you actually expect me to *pay* you?"

"Sir?"

"*Sir* what? We're you about to call me an asshole?"

"I'm sorry, sir, that word isn't in the Canadian lexicon or vocabulary." The boy wasn't completely devoid of charm.

"All right. Tell you what, kid: If I manage to nail you in the head with this cork, I'll give you fifty bucks and we'll call it even Steven. Sound good?"

"Um, I'm… uh, not sure this is such a good idea—"

"'Course it is. Here goes!" Jack popped the top, exploded in Champagne, and buried the cork deep in the bellhop's left eye.

The boy dropped to floor like a sack of rotted potato spuds. "Ffffffffffuuuuuuck!"

"Holy smokes! I really nailed ya, didn't I?"

"Yes… yes, sir, you did. Mr. Mitford, sir."

Jack drew the bottleneck to his lips, gulping victory in smooth belts. "Shit, man, that must really sting! Hurt, even—"

"Yes, yes, sir, it does."

For a second, maybe two, he did think about helping the poor kid up, but Jack had a few more sips instead, and then spoke. "Wow! That was classic, what a shot! I wouldn't be surprised if that thing closes shut and gives you a real shiner, Nancy. Yeesch sucks to be you."

"At least," the boy struggled back to his feet, a noticeable welt of fleshy round pulsing on his stupid, once smug face. "I look better than you do."

"You got me there, shitstick." Jack dug out a bill from his pocket, staring at his own face in the hall mirror. It *was* true: he still looked like a body-double for the elephant man, Quasimodo with Kyphosis of the vertebrae. "Here you go, kid. No hard feelings?"

"What's this?" The bellhop looked down at the money in his hand with what might accurately be called disgust.

"It's only a 20, I know. But it's all I got on me right now. I'll hit you back tomorrow— agh, gee, sorry pal, poor choice of words… look, don't worry, I may be a letch, a drunk, and an occasional liar, but I'm a man of my word."

"N'ah, dude, that wasn't the deal! That wasn't the deal at all!"

"Well you don't have to be a baby about

it."

"50, we said 50 bucks. Now, cough it up, fucker!"

"Look, that's all I got. I swear. I'll get you the rest tomorrow, promise. I'm here for at least one more night."

"This is total bullshit, Mitford! And what's with this Canadian cash, eh?"

"We *are* in Canada, aren't we?"

"Hey! Need a hearing aid, grampa? Get me some real money, goddamnit! I'm talkin' 'bout Benjamins! Understand? Or else!"

Jack did his best to keep a straight face. "*Or else?*"

"That's right, or else!" The room service rookie moved towards the door, holding the side of his face. Jack, meanwhile, winced as he maneuvered to pull his dwindling vial of Demerol out of his pocket as a sort of peace offering:

"Here, kiddo, pop one of these. You should be feeling better in no time."

"What are you, some kind of pusher now? This isn't cool at all, jerkface!"

"Hey take it easy, man. I'm just handing you an olive branch here."

"No you're not. You're handing me narcotics! I know my rights. My brother-in-law's a cop with the RCMP in Saskatoon. I could have you busted for this, bub!"

"These are prescription pills, you nitwit. And no one's forcing you to do shit, Doris, so just zip it!"

"Listen, mister, if you don't have the rest of that dough tomorrow, I'm turning you in, end of story." The neotenic boy cupped the entire left side of his face now, rocking on his heels. "You'd be in BIG trouble then. I've seen the CBC documentaries, and you don't want to see the inside of a Canadian jail cell, believe me!"

"Why? Are they cleaner than the rooms in this fleabag motel?"

"I'm telling!"

"Telling? What are you, five?"

"I'm telling the shift manager you said that! You're bad news, Mitford, I knew it from the moment I first saw your ugly, American face! You Americans are all the same!"

"Would somebody please explain to me what that means!"

"Means y'all think you're so darned superior—"

"I can't imagine that's very hard. At least not where you're concerned."

"You're fucked, buddy, fucked! You hear me!"

"The whole hallway heard you, you filthy sodomite, now beat it!"

"What d'you call me?"

"Oh, great, and uneducated, too. Here, let me put it this way: you best shut your damn mouth about all this, or *I'm* the one who'll be talking to your shift manager. I'll tell him about how you broke in here wearing nothing but a bra and whipped cream on your dick, you sicko!"

"You wouldn't dare!"

"Try me, asshole. And then think about how much fun it'll be working around here. I'm out of here in a couple days, but you have to keep working in this depressing, miserable shithole. What's your name, anyway?"

"Pete."

"*Pervy Petey*, they'll call you."

"No, please. Please don't, I need this job! I'm, I'm puttin' my mother through night school—"

"Of course you are—"

"Please! I'm begging you…"

"All right, all right, settle down, chief." Pervy P stopped groveling and stood there, forlorn. "I'll have the rest of your cash by tomorrow—when's your shift start?"

"6 p.m. But let's just forget it, okay, Mr. Mitford? We had a misunderstanding, that's all. Can't we just leave it at that?"

"No, absolutely not! You won the bet, fair and square. I'll pay-up like I said. I made you look like a one-eyed butt pirate; the least I owe you is the cash to go with it. You'll get your money at shift start, just come up here and see me. Now get the hell outta here, understand?"

Jack smoked three cigarettes in the aftermath: one out of guilt, the two others from sheer exhilaration. The taste of the *Crystal*, as it mixed with the smoke, made for memorable palate overtones. Rocket to Reno, folks.

    The entire bottle went down slowly, giving Jack's thoughts the time to sweep up in cascading arcs, fluttering in minute moments of being before dipping off in glorious, downturned deaths. Thwarted, he still raced towards the cracks Rabinowitz provided, the conversation with Monty flashing in opaque fragments. Jagged, and unclear, the sharp inchoate shreds rubbed together in discordant arrangement of puzzle pieces. It was like trying to sift through a cloud. With no concrete spaces to latch on to, there was only possibility, sodden conjecture, and the ruins of something now long dismantled.

    There, sitting shirtless in bed, his lungs wheezed to breathe. Strips of fuchsia were filleted across his upper body, matching the eggplant explosion of his cheek. The more he sipped, the more the external world dissipated. The pain capsules also helped, playing a sunset symphony of delirium across the horizon of an ominous sky.

    Once all the champagne was gone, Jack's nose was back in the mini-bar. Rather than pretend to be responsible, he immediately poured out five mini bottles into a large glass and turned on the boobtube. Because of its built-in digital rabbit's ears and lips, thousands upon thousands of luxated images fluttered fast on the convex screen.

He called down to have the front desk connect him with Clint. One of the Hampton house servants answered, but it didn't take long for Clint to get to the line.

"This is Richter."

"Clint? It's Jack."

"Jack, it's one o'clock. Is everything all right?"

"Sure, everything's fine." Jack took a long draw of the booze blend and looked for his pack of cigarettes, which were sleeping in the folds of his sheets. "I didn't wake you, did I?"

"Shit, no! I'm a night owl."

"Me, too."

"Sometimes I'm a nightgown."

"What?"

"Joke. As a matter of fact, I'm busy building scale models of French Revolution scenes, a hundred-and-fifty years before the bastards became cheese-eating surrender monkeys—give or take."

Jack found his duty-free pack and lit up. "So what, guillotine executions and cake parties?"

"Actually, right now I'm working on a mock-up of the martyred teen revolutionary, Joseph Bara, one of Bonaparte's boys. He died with a bayonet to the crotch, supposedly crying out: '*Vive la République!*' Now I don't know about you but, personally, I think that with 11 inches of steel thrust through my balls I would

have shouted out something slightly different...
Anyway, did Bobo set you up with everything tonight, you feel you got what you wanted from the tour?"

"Yeee... aaah, I guess."

"And you're still planning to fly back on Friday?"

"I am still coming back as scheduled but listen... how do I put this? I'm—I'm not sure that I really 'got' much of anything while I was up here, except for a beating and maybe the clap from a prostitute."

"Sounds like my kind of trip—"

"It's just... I'm not sure I can justify—"

"Look, don't sweat it, Jack. Like I said, I already have all the pertinent info here in my notes. You can't see *now* what it was like *then*, can you? Besides, hell, the section about the Hangar is damn near done to polished form, except for typos. I just wanted you to get a feel for things, the place."

"Doesn't mean I don't feel any less... ridiculous on this recon mission, if that's what it is. I'm nothing more than a useless, accidental tourist."

"A tourist is exactly what you are—for now. Revel in that tentative jeopardy, in those intoxicatingly imperiled improvisations. But you're not useless; you're my eyes and ears on the ground. Oh, speaking of which, did you take any pictures?"

"No."

"Really, none?"

"You specifically told me not to."

"Oh, right."

"But Monty said he'd forward some along."

"Great! Buffie kid, in'he? Me and his old man—'Nignog,' as we've always called him—go way back." Jack heard the tinkling of cubes from Richter's receiver end. "And so whadd'you think a' the mega Megalopolis up there?"

"Here? Kind of a provincial pisswater."

"Full of provincial lies, which is what makes it dangerous. They buy and sell nothingness there like a hot convivial commodity—D.C. miniaturized. Everybody thinks they've hit the big time. They're so utterly up to their necks in mellifluous mock manure, no one can smell the real thing anymore." Clint paused, taking the time to finish painting a small section of brickwork on the wall of the Bastille. The color was proving more problematic than he'd anticipated, and the blood spatter was ruining the effect of the brown hues. "Listen, Jack: I called you the other night—seven or eight times."

"I know, sorry about that. I got tied up having a philosophical exchange with some friendly local sailors. What was it you wanted?"

"Uh, well, this may seem a little New Age sensitive of me, but… I wanted to apologize for yelling at you."

"Please. You had every right to, Clint—"

"I realize that, but I still feel like a heel. I hired you to do the job, and I should let you do that at your own pace. It won't happen again."

"Don't worry, really."

"Anyway, what I'm most sorry about is that you weren't in. I had Springsteen over here, and I was going to get him to belt out a few requests for you over the line. We were just shooting the breeze, catching up over Montecristos and Lagavulin, and I figured it was the least I could do to apologize—"

"The Boss?"

"You like him?"

"Are you kidding? I've loved him ever since my dad took me to see him and the Big Man at the Palladium."

"Yeah, Clemons was here, too, in spirit at least—may he rest in peace. Boy oh boy, did we ever tear one off! Watched the sun come up in our underwear! You missed a good one, a real barn burner—"

"Seriously?"

"Ah, well, too bad. Next time, though, huh?" A deep-pit despair struck at Jack's marrow. It hurt worse than the recent beating. For a second he felt like retching, ga-ga-gasping for air with staccato sucking sounds. "Jack…? You still there?"

"I'm. . . I'm here."

"Listen, the paint's drying unevenly on

this fuckin' model here. I should go. Call me when you're back in the City. I'll have a car come out and bring you by the house. I have about five or six other places I want you to go check out for me. Unless this first leg's tuckered you out already?"

"More traveling? When?"

"Don't get your panties in a bunch, it's nothing major. Two weeks tops, and on home turf this time, too. At least on the intra-national inspection you won't have to worry about the goddamn foreigners as much."

"We'll—we'll talk about it when I get back. I mean, I'm not even really doing anything so—"

"Oh, believe me, you are, Jack, you are. You just can't see it yet, that's all."

"Fine."

Suddenly, Richter got caught in a sudden, chaotic coughing fit. Epic was one way of describing the sound, a deep-lunged and kidney shattering lurch courting death. Eventually, the old boy recovered. "Grrrrh! Sorry 'bout that, too many damned cigars the other night. By the way, I dropped a whole wad into a special account I set up for you over at Manny Hanny."

"Where?"

"Fuck, I gotta stop calling it that. Sorry, I meant Chemical Bank—"

"But I bank with Chase Manhattan."

"I know, and I thought about using them,

but they're a pack of racists. The whole Standard Oil/I.G. Farben/Holocaust thing has always put me off, plus their logo does look like a screwy swastika."

"What?"

"Anyway, the funds'll lay dormant—in what's known as a monkey-puzzle, offshore account—until the whole job is done. Is that incentive or what?"

"You mean I can't touch it?"

"Right, but not to worry, neither will your battle-axe bitch of an ex—if you'll pardon my Polish. She won't see a cent, and her dirtbag lawyers down at Inverarity, Supercilious, Snollygoster & Lickspittle will never even know the boodle exists."

"Um, great."

"You bet it is. Got to keep doing our part in keeping the Boyz Club intact. Oh, that reminds me, I also took care of things with your hotel up there, too. They have my card details for incidentals and such when you checkout. So be sure and treat yourself, have some peanuts from the mini-bar or something."

"Will do." Jack ate every bag of peanuts while finishing all the miniature bottles left in the fridge—gin, vodka, rum *et al.*—within an hour of hanging-up. He thought about calling up the pro from the first night, Colleen, to help take some of his pain away, but his wallet was still empty. Instead, and for a reasonable 673-dollar "after-hours service fee" (billed to the room, naturally, and that on top of the $429 for the actual booze itself), Jack managed to have the mini-bar entirely restocked, which enabled him to push through the night drinking and smoking until sufficiently sated—i.e., passed out.

    By compensating for the dulling effects of the alcohol with well-timed doses of Demerol, Jack achieved an equivocal threshold of numbness. It was a momentary plateau, where nothing around him seemed to matter. All the mistakes of his life, all the truths he'd taken for granted, all the wires he'd got crossed, and all the moments he'd been sure would never disappear, vanished under an ephemeral blanket of white. It was his luminal liberty; his liminal liberation.

Digestive Divertimento

In the light of day, all was lost anew. It was a cruel come down, as every substance surfer knows. The wave was crashed, man, way crashed. And, of course, with that too came regret. Looking at the dead soldiers on the carpet—33 mini bottles at quick glance, and two packs of Pall Malls—repentance went straight to Jack's born-again head. He looked at the clock. It was already mid-afternoon. Why even bother getting up? His bladder, for one, did make a good case however. And so up he went to the ceramic tile. A feeble stream of cloudy urine filled the bowl. At least the blood was gone.

Jack ordered up some coffee, juice, and croissants ("The Continental," priced at a moderate $176 bones *à la carte*), and lit a cigarette while he waited. With no cash in any of his pockets, he hid from the delivery. Pathetic as it was, he waited a full quarter of an hour after the room service knock in order to retrieve his tray of food from the corridor, half of which had been mercilessly scavenged by skulking hall rats.

Adding a dollop of gin to his freshly squeezed orange juice, Jack calmed his nerves—the poor little things. Two important chores needed to be accomplished today, and Jack wasn't sure he'd survive the strain in a sober state. To begin with, he needed to pick up some bank cabbage in order to settle the score with that unremitting and industrious hotel troll, Pete. Secondly, he was hoping to fill one of the scrips Ernesto had written out for him. Needless to say, it was a big day ahead.

Despite inadvertently falling into an unrestrained cycle of pill abuse recently, Jack *was* indeed in mild to severe pain. In fact, he probably still had some internal bleeding; so if he wasn't going to see a doctor about that, the least he could do was self-medicate. It goes without saying that already the effectiveness of Gabby's Demerol stash seemed to be lessening. How archaic it was to endure malaise unnecessarily. Pill-a-phobes and pharma-naysayers were out of their minds, and clearly jealous of drugstore cowboy freedoms. Anyway, weren't pharmacologists bound by the Hippocratic Oath? They were here to help, you ascetic asswipes, not to harm!

After washing down a duo of Demmys with his juice, Jack smoked a chain as he watched the images flicker on the screen. He wondered if the hotel had cash machines somewhere along its wide concourse, as well as a druggist, that way he could kill two little birdies with one toss. If this were back home, in a properly civilized city of convenience, then no problem. Chances up here in the boondocks were 50/50, eh.

Almost buzzed back to normal, Jack ventured down to the lobby with the help of his mopey moose cane. He was in luck. After ensuring that the front desk restocked his mini-bar again, Jack convinced the clerk (Clyde on his nametag) to give him cold hard cash back from the card on his room file, Clint's card. The clerk had been tough, even reticent at first, until Jack insisted Clyde should skim $500 for himself as recompense for his considerable efforts of punching keys on a keyboard. Armed then with a mittful of colorful bills, Jack hobbled across the hotel's delightful shopping concourse to talk to Mister Jimmy about getting his prescription filled. His plan was in full effect, and, after a cherry-red soda, Jack was back in his room, once more on the precipice of a decently colossal escape.

    The Nembutals he'd scored from the hotel pharmacy flickered magically. It was a new sensation, an entirely new prescription, so he'd started with one, just to be cautious. The yellow jacket had set his heart aflutter in measured ticks. He could feel his blood thumping through veins, soon forgetting about the aches from his bruises. Time lost meaning in this comfortable void.

    When Jack heard the knock—an incessant echo ringing in his ears—he straightened himself out as best he could. Had he fallen asleep for a minute, longer? He splashed water on his face, ready to greet the kid come grubbing for the rest of his cash. The second knock was soft, but firm. Jack ripped the door open in a sweep, but the boy was a girl:

"Hey, Jacky-Boy."

"G—Gabby... hi." Her face was lit in makeup, subtle around the edges. The hairline fractures of her age were timid and inconsequential under paint. She was wearing a ruby sequin dress under the folds of her coat, its regal piping a deep Mars red. She had a package tucked under arm and something was slung over her shoulder.

"You look better, Jack."

"Hi... hi. Thanks." He stayed propped against the door. The smell of trapped smoke wafted out into the corridor, filling the air with a sickly-sour scent. "H—how d'you, how did you find me?"

"Why? 'Cause you lied and told me you was staying up at the Westin—?"

"Yeah."

"You talk in your sleep. Look, can I come in or what?"

"Oh, well I, I mean it's—uh—it's, not what you'd call, or accurately call a, ah—"

"Are you high?"

"Uhm, yeah. Actually."

"Really? On what?"

"Some of those horse tablets you gave me the other day, and something called, ahh... Nembutal, I think it is."

"Sweet! Hook me up, Major Tom. I never say no to some moon dolls." Tired of waiting for an invite, Gabby walked in to the room while Jack went to the washroom for the pills. "By the way, groovy room number."

"Hmmn?"

"*The Graduate*, right? Dusty Hoof-Munn and Mrs. Robinsong boning bad in the big room? Someday I think I'd like to do it in a pool, wearing scuba gear."

"I can't stand Hoffman."

"Who can?" Jack came back with a pair of pellets, palms up. Gabby placed the package down on the hall table and dropped a dry cleaning sash to the unmade bed. She grabbed the yellow capsules, swooshing her head back. "Mmn. Before I forget, can you make sure this gift makes its way to Clint? You shouldn't have too much trouble with customs, if any."

"Why, what is it?"

"Nothing the border clowns would kick up a stink about. Trust me."

"And what's that, on the bed?"

"Your tux."

"My—?"

"You're taking me to this thing in the banquet hall downstairs tonight."

"When did you rent this?"

"I didn't. I took your measurements while you were passed out at my gram's the other day and had it made, as a sort of apology. It's yours."

"Why?"

"You'll need it for the fundraiser—black

tie. It'll be the usual cocktail for rich, open-minded retards, but the after-party is what I'm banking on. Believe it or not these stuffed shirts have the hang of cuttin' loose in the vespertine—that means nighttime, in case you ain't a Björk fan."

"I, I, I… can't go to that—"

"Why not?"

"I have a plane to catch tomorrow."

"When?"

"I don't know, morning sometime—"

"Oh, well this thing should be done by then. Or not. Stay up all night, for gosh sakes. Live a little why don'tcha!" Jack's skin was sweaty. He was having trouble focusing. The television twirled persistent images. "Say, palomino, what does a girl have to do to get a drink around here?"

"You thirsty?"

"Always." They shared a drink—gin gimlets in a cup—and one thing led to another. The maneuvers were largely unplanned. Everything just seemed to happen without warning. They kissed, distractedly, the sheet of the mattress farting in cascades. It was a thoroughly unpleasant exercise at both ends, and sobering. The whole coital ordeal lasted about ten minutes, which was ten minutes too long.

Sitting next to each other in bed, smoking side by side in the wake, Jack watched the flickering of the silent images in the cold afterward. Here's where boredom leads, swathed in the bland blankets of venery.

"Would you like another drink?" Jack asked, stepping off the bed.

"Sure." Gabby watched him as he carefully slipped into his boxers, the hair of his lower back crawling up in shelves to his fuchsia-stained shoulders. "You know, Jack, I have to say: that was pretty fucking terrible. Downright awful, as a matter of fact."

"Agreed."

"What were we thinking?"

"I don't know about you, but I'm not *thinking* straight at all right now, if you want the God's honest. Heartbeats—my heartbeat—that's mostly what I was thinking about. I'm talking about fast, fast, fast, fast—"

"That you were, tiger."

"These pills are taking a real whack at my metabolism."

"You're half in the bag, practically stoned off your ass, and you couldn't do any better than that? Shit buster, your flag was up for like three, four minutes—tops. I mean, I knew not to expect much by way of length or girth, but I didn't think you'd be so freakin' premature."

"Supposedly it happens to lots of guys—"

"Are you kidding? It happens to no one. Not even preemies are as premature as you were, ugh! That was a truly painful, pitiful, pimply pubescent show by any standards. Like, high school under the bleachers bad; back seat of a Pinto bad; band practice room with half a clarinet bad. We're talking amateur hour at the Apollo every step of the way here, chum. Christ, you damn near tore my dress and my bra is still on!"

"I know."

"Don't you like titties?"

"'Course, I do."

"You sure?"

"Yeah."

"Could've fooled me." She stubbed out her cigarette, puffing up the parts of her hair flattened by the headboard. "Well?"

"Well… what?"

"Go ahead then, apologize for being a limp-dick, let down."

"Hey, I wasn't limp-dicked, Gabby. I was fast, all right, but we both know that's not the same thing."

"It's a figure of speech, Jack, an expression. You *were* a letdown."

"You should take my overeager enthusiasm as a complement." Jack poured the last seven mini-bottles of gin into Gabby's cup, hoping to cheer her up. "Here you are. You're not suggesting we try again, are you?"

"Absolutely not! You have no idea what you're doing when it comes to women." She took the drink and had a sip to clear her throat. "Mm, thanks."

"You're welcome. Anyway, I think I've

had enough sex to last me a year—"

"On behalf of women everywhere, Jack, I thank you. And for the future, may I suggest abstinence!"

"I'll go for Absinthe, instead." The two shared a good laugh and dropped the matter. Talking about the whole clattering incident had been much more fun that the actual act itself and taken almost as long, if that can be fathomed by all those blissful couples out there with healthy, satisfying, and meaningful sex lives.[10]

Jack drank water and dressed while Gabby slurped her gin. The tuxedo she'd bought fit him like a glove, a very expensive and well-tailored glove made in the shape of a tuxedo.

When Jack heard the door again, he remembered all about the bellboy. It was almost seven thirty, according to the bedside clock. Gabby took the opportunity to sneak into the bathroom and shake one loose.

"You're late," Jack said to Petey, who looked like a deformed raccoon wearing an eye patch. "Over an hour late! And you look ridiculous, by the way."

"Sorry, Mr. Mitford, sir. I've been really, really, really busy—got a lot on m'plate. Plus, the Shift Manager sent me out to clean the downstairs

---

[10] The rest of the planet hates you, by the way, and God will never forgive your copulatory gloating.

dumpsters and I lost track of time."

"Dumpster diving, that's some excuse! By rights I should dock you some of this cheese, Petey, but I won't. A bet's a bet."

"Yes, sir. Thank you, sir."

"Well, don't just stand there like a mook, take this." Jack gave the kid $40. The extra ten was for the misunderstanding and added mental distress. It was a fact, Jack truly was a prince among men and minions.

"This is too much."

"No it isn't."

"I hate to contradict you, Mr. Mitford, but it is. Ten dollars too much."

"Call it vig on the skeet, all right?"

"What?"

"Interest, kiddo. Anyway, I couldn't get my hands on any real money, like you asked for, so let's call this an exchange-rate bonus, cool?"

"Gee, thanks! My mom'll really, really appreciate this. It'll probably cover next month's tuition! Wow, if there's anything else I can do, anything at all, please don't hesitate to—"

"Actually, Pete, there is one thing."

"Name it, sir."

"I'm going downstairs to that banquet event—"

"You look great in that tux, by the way."

"Oh, that's so sweet of you to say, thanks." Jack stood, smiling, lost somewhere in incomplete synapse.

"So…?"

"Mm, right. Sorry. I, uh, I wondered if you could make sure the mini-bar is fully, uh, restocked by the time I get back—"

"Again?[11] Mr. Mitford, sir, I should advise you that there's a mandatory (and hidden) $775 service fee every time you request that particular amenity, plus whatever else the Duty Manager feels like charging on top of that."

"So?"

"And, uh… well, quite frankly, it's also a complete hassle for everybody involved, if you want to know the truth of it."

"What makes you think I want to know the truth of it?"

"I could provide you with regular sized bottles instead, at a much cheaper rate, from one of our licensed suppliers. This mini-bar thing really is a scam."

"But I happen to like the little bottles, they make me feel like a giant."

---

[11] The kid's tone could be excused, largely on account of his naiveté, and the inflections in his voice did seem to stem more from genuine concern than flippant moral judgment. As a side note: unlike all the no-good, drunken liars down at the Betty Ford clinic would have you believe, alcoholism is a life choice and *not* a disease. It might be best to bear that in mind as we trudge along.

"Just trying to be helpful."

"Don't be a loaf."

"All right. I'll get it done, Mr. Mitford, with pleasure."

"Great, Pete. Thanks. I appreciate it, okay? Here's an extra 2K for you and your mom on top, sorry, but that's all the cratch I could get a hold of downstairs. Make sure she goes to college, all right!" An ever so slight trickle sinew of urine ran down the kid's leg. "Oh, Petey, can you also see if they have any Frangelico? That stuff's just delicious, isn't?"

"Simply divine."

The banquet downstairs was in honor of a freedom fighter named Jonas Kramba, who'd died in a recent suicide bombing. Originally from Angola, Kramba had been leader of the rebel group Fighters In Search of Trouble (FIST), and as a martyr he'd become an overnight sensation—in diplomatic circles at least. He'd successfully detonated a blast at the latest Southern Africa Convention of Despots, and the explosion had annihilated the inner circle of several dictatorships, including what Jack overheard one banquet-goer describe as "some really, really bad ones."

FIST was a decidedly socialist organization—albeit a violent, non-humanitarian one—backed by respectable left-leaning governments of the New World Order. Think of them as the pseudo-antithesis to the Lord's Resistance Army in Uganda, led by that despicable Joseph Kony guy, the one who'd managed to obliterate bi-partisan politics here in the west for about 15 minutes and get good people tweeting again. The FIST motto was a pithy reworking of a time-honored Hells Angels credo: "Three can keep a secret as long as two of 'em are dead."

Gabby dropped Jack soon after they arrived, mingling well with the bald-headed masses in bloated suits. The banquet was a regular romp of comfortable liberals (corporate and tax lawyers, mostly), crepuscular cads, and thinly removed Marxist intellectuals. Such culpable, reactionary progressivists were embarrassingly earnest and always felt better once they'd given inordinate sums away in an enthusiastic hog toss—success was their religion of contrition. Like most rational human beings, Jack was a Groucho Marxist, that witless wit of ages, which rarely got him anywhere with folks of this ilk, unable as they were to appreciate any sort of off-color crack, jibe, yarn, or perorated gag properly.

Even the bartender was a downright stick in the mud, but at least he had a loose elbow; after unfurling their checkbooks ($15,500/plate) with great celerity, that's all the attendees really expected for their philanthropy, and they made damn sure to make the most of it by getting absolutely shitfaced on the superior staves. Plenty a' wawa to keep 'em gaga as they posed for various society-rag pictures, their perfectly blanched teeth (one of only two bleached body parts) coated in smears of dolphin pâté, Wagyu steak morsels, White Alba truffles, and *fromage frais* made from the milk of virgin unicorns—say cheese!

    About halfway through the evening, though, Jack realized that he'd been completely mistaken in his prejudice about the guests—they were actually a laid-back, down-to-earth barrel of monkeys; they just had better bank accounts than most folks, that's all. The real clincher came when a boat race broke out with magnums of *Veuve Cliquot*, which busted the evening wide open and put the "fun" back in fundraiser.

    Eventually, impromptu games of strip poker, socio-economic speed-dating, and pin-the-tail (a 12" brown anaconda dildo) on Hilary Clinton were being played everywhere, while beautiful breakdance karaoke renditions of Dolly Parton gems "9 to 5," "Hard Candy Christmas," and "Islands in the Stream" echoed through the hall. It was an entertaining circus thrall to be swept into, and the more the wealthy socialites fumbled over themselves, the more Jack found he was speaking their language.

    Gabby was barely standing when she found Jack again. But luckily for her, two kindly gentlemen named Rick and Hassan were keeping her propped-up with highballs of Stoli. "Hiya Limpy," Gabby shouted at Jack, drool bubbling from her lips. "I'm totally zoolooed, you?"

"Hanging in there, barely."

"C'mon, Jack, follow us!"

"No, no, that's okay."

Gabby shimmied her hips, purposely rubbing against the crotches of both her pillared companions. "Aww, come on, you *have* to come with us, Jack. Seriously!"

"Nah, I should be getting back to the room." Both Rick and Hassan seemed in full agreement. "I've got a plane to catch—"

"You don't understand, there's a Furries convention going on in one of the conference rooms next door. Furries, Jack! You cannot pass up a chance to check out these furverts first hand!"

"These what?"

"Furverts![12] They're those freaks who dress-up in furry animal suits, na mean? Come… on! Puff the Magic Dragon, Ahab! Who knows, it might even get some blood pumping through that limp little noodle a' yours, a-ha!" She half turned to the boys, thumbing back in Jack's direction: "You guys'll never believe what a quick shot this fucknuts is in the sack!"

"Gabby, please—"

---

[12] Try saying that three times fast with a raging, boozed-out slur. Dare ya!

She turned around in an uneven sway. "Aww, lighten up, Jack! It's just a joke. Jeez! Working for my father really has your sphincter clenched!"

"Father? Wait, what? Clint's your father?"

"*Step*-father, technically. Thought you knew that, dumb-dumb."

"No."

"Next of skin, all right! Who d'you think paid for our plates of Almas caviar tonight? Bought that ridiculous penguin suit you're wearing? Or sent me along with a relief-sized check for whatever this evening's for? Yep, that's the Great Clint Richter: philanthropist, philanderer, philogynist, and panderer extraordinaire."

"Weird, I had him pegged for a scummy Libertarian—"

"Panacea of the People, not to be unraveled! He's a mystery wrapped in an enigmatic corpse, ahoy-o-ho! A woman in every port, Sailor Jerry! Got 'em scattered all over the world. Sucks for him to have gone the A-gory side of phobia, though, stuck in his dirty Hamptons hamster cage like he is now. Boo-hoo, boooo-hoooo…"

"*Really*? Your stepdad huh, no shit? How did I not see that one coming?"

"You're kinda slow on the uptake, ain't yaw? Come on, Casanova, I'll tell you about it if you really want, but first you'll have to trade that tux in for a bunny suit."

After weaseling a few more spotty details from Gabby, Jack managed to give the threesome the slip on the way to the after-party. He waved his cane as he passed the pinch-nosed maggots manning the night desk, hobbling onto the main elevator bays in a litter of excess. Drunken conventioneers groped each other in the back hallways and waiting areas, their slobbering and inappropriate end-of-the-world debauchery politely ignored by the invisible graveyard shift cleaning staff. The marble was not the only thing being buffed.

As soon as he was inside the elevator, Jack let out a terrifically terrified yawp as he bashed his cane against the copper paneling—its space-aged design snapped immediately. Sweet Christ, he'd slept with Clint's daughter! Not only that, but it had been horrible, downright ghastly. He couldn't help but wonder what kind of repercussions this would have. Surely she was off somewhere right now, erasing her earlier Jac(k)obean mistake by playing stuff the donut with one or both of those whacked-out weirdos, double pen style—did that make things better or worse?

Selfish self-preservation overtook Jack's mind, his survival instincts suggesting he bottle everything up. And so, back in the room, he tried not to think about the bigger picture; anyway, he hated it when people did that. Instead, he concentrated on rehydrating himself with the Frangelico minis, one by one. By the time the sun came up, everything was pretty much a blank. He'd emptied the entire fridge and was at least three-fourths drunk, with fifty or sixty little friar bottles littered at his feet. It was a unique, Canadian sendoff. Happy *hapax legomena*, hosers!

    A maid slipped a copy of the bill under the door as Jack was stumbling around the room, trying to decide whether to pack his things or just leave them behind. Personal possessions were becoming overrated he'd come to learn, thanks to Merrick, who'd systematically been taking his things away in a slowed progression defined by a simple, snide kleptomania. It actually wasn't a bad way to live. Reinvention was priceless.

    When Jack opened the invoice—which had already been paid in full—he nearly fainted. You could buy an economical luxury car with the total of his tab for the week, or a small island somewhere in the lesser desirable section of the Caribbean. He crumpled the paper tossed it on to his unmade bed, its sheets still ruffled from the fumbled tryst.

    He scooped the package Gabby had wrapped for Clint, and exited the room with only the tux on his back, a pack and a half of smokes, and a slightly dented vial of Nembutals. No doubt Jack was going to pay for this one, some way or another, but for now he was going home.

Frenemies, Domestically Foreign

Home isn't necessarily where the heart is. For Jack, the apartment he'd left was as empty, disused, and disgusting as before; stripped to its bare necessities, you might say. Ever have that feeling? Things looked just as you remembered them, faultlessly matched in fact, but you were convinced something was different—like a simulacra of same? Well, this wasn't that. Merrick had been around; a note confirmed her snoop:

Babyboy—You on Vay-Cay? With what? If you're sneaking ma-ma-my-moolah somewhere, bet you're A$$ I'll find it! Toodles, M.

She'd been up to her usual tricks, too, as a means of driving the point (away from) home. To that end, she'd removed the toaster, some pots and pans, as well as all the pertinent cutleries. Items Goodwill bound, surely. All the frames had also disappeared from the living room, the shower curtain was missing, and the toilet seat was covered in dried piss; it was the old double-reverse standard, which Merrick found hilarious. There was no malice or fury in the hellish conditions she sought to subject Jack to, but a certain love behind the madness—the kind of love, perhaps, that a laboratory lazar shows to her cure mouse in a maze.

A pouch of Latakia tobacco, with its pungent pepper aroma, was the barter for Merrick's sedulous persistence. She'd left it in the freezer, next to the peas. Jack rolled a few sticks of the Turkish delight as the last of the coffee brewed. He spent the first hour of his first morning smoking and drinking on the balcony.

New York in the late fall this year, said the radio, was abnormally warm. Below Jack's third floor perch, a dead mangled pigeon lay spread in a liquid pool on the edge of the sidewalk—black bloody water mingled with motor oil, gum, and people's spit. They too, the rushing bodies soaring up to the sun's heights with wax melting, avoided the death beneath them.

The apartment telephone—inconsiderate, insidious, and intrusive little device that it truly is—started ringing:

"What's going on?" Richter said, when Jack finally answered.

"Nothing."

"Well, what in the hell are you doing?"

"Reacclimatizing."

"What is that, some sort of hippie shit? I'll have a car out there in an hour. We gotta keep moving on this hot potato." Had Gabby told him? If so, Clint wasn't letting that stand in the way of furthering this pointless endeavor.

Clint's case was by no means unique.

Save for the independent wealth of his funding, his delusions of grandeur and overblown self-importance were typical affectations of the memoirist. Obsession inevitably infested this cognizant being, consumed him with an unrepentant need to leave a piece of himself behind, a distinctive smudge on life's brief flash.

Under normal circumstances, Clint would have been advised to drop the multi-national cabal exposé, with its overt and wildly accusatory conspiratorial tones, and told to focus instead on the party aspects of his padded socialite past. Glamour and gossip were the ticket in the trade, guaranteed big-money in the saucy references to the coked-out glory days at the 82 Club, the Roxy Roller Rink, the Copacabana, Le Jardin, Pravda, Erotic Circus, Studio 54, Danceteria, Plato's Retreat, Xenon, Infinity Disco, and the Mudd Club, especially with the likes of Christo, DeeDee Warhol, Veruschka, Steve Maas, Basquiat, Spider Webb, Delia Doherty, Roy Cohn, Alice Aycock, Sam Shepard, Bianca Jagger, Appolonia von Ravenstein, Diana Vreeland, Halston, M & M Hemingway, Steve Rubell, Grace Jones, Truman Capote, Olivia Newton-John, Rudolph Nureyev, Louise Bougeois, and clasping cinema relic Gloria Swanson.

But, Clint didn't need advice or a pushy publisher, what he needed was a forum; for that he would overpay for the Lincoln Press imprimatur, which was worthless enough to be bought. It was a self-publish scheme for the bored and over-privileged. This was, unmistakably, Clint's show. So far, Jack wasn't being paid to ask questions, nor was he required to fulfill expectations whatsoever. Shit, he wasn't even writing anything down! In point of fact, Jack had absolutely no idea what Clint was having him do, or how long this ridiculous ride would last, so he figured he might as well do his best to enjoy it. Sometimes, Houdini once said, being in the dark was a comfort to crawl.

    A 1934, burgundy brown Hispano-Suiza J12 picked Jack up early in the afternoon. Ol' Pappy was driving. They rode out to Clint's fiefdom in style, top down. Richter was on the front lawn, wielding a shotgun, when Jack arrived. A jaunty Jolly Roger flag flapped high atop the front lawn mast. The old man was in fine form and semi-oiled, dressed in a well-brushed pink camouflaged coat, hunt boots, and spurs fit for a big-game hunt.

    "Hey kid!" Clint said, as Jack stepped from the car with a slight limp. It was a winsome beginning, which suggested Richter was probably still in the dark about the whole Canadian hanky-panky business. "What happened to your face?"

    "Tai Chi accident."

    "Bummer. Wanna shoot?"

    "Uh, not right now, thanks."

    "Suit yourself." Clint squeezed off a few rounds, destroying two skeets as they were flung to the air. Several hundred yards in the distance, a pair of elderly black men dressed in Confederate Civil War uniforms manned the arcane machine.

"S'uh?" One of them bellowed.

"Swanny!" Clint yelled back, "Send off some of them 'Pelosi' pucks, some 'Quisling' and 'Mao' models, and more of those 'Hammarskjöld' and 'Boutros-Ghali' targets, too!" Richter took a swig of orange liquid from an unlabeled bottle and passed it over to Jack. "Bourbon?"

"Sure." Jack tucked the package he'd brought down from the Land of Bland under his arm as he drank. "What's with the target practice?"

"Keeps me on my toes. I have the boys make up different sized clay pigeons. They experiment with the consistency of the materials, the mix of the pitch, and the shapes of the targets to get more lift and thresh. They like painting faces on them, just for the heck of it, so I let 'em have their fun."

"I take it they're on a bit of political curve?"

"Pull!" Seven pigeons went flying, and in the ensuing enfilade Clint missed all but one. "Fuck! The neighbors are gonna kill me if I keep landing full disks through their windows—especially if they're painted with goddamn liberals." He started reloading. "Had a local gunsmith make this for me the other day, and it's got a real tight choke. Inn't she a beaut? Or would you say she's more of a dandy?"

"I don't know anything about guns."

"Me neither, except which way to point 'em. This one's got an eight-round tube magazine."

"Is that good?"

"If you got eight people to kill real quick, sure. It's not regulation for this sort of stuff, but I don't give a shit. Say, you hungry, Jack? I'll have Auntie J prepare her famous Cajun Mac-'n'-fromage for us as a snack. I don't want to keep you long because you'll probably want to get back to the City and pack—"

"Pack?"

"Yeah, you're leaving tomorrow."

"But, I just got back fr—"

"I got your next few weeks planned out. It's a bitch of a whirlwind, but you'll be back before Thanksgiving."

"Wait a sec—"

"Pull!" Clint swung the barrel across Jack's head and offloaded five shot patterns at the throws: 0 for 5. "Shit! Total bullshit! Five birds away, this just ain't my lucky day... Hey, Cornmeal!"

The ancient, grizzled dodderer stepped away from the mechanical trap and answered back in a croak: "Yass'uh!"

"Take a time out and go tell Jemima to whip up her lunch specialty, would ya?"

"Yass'uh!"

"And make sure she cooks extra grits and hushpuppies this time, too, the dogs can't get enough a' that crap! Oh, and bring out more bourbon!" The man wobbled inside as fast as his bowlegged limbs would allow. He, too, looked more than semi-oiled.

Jack cupped his hand to the winds as he lit a cigarette. "What happened to the chef you had before?"

"The Greek hippo, Panayotis?"

"Mn, right."

"I fired that fuck." Richter started reloading. "He couldn't cook for shit—ahh, no, that's not true. He was a helluva cook, but he was one of them quirky sons of a bitches. He always walked around in a toga or a pallium and every other day I kept finding him in dick-measuring contests with the statues on the back lawn. Besides, we had a huge fight about Onassis that I just couldn't let slide—"

"Oh?"

"Yeah, called him a bloated Blofeld and accused him of having an affair with Kissinger. We've all heard the Howard Hughes kidnapping story, of course, but the truth was they were fishing buddies. I mean shit, Aristotle could be a right ole prick at times, but he wasn't no terrorist—not in the textbook definition anyway; and above all, he was a friend. No way some dishpig, dipshit toad was having his say like that.

Jesus, fuck! What's the problem here?" The man left standing at the projectile machine looked confused, lost. "Swanny! You okay?"

"Yez, s'ah!"

"You all right to man that trap alone?"

"Yez, s'ah!"

"Great. Gimme a few minutes to finish reloading, and then send off the Roosevelt cluster of turkeys: *Prosperity at Home, Prestige Abroad!*"

"Aye, aye, Cap'n!"

"It's *Colonel*! Christ, how many times I gotta tell ya? Captain's for those deck-swab yahoos!"

"Sorry, C. Figure a' speech, s'ah!"

"At ease!" Clint turned, shaking his head. "The man's been with me since I left Ft. Bragg over 4 decades ago, you'd think he'd remember. But no, every other day he keeps bustin' me down grades in a sort of anti-brevet. Can't blame him much, though, he's a tarnished innocent. The only book he's ever read is Monsarrat's *The Cruel Sea*, which some say is all you need in life. Here, listen to this: Sailor!"

"S'ah, yez, s'ah!"

"How long've you been in the Navy?"

"S'ah, I been in da nay-vee all m'uh bloomin' life, s'ah! M'mama wuz a muh-med and m'papah wuz Kin Nep-toon. E'ree bone in m'bodee's a spar, an'a when I shits, s'ah, I shitz tar. I's hard, I iz, I am, I are!"

"The ole *schvartze* bugger's always had a thing for Annapolis and the British Royal Navy, God knows why! Guess he's got it bad for bellbottoms and porkpie caps. Poor shithead's as senile as a Gabor sister—"

"Must be harder and harder to find good help these days?"

"So they say, but I've been a blessed man." Clint picked up the bottle and took another long sip. He winced, slightly, before talking again. "So, Jack, everything went fine up north?"

"I guess."

"The hotel bill was a dead giveaway. Shit on a stick, son, you sure know how to spend!"

"Too much?"

"Not a chance. I believe in spending the money I have, not hoarding it. I see now that you feel the same way, even if it is *my* bread."

"Well—"

"No need to explain, Jack. I admire someone who spends another man's money with such abandon, such gusto." Richter's glint was a proud beam. "And the eleemosynary banquet with Gabby, you two got along?"

"Yeah. I wish you'd told me she was your stepdaughter, though."

"Hmm? Oh, I thought I had."

"No, you didn't, and I felt like a bit of an idiot for it. Plus, not knowing her name almost got me killed—"

"At a charity dinner? Who's being

paranoid now?"

"What? No, I'm talking about something else." Jack took a drag from his smoke, sifting through the things best left north of the border. "Oh, before I forget, Gabby gave me something for you…"

Swanny suddenly bellowed, "Reeeeeaaadddddeeeee!"

"Pull!" The birds were instantly catapulted, and Clint hit half the targets.

Jack's ears were ringing from the close proximity of the gun blasts. "Jeeee-suuuzzz Kiiirrreyezzzt!"

"Loud, huh?"

"How come you aren't deaf?"

"Earplugs."

"Any spares?"

"Nope, sorry." Jack handed over the package Gabby had given him. The wrapping was disintegrated, somewhat. "You opened it?"

"Absolutely not. I respect a man's privacy."

"That's why I trust you, Jack. Was in your eye, the first time I met you."

"I was drunk and stoned when we first met."

"Is there a best time to test the theory? *In narco veritas!*" Clint's fingers toyed with the edges of the wrapping paper. "So you two had some fun, huh?

"W—what d'you mean?"

"How long did it take for her to make a pass?"

"Uh...?"

"Hey, I know what you kids are like today. You're like polygamous rabbits. I figured you two would hit it off."

"If I said we, uh... fooled... around—a bit—would that get me fired?"

"Hell no! Have your fun, I say! We sure as shit did back in the seventies! Besides, Gabby's practically a grown woman." Richter smiled then, with a hint of the Cheshire cat in him—it was an expression difficult to interpret, and somewhat perplexing. Knowing the old man, though, the sentiment was probably genuine (or not). "Swanny! Hold off for a minute! I'm opening a present."

"Yez, s'ah!" Clint put down the gun, its barrel pointed straight at Jack's groin. Before opening the gift, Clint wiped away a titanic gob of snot with his sleeve, the buttery yellow goo blending in with the camouflage of his pink jacket. In one swoop, he tore off the gift's wrapping.

"Oh my God!"

"What, what is it?"

"It's a purple pelt Timberwolf! A rare interbreed strain blended and bred from the Northeastern wolf (*Canis lupus lycaon*) and the elusive *Canis rufus* (Red Wolf), now found mostly in Texas." Clint ran his hand along the fur, its bristles shimmering a slight lavender hue in the sun. "See those plum tones? Amazing."

"So, wolf fur? That's what Gabby had me lug down here."

"Not just *any* wolf fur, Jack. Researchers think that this unique strain happened some time during the Upper Pleistocene period and managed to stay alive, somehow, secluded in certain remote parts of the arctic watershed basin in the Northeast. Supposedly, there are fewer than twenty-five of these living lilac babies in the wild—well, 24 now. We're talking top-level of the Critically Endangered List. Shooting one is considered a real IUCN no-no."

"I-U-C-N, what's that?"

"International Union for the Conservation of Nature and Natural Resources. It doesn't quite fit with the acronym, I know, but I guess it was the best those bureaucratic clowns could come up with. They wield enormous power in the wings, as a shadow organization, a sort of secret society for modern times; but they've got no inner moral compass, you see, which is what makes them much more dangerous than classics like the Templars, the Chevaliers of Malta, the Trilateral Commission, the Rotary Club, the Freemasons, the Teutonic Knights, the Rosicrucian Order, the Croatian Coven, the Bohemian Club, the Illuminati, the Zapruder Card Sharks, the Bilderberg Group, the guild of North African American Corporate Practitioners (NAACP), the

Ordo Templi Orientis, the Council of Foreign Relations, and the Shriners—all of which I belong to, by the way."

"The dues alone must be murder—"

"Tell me about it, but it's all in good fun. Anyway, nowadays, none of those old school clubs can hold a candle to snot-nosed upstarts like the IUCN—their priorities and agendas are way, way, way out of whack and they've made serious inroads with the collective psyche of the dominant first world ethos. I mean forget about introspection! These are the people who would rather see your cock chopped off than hear about a baby beluga getting its head smashed in by those North Pole Eskimos."

"They prefer Inuit, now, I think."

"Is that so? Huh. Anyway, the 'who' doesn't especially matter to the IUCN, the act is just as bad when ol' whitey's doing the bashing of the skulls, too. Except for celebrities, mind you, they're immune. Like when that boring rubber-faced McBeatle—Angela Lansbury—went up there with cricket bat in hand to spazz out on some seals with his peg-leg lass, Heather."

"Did we get off track?"

"Not really."

"Well, back to that pelt in your hand then, Clint. Isn't it illegal to be caught with the skin of an endangered animal, much less cross borders with one in a backpack?"

"Oh, you bet. Absolutely! This is

America's Most Wanted type stuff. These days they treat pelt smugglers worse than they used to treat terrorists like bin Laden, or Abu Abbas of the PLF. These environmentalists got mad skills in the torture chamber, too, better'n any nail-ripping Gitmo grunt I ever saw. What's brilliant about the IUCN is that they use the EPA as a piggyback front, and their yearly operating budget is something like twice that of Homeland Security. It's perfectly understandable, seeing as the public's got nothing but support for the mutilation of monsters that poach any near extinct animal species for cash. Hell, I wouldn't be surprised if the head of PETA herself hooked your balls up to the car battery and got the Animal Liberation Front to chip-in for the pliers."

"Are you fucking kidding me?"

"Not at all. You saw what those nuts at PETA and the ALF were saying when the big one hit Haiti—forget the hundred thousand dead men, women, and children, who's gonna speak for the poor voiceless little fluffballs? Give me an effing break. Imagine, being so obtuse to all that human suffering—"

"But what about this pelt!"

"Oh, right. Well, we'd have to ask Gabby where she bagged it exactly. No matter what, she always sends me the best pieces for my collection. You've seen some on my walls, in the study, right?"

"You had me haul that thing across the

border? I could have been arrested!"

"And worse, no doubt."

"Worse?"

"The lock-up ward of child molesters and rapists, probably. In the penal system, you see, animal poachers are hated by the gen. pop more than the pedophiles. So, in turn, those sickos hate you guys worse than anyone."

"But I'm not a poacher, Gabby is! You *almost* set me up."

"Hey, how was I supposed to know what was in here? It's from Gabby *to* me; it's obviously meant as a surprise. Who knows where it came from?"

"That's for damn sure! Is that the reason you had me go up there?"

"Don't be ridiculous." Clint pulled the cork off the moonshine bottle with his teeth, sipping slowly to wet his throat. "It was only *one* of the reasons you went."

"Christ! I can't believe it. You used me as a mule."

"Look, calm down."

"You blindsided me with all that conspiracy nonsense!"

"None of which you believe. You were innocent and unaware, there's nothing more trustworthy than that. It's not as if you can UPS this shit any more. Besides, that was merely a... fringe benefit, as they say. I really did want to send you up there to have a look at the Hangar."

"That place is a joke, man, just like you! It's a storehouse for rotting shit, junk!"

"Listen," Clint put his hand on Jack's shoulder, in a paternal pat. "I'll pop off a few more rounds, we'll go inside for a bite, get a good buzz on, and chat about the upcoming tour—"

"Are you insane? I'm not going on any more stupid fucking pointless errands, putzing around for you like some shameless indolent schmuck—"

"Why not? I've already got it all planned, and you'll be back in a couple weeks, tops. You'll have more fun on this one, guaranteed, and we'll get a book out of it."

"Forget it! You manipulated me, man, with… with—"

"Nothing. I didn't manipulate you at all—not much, anyway. I sent you on a working holiday, that's it. You had plenty a' fun at the expense of my bank account, right? You may not know what you're doing, but I do. So why d'you care? I know why, because as cynical as you *wish* you were, you also want to believe in things, in deeper truths hidden beneath the surface. Right? Well, join the club, mac!"

"I don't even know what you're saying."

"I'm saying: chill the fuck out, Jack, have a belt of this, and let's go talk about the rest inside. A gorge sound good?"

Jack's defenses were down, and his weaknesses ably appealed to. What was there, really, to resist? Nothing in his life had worked out the way he'd planned, and with Merrick gone, nothing remained of his past. He had nothing left, and nothing to lose, so why not keep doing nothing and get paid for it? The dilemma was timeless. Ay, there's the rub: inimitably trapped between the perchance dream and the suffocating incubus of the mundane. Faced with the permanence of the undiscovered country, choices truly were few. "All right, Clint, lead the way."

"Attaboy! There's the winning spirit. Believe me, we're riding a wave of privilege here, son." When Jack got home, hours later, he barely remembered the rest of the afternoon. Richter had managed to calm him down with some no-harm-no-foul drivel, plying him with copious dishes of food and endless wine. After taking three Nembutals, Jack floated in flashes.

At least Clint had provided some concrete notes on the places Jack was meant to visit this time around, instead of just epigrammatic rhetoric gnomes. The itinerary was a tightly scheduled, east-to-west sweep starting down in Florida, through Texas, Arizona, and California, with coffee breaks in Seattle and some as-yet unnamed, nameless Midwest towns. The organ grinder's wheel once again turned.

Part III

he winged away on a wildgoup's chase across the kathartic ocean and made synthetic ink and sensitive paper for his own end out of his wit's waste. You ask, in Sam Hill, how?
—*FW* I.vii.185

Meaningless Rigor Mortis

The morning after Clint's, Jack was groggy, a feeling he was now thoroughly used to. His Nembutals were becoming a good safety-net rebalance to such excess, especially with Gabby's Demerol stash now almost completely dwindled. Jack planned to hit the *farmacia* around the corner before he left and get Manuel to fill his Adderall scrip. He wondered, as his first urine stream dribbled into the bowl, why it had taken so long for him to get on this miraculous pill-popping train. Who'd been holding the schedule?

Packing for this next trip was made simple for two reasons. On the one hand: Jack no longer owned any clothes in his closet that could be deemed "wearable." Merrick had whittled away his wardrobe in an endearing bi-part plan defined by: a) Burning his best suits with kerosene in the empty barrels of the alley behind the building; and by b) Ensuring that 72.5% of Jack's shirts, sweaters, pants, coats, hats, and shoes (dress and sport) were donated to the local mission. The number was a fair, perfect match to the percentage of his pre-Clint Lincoln Press paychecks she'd commandeered.

On the second (and more important) hand, Clint had just dropped thirty large on Jack, cushioning the blow of his being otherwise broke

(broke on paper, anyway). Most of this so-called walking around money Jack planned to spend irresponsibly, on expensive throwaway get-ups, pricey cocktails, or useless trinkets that he could hurl from his hotel room balconies—brief flights of sparing glory into the wild blue yonder.

    The rest of the apartment prep for his departure was non-existent. He had no plants or fish to feed and, except for some take-out food condiments and a black tomato that had become the mascot of his shelves, the fridge was utterly empty. There was nothing else to do but wait for the limousine to come pick him up, so Jack nervously fiddled. He left a note for Merrick on the kitchen table—*GONE FISHIN'*, written in bold ink on a scrap of paper—then abused himself with the help of an old Sears catalogue from 1986, put on his traveling tuxedo, made coffee, and afterward paced around the place, smoking.

    In the final moments before departure, the air settled into a strange calm that suddenly broke. The phone was ringing. Maybe Clint had changed his mind? Maybe the driver was late, stuck in traffic?

    Jack answered in a soft, calm tone: "Mmyallow?"

    "Jack?" Shit, it was his mother. Something was up, definitely. Out-of-the-azure was not her style.[13]

Jack hadn't heard from Muggins in years, not since she'd boycotted his marriage to Merrick. The apology she'd sent cited a previous engagement at "Ramanuja Ranch," a Yogi-Barn bubble retreat outside of Santa Fe. Her appended congratulatory message, nebulous aphorisms

---

[13] A quick background sketch: unlike what Jack supposed was the common operational modus of most maternal units the world over—nagging, pestering, coddling, caring, henpecking, urging, teasing, cherishing, tormenting, coaxing, scolding, harassing, indulging, cajoling, hectoring, tormenting, reminding, spoiling, fawning, flattering, feigning, manipulating, inveigling, persuading, soliciting, teasing, wheedling, cherishing, nuzzling, doting, emoting, worshiping, stellifying, attending, furthering, monitoring, nourishing, proctoring, rearing, protecting, nattering, providing, nursing, heeding, and, yes, even mothering—Jack's mother was regimentally indifferent to the common course of motherhood and selfishly removed; or, to be kind, she'd always focused concern on her own well-being over that of Jack's piece of mind. She was a vindictive, ill-mannered, fair-weather parent who constantly picked sides—and that side was always Shelley's, Jack's sister, yet another opportunist of the highest caliber. Anyway, back to Mother Marion, known to all simply as "Muggins."

really, were laconic shards of transcendental mumbo jumbo mostly cribbed from Shirley MacLaine's character in *Terms of Endearment*.

Muggins was much flightier than Jack, straight from the birdcage, and a force of light. Her fierce independent spirit was admirable, even though she needed to be perpetually married to assert that independence. Hard, was one way to describe her; but her muffled personality had been softened by two decades of sitting under the Arizona sun, eating bean sprouts, and writing trashy romance novelettes under the *nom de guerre* Debra Wingnut. She was a Southern Simenon, prolific in an enviable yet repugnant way. She was also a censorious sensor ray for poor social behavior. Her smell, for as long as Jack could remember, was a sweet odor of wine-tipped cigarillos and rubbing alcohol. She'd never suffered from the costive curse but owned instead a great talent for babbling on endlessly, using disparaging dubiety as a smear-all handkerchief. Muggins was, along with many other things, one of a kind.

"Hello, Muggins."

"Jack! Christ, I can't believe you answered your own phone. I was expecting to talk to that wife of yours, what's her name again?"

"Merrick."

"That's right. I remembered it was something stupid. Who ever heard of such a name! Actually, know what? I should put her in this next piece I'm working on. I've got a real odalisque-slut character still in need of a handle. How is she—your wife I mean—by the way?"

"Not sure. We're divorced."

"Great! Outstanding! Guess she won't mind if I use her moniker then—"

"Go right ahead."

"Cripes! This call is already much better than I expected!"

"Glad to hear it."

"Oh, before I forget, have you talked to Shelley by any chance?"

"No. Why would I?"

"You really should. She and Allan are doing very, very well!"

"What is it you want, Muggins? I've got to get going here soon—"

"Why d'you even pick-up the fuckin' phone then, if you were in such a rush?"

"Look, I thought it was someone else, okay?"

"Don't you have that panel deesplay, or whatever it is they call it? Your entire generation is obsessed with having to know who's calling. *Who's calling! Who's calling?* For decades, we just picked up the damn phone and none of us died from it. This new technology shit is an invasion of privacy! How are you supposed to prank-call anyone anymore?"

"I don't have caller ID, all right? And I *am* running a little late, so—"

"Fine, I'll get to the point. As if a mother needs a point to call her own son—"

"Or even needs to call her son at all, for that matter."

"That's not fair."

"No? I think it's perfectly goddamn fair."

"What? I stay in touch. I call."

"Beyond that, that—let's face it—downright weird RSVP note you sent to the wedding reception, I haven't heard from you in almost four years."

"See, there. That's keeping in touch, isn't it?"

"I don't even know why I'm getting into this—"

"Exactly. I mean, if it *has* been such a long time, as you say, you'd think a little more effort could be made when I do call."

"Is this going to take long? I have a plane to catch." Jack took out his pack of cigarettes and lit one. The smoke came out in a loud exhale.

"Are you still smoking?"

"Yes."

"Good! Don't let them goody-goody New Yorker assholes try to convince you to clean up your act. What's all this jazz I hear about them not letting you light up in Times Square now? That's complete and total bullshit!" She enunciated with bravado, as ever, which was strangely comforting. "So, where is it you're flying to anyhow?"

"Florida."

"Florida? That gator-infested swamp! Why?"

"I'm going to an Ernest Hemingway look-a-like contest in the Keys."

"Really?"

"No."

"Would you be serious for once? You were never serious about anything, not even your writing. Why d'you think your 'career' tanked?"

"My career didn't 'tank,' Muggins. I left voluntarily."

"Ow, right. More like voluntold to take a bow."

"Can we *not* talk about this, please?"

"What are you doing with yourself, then, still wasting whatever shreds of talent you have by ghostwriting garbage for other people?"

"Yes."

"Why?"

"I'm hanging up now."

"Wait, wait, wait—"

"What, what is it?"

"Why don't you come by the house? We could talk in person. That is, once you're done slumming it in the Conch Republic Micronation sippin' on Mint Juleps—"

"I'm pretty sure that's a plantation drink. Budweiser is more Florida's speed, and NASCAR."

"Well, whatever. Just come visit. It's not

that far to the Old Pueblo from there."

"Ah-huh," an irrational, clouded dread leapt into Jack, as if he would somehow happen to bump into her while slashing through Arizona, doing whatever in the hell it was that Clint had in mind for him. Even though he couldn't care less for Muggins, or her life, he also didn't want to take the chance of hurting her feelings. Was that odd? "I, I—you know—I might just be able to make that trip, as it turns out."

"Really, you'll come to Tucson? Just like that?"

"Why not?"

"I can loan you the money—at 83% interest—if you need it?"

"Nope."

"My, aren't you a thoughtful son!" After Jack hung up, the falsity of her words continued to ring. When had she ever said anything like that? Even when Jack was a child, she'd specifically gone out of her way to *not* complement him; or else, she'd complement his sister, who never did anything of real value and never has. Shelley Sadsack, as she'd always been known, and her no-neck husband—both entertainment lawyers by trade—loafed around their Kenilworth, Illinois house (an impoverished suburb of Chicago) in sweat pants, doing nothing else but stuff their fat red faces with cheese puffs, Cherry Garcia ice cream, and maple-syrup Ding Dongs while watching endless pay-per-view programming. They were the epitome of useless human boobs, consuming but for nothing.

And maybe that's what Jack did too, but at least he'd contributed, culturally, at some point. In his mind, it wasn't completely inconceivable that someday some English professor, probably at a third-rate college somewhere, would teach a class on '90s literature or literary one-hit wonders and would include Jack's work. That would be his legacy, whether acknowledged or not; that would be his permanent period.

The conversation with Muggins completely ruined the first leg of Jack's trip. It was hard to put out of his mind. The call was too coincidental to be coincidence; something deeper, weightier, marinated obscurely below the shimmered surface. The enormity of possibility was perplexing. Predictably perhaps, he appeased his concerns with Nembutals and whiskey, mostly.

The one careful lesson Jack had learned from Muggins, long ago (and what he perhaps emulated without necessarily being conscious of), was the constant quasi-inebriety that she carried so well. The genetic equation for imbibition, therefore, is: Mother: Son; Apple: Tree. But was perpetual, dependent, despondent non-social drinking well and truly hereditary? The 12-step AA converts would give a vehement affirmative yelp to the query, but no one takes any of them seriously. They are just a bunch of drunks, after all.

Soon, a greater curiosity overtook Jack's concerns. In Florida, Clint had him follow a very specific set of map points, explicitly detailed. The locations, Clint claimed, were once cold war training facilities, black-op insurrection launch points, and tactical torture chambers for the interrogation of illegal foreign nationals. These torment complexes utilized methods now generally regarded as either unlawful or unsportsmanlike (except under the legislative legerdemain of Dubyah's PATRIOT Act), and usually involved a smorgasbord of bullying, name-calling, browbeating, *agua*-boarding, finger pointing, intimidation, and all-purpose hazing of those unwilling to bend to the Good Ole American Way (GO-A-Way!).

Clint insisted that Jack follow his itinerary route to the letter. And this insistence bordered on maniacal obsession, which defined the *modus vivendi* of the entire "fact gathering" mission.[14]

The refulgent Sunshine State circuit was as follows: land in Miami, pick-up an exquisite

---

[14] Jack didn't make much of the old man's insanity at first, but follow along on your road maps at home and later down the line a clear pattern will eventually emerge for you, as well as for Jack. Meanwhile, here's where the infernal maw of the road swallows us whole…

ragtop '67 Mustang rental, and flow up the I-95 North. Past Fort Lauderdale, Palm Beach, Fort Pierce, and Rockledge, Jack was told to veer west on the 528—the old "Bee Line Expressway," now renamed for some dirty-deed developer—to Belle Isle, Sky Lake, and eventually stop just short of Sea World. At that point, instead of taking the more efficient option of Interstate 4 up towards Daytona, Clint had Jack retrace his Bee Line path back to the I-95 North.

As any diligent traveler will note, upon looking at a roadmap of the state, this was definitely the long way around. Not only that, but the coastal intersection placed Jack squarely on the state's launch pad to all things space related: Astronaut Memorial Hall, the Planetarium & Observatory, Valiant Air Command Museum, U.S. Astronaut Hall of Fame, Spaceport USA, Cape Canaveral (including its Port Authority and Air Force Skid Strip), and, of course, the Kennedy Space Center and National Wildlife Refuge, which must benefit enormously from all improperly dumped rocket fuels.

Jack had to find a payphone and confirm the morphology of his orders:

"Should I *not* be going to visit at least some of these places, Clint?"

"No."

"Why? Seems to make a lot more sense to me—have a lot more to do with your astronaut days, for example—than going to some stupid warehouse up in Canada!"

"Too bad, that's the way it is. Ain't nothing for you there."

"Nothing for me here? I'm a kick away from Merritt Island, the hub of American space exploration."

"No it ain't, that's in Houston! What you're talking about is a museum of fakeries and near misses. It's like Disneyland, except everything sucks. I don't need you to check that out for me, I already know it's a bullshit political quagmire."

"Fine. Whatever you say."

"Follow the damn directions, Jack. No questions asked! That's what we agreed on if you're gonna be on my dime. Right?"

"Right."

"Do you need me to run down that list for you again?"

"No."

"Well I will. One: Only go to the sites I put down. Two: Make a note of what the building is used for today. Three: Take approximate measurements of the structures and document any unusual features. That's all, a piece a' piss. Can't be any easier than that. You got it?"

"Yes."

"You sure?"

"Yes, I said!"

"Then do the damn job like I asked!"

Jack continued his shoot up the coastal

spine, past Daytona Beach, and on to Jacksonville, where he eventually got on the I-10 all the way to the Pensacola Panhandle, America's First Settlement. You should be able to guess, by now, what letter his trajectory revealed.

The trip was done in two days, at a leisurely pace, inspecting the seven sites Clint had identified. It didn't strike Jack until about the third or fourth location that every modern incarnation of a supposed covert, underground installation came up as a Burger King outlet: *Where Kids, Freedom & Angioplasty rule the Land!* Each location, it was also semi-important to note, was a stone's throw away from airstrips originally used as bases (known or unknown) before and during the Second World War. But, that was probably just coincidence, Jack decided.

Predictably so, Jack felt the urge to order a little something when walking in to these franchises, which was the least he could do while taking measurements and jotting down notes. He usually used their washrooms, too, flapping fantastic flatulence at the fast-food walls while listening for the distant, faded sounds of bygone brutal torture or cleverly encrypted radio broadcasts. When Jack related his preliminary BK findings to Clint, Richter simply answered with "Huh, really?" as if this were an unsurprising fact.

The reconnaissance was a well-planned goose chase. Again, Jack couldn't help but feel played like a pawn, a half-wit marauder investigating empty avenues. Previously covert Americanizations now modernized into overt ones, with bone cutters, Catherine wheels, and polygraph devices seemingly replaced by deep fryers, mop closets, and Drive Thrus. And just to add a bit of zip to the special sauce, the common conversion spices of *Jus soli* (law of the ground) and *Jus sanguinis* (right of blood) had been mixed and peppered and served on a tray.

The precise seven-point route went as follows, starting outside Miami, just off the Avenue in Opa Locka (1), then continuing on Consulate Drive, at the meeting of the 528 and the Rockin' Ronnie Reagan Turnpike (2), on the East Highway in Flagler Beach (XFL (3)), a skidmark away from the Daytona International Speedway (4), then off Normandy in Herlong (5), on Tennessee Street near Dale Mabry's Fields (6) and, finally, at Bayou Boulevard in Pensacola (7).

Jack had only been on the road for two days, and already he was exhausted. Pills did what they could to take Jack's mind off things, but, no doubt, he was once more neck deep in a mire of Clint's bullshit. He only had himself to blame of course, or maybe Merrick, who'd drained all options along with his bank account; and now, on top of that healthy dollop of self-loathing, he was being watched.

At first, Jack figured Richter had simply put a tail on him. The move fit Clint's style perfectly: pay one schnook to bounce around Point A to B to Z, for sheer entertainment value, and pay a second schnook to keep an eye on the first one to make sure he was more or less conforming to the psychotic plan. Results were inconsequential in such a senseless scheme, where only the game of it was of any substantive matter. Yet, the concept of "more or less" was of primordial importance in a mysterious, metaphysical meander such as this:

Clint was too rich to do his own dirty work (that much was clear, even when discarding the whole absurd and asinine premise of the Agoraphobia angle), but the root causes went deeper than that. Clint's entire Baby Boom Generation had been unwittingly caught in a long-fought, downward spiral, retirement trajectory to the finish line. They'd been raised on constant conflicts, hardened on Cold War promises, and embittered by the dragging inaction of a never-ending South-East Asia war initiative. Their character had been forged, and they'd had absolutely no say in the matter. In that type of zeitgeist, things had indelible and inherent value: a man's word was his bond, and a handshake was better than any piece of contractual scrap paper could ever be.

None of those beliefs disappeared as time wore on, but they softened in a world where applied rigor was no longer the predominant point of view. For Richter, this was ostensibly tempered not only by a generational question, but a socio-economic one as well. In a Camelot-like environment, therefore, it was natural to careen through the milestones of life at the helm of your yacht, natural to rub elbows and bump uglies with celebrities, natural to assume that the halls of power were yours for the taking (by any bribery means necessary), natural to have people wait on your every whim, and natural to assume that 99% of the world population was inferior to you in some way, shape, or form. This variety of ablative philosophical outlook was not vanity, but a simple belief that lived deep in your heart.

So, here we bend sinister back to the More or Less. If those of Clint's ilk needed things done in a certain orderly way, why hire one stooge when you could just as easily hire two? It was an elemental algorithm of the upper class, a practical equation that balanced the surface with the nitty-gritty and covered all bases without seeming too needy.

This quadratic theoretical component Jack had managed to work out and come to terms with, but the very real threat of imminent danger from his newly acquired shadow presence was infinitely more problematic. It was downright unnerving having a spook on your shoulder like that, and it was next to impossible for Jack to keep from taking the undercover tactic personally. When, in the plush of his Pensacola hotel and well past half-in-the-bag, Jack confronted Richter about his postulations, the results were inconclusive:

"So, Jack, you settled in fine down there, get a good look at all seven points I had notes on?"

"Yep. All Burger Kings, like I said."

"Doesn't surprise me, really. What better cover than to sell out to an All-American icon. Burgers, I mean, not that particular chain of artery cloggers *per se*."

"I suppose."

"What about Pensacola? Sure is a pulchritudinous spot, ain't it? D'you enjoy your so-called day-off?"

"Yeah. Listen, Clint, you wouldn't happen to have someone tailing me right now, would you?"

"Don't be ridiculous! That's—that's... I think you're buying in to your own paranoia, Jack—"

"*My* paranoia! I didn't believe in paranoia until I met you."

"Well, don't sweat it. People always feel strange when they're out on the road, comes with the territory. Why d'you think I went for the shut in life?"

"You're about as shut in as the Pope."

"What can I say, Pope's gotta shit in the wood some time."

"Wha'?"

"Look, my advice is to put it out of your

mind. Just try and enjoy the assignment, no harm in that."

"Enjoy it? I found a knife stabbed into my pillow when I got back from the bar late this afternoon—"

"Really?"

"No. They were mint chocolates, but they could just as easily have been a switchblade."

"You're letting things get to you; it's understandable." Clint paused to clear his throat and in the background it sounded like screeching women.

"What's that?"

"Pillow fight. Anyway, what were you doing in a *bar* this afternoon?"

"What do you think?"

"You're supposed to be working, even if I did give you a day off."

"I *am* working."

"If someone were trying to kill you, doesn't sound like you're making it too hard on them."

"Speaking of that, I'm positive the bartender downstairs is my man. He wrote some shit on the bathroom wall down there and I also found a note up here on my desk, in the same chicken scrawl, saying *We Are Watching Again*."

"So? That's probably just the hotel's slogan."

"And my suitcase has been riffled through. If I owned any clothes, I guarantee they'd be all over the place as we speak, probably ripped to shreds."

"Bah, that's an easy one. Sometimes the maids in these fancy joints throw 15-minute benders in the guest suites and then take the party to another room. They used to call 'em Pussy Parties in my day; I'm sure they've got some ludicrous techno name for them now. Check for used condoms and syringes on the ironing board in the closet; or, better yet, look inside the mini-bar, that's usually the sure-fire test—"

"Mini bar's almost empty."

"See, whad'I tell ya?"

"I did that."

"Oh."

"Look, just be straight up with me: is someone following me?"

"No one is trying to kill you, Jack. Get some rest, okay? Sounds like you need it."

Five Flag Play-by-Play

The menace Jack was feeling in Pensacola was real. He knew that much, at least. He'd sensed the shadow presence building around him ever since his visit to the Panhandle Pub, this morning. Amidst the peanut shells, foul beer reek, and blaring sports televisions, a looming weight lingered in the grass. At that early stage, mind you, the menace remained bleakly imperceptible:

Following four Tequila Sunrise doubles and two Nembutals for breakfast, Jack had managed to take a good portion of the edge off. He was on a Richter-sanctioned day-off, after his two-day drive, and Jack was determined to make the best of it.

As any visitor to Pensacola well knows, there is so much more to this pocket paradise than meets the eye. Thanks to Hurricanes like Eloise (1975), Juan (1985), Opal (1995), Ivan (2004), and Dennis the Menace (2005), the place had been whittled into a true emerald coast to be desired. But dive bars, the Blue Angels flight squad, and the University of West Florida cheerleaders were the real draws of the town.

Carrying a slight buzz, Jack ambled through the eighteenth century streets down towards the Gulf Coast waters, getting grit and sand in his teeth—now bared in a steely, unfamiliar rictus. Well-fed Floridian cicadas persistently chirred. Amongst the numerous beach offerings, he opted for a long swim with an uneasy school of Kemp's ridley turtles and then set his mind on turning his tenuous haze into a full-blown bayou brownout.

In a tiki watering hole called *Slim Pickens,* Jack met a female Lieutenant from the local Air Station, and he bought the fine-figured woady a Martini to add to her collection. She repaid him with a few dirty looks and some choice wisecracks. It felt, for a time, like he was getting somewhere. Then, the inevitable:

"So, what are you doing in the Cradle of Naval Aviation, Jack?"

"Just passing through."

"You had a chance to play tourist up at the NASP?"

"No. The Armed Forces isn't really my thing. That's more my boss's deal."

"He sounds like a smart man."

"He's a certifiable yo-yo—"

"Did you know that John Glenn flew out of here?"

"No, I didn't. Who's he?"

"Seriously? He was the first American to orbit the earth."

"Mmn, cool."

"Glenn said this place was what gave him the courage to go into orbit."

"Is it that bad?"

"Neil Armstrong said practically the same thing, about the first lunar mission. I doubt I have to tell you who he was—"

"Nope, you sure don't. But I'll tell *you* something you might not know about the Giant Leap For Mankind—"

"Oh, what's that?"

"Buzz Aldrin was actually the first man on the moon."

"Excuse me?"

"Hand to God. Only problem was: those NASA clowns couldn't get the camera rolling when they were up there—something to do with the film speed and the earth's gravitational pull, I think it was—so they had to re-shoot the whole damn thing when they got back here to terra firma." That look crept in to the Lieutenant's eyes, the look you get when you fall off your rocker. "You laugh, but I've seen the inside of the honeycomb—"

"Uh-huh."

"They've got this place up in Canada, see—?"

"You're nuts, bub!"

"Wait! Don't go, it's true! Aldrin lost this high-stakes poker game the night before the re-shoot and he…" Well, at least she forgot to finish her drink. Jack drank it and left. No sense in wasting someone else's perfectly good money.

It was around this time that the ominous, looming presence Jack had felt since the morning, intensified. While stumbling his way back to the hotel, he turned around quickly—on several occasions—to see if anyone or anything was lingering behind. He peered around palm tree trunks, he peered behind mailboxes, he peered (creepily) at men reading newspapers on benches. But the espionage/counter-surveillance game wasn't Jack's bag, being too conspicuous and vulgar. Besides, who would be following him for a few, meaningless covert operation cum-Burger-King locales? Much less want to kill him for it, right?

He dropped the idea until he got back to the hotel lounge, around dinnertime. He'd taken a couple more yellow pills to even out his buzz, and the combination was working well. These pills were an absolute miracle, and Jack loved the way his body reacted to the mixture of them with booze. It was still early, and if he wasn't going to get any tail in this pisswater of the panhandle, at least he might get a chance at a good night's sleep. He ordered a pint glass of Kentucky straight from the barman and popped off to the toilet to drain the main vein. It sounded like someone was snorting lines of "Billy Idol" in the stall, which was always a classy sign. In front of his urinal Jack noticed the warning, his first concrete clue: *Jack! Stop following the Path!*

The message got Jack thinking, but not for very long. Halfway through his pint of whiskey back at the bar, his mind went reeling in other directions. Movements got tight, labored. His speech patterns began to slow. The rocket from the Nembutal slingshot was coming crashing back at terminal velocity. Maybe it was time for him to retire upstairs, but he seemed to be in the middle of a conversation with the barman. It was hard to figure where they were at in their talk, the pharma-buzz once more winning the battle. Was it Jack's turn to speak? He took a chance:

"Sorry, what?"

"I said, you here 'til the weekend?"

"I'm leaving tomorrow."

"Too bad, you'll miss the BYOB party hosted by the BBYO."

"What's that?"

"The B'nai B'rith Youth Organization. I'm on the committee. I just do this moonlighting gig to pay for college."

"Good for you—"

"We throw one hulluva fuckin' party!"

"Oh yeah?"

"For sure. Usually we have keggers, but we're trying to tone down our party image. Know what I mean? Anyway, if for some reason you're not back on the path, stop by Beth-El Temple."

"Why did you say it like that?"

"Like what?"

"Did you write that stuff in the washrooms? Are you the one who's been following me?"

"I'm sorry, sir, I don't know what you're

talking about."

"Bullshit, kid! Richter put you up to this, didn't he? Didn't he! It's completely fucking insane!"

"You have to calm down, sir, or I'll have to ask you to leave."

"What's in this glass?"

"Whiskey. That's what you ordered."

"How do I know? I didn't see you pour it! You could've... you could've put—"

"Sir, do you need help up to your room?"

"Absolutely not! That was your plan all along, wasn't it? You're sick, man!"

"Sir, please." The few couples in the darkened lounge started whispering, shooting furtive glances over to the bar. Jack stood up in a rush, forgetting that his glass was still in his hand. "Sir, you can't take that with you—"

"This man is trying to kill me," Jack yelled at the room. "First, he followed me around all day long, and just now, he propositioned me! He wants it both ways, the sick fuck—!"

"Sir—"

"I'm on to you, buster! Stay where you are! Everybody, stay calm! Keep an eye on this— on this... degenerate mercenary! Watch your drinks, too, he told me he puts roofies in there!" A woman at one of the tables echoed with "That's the date rape drug," adding a concerned scoff. She and her husband immediately stood from their table, and Jack knew he was making headway. He dropped the glass that was in his hand, which smashed to the marble tile in a thousand dirty pieces.

"Don't worry about that, sir, I'll have the staff clean it."

"Beware, everyone! This man's a pedophile, a convicted sex offender! He just finished telling me that he distributes kiddie porn!" All the couples were up now, but it wasn't clear why. Were they afraid of Jack, the man behind the counter, or the mere ignominious disaster of the scene itself? Sometimes shameful public accusations were enough, even if they came from a hopped-up, deranged paranoid.

At this stage, Jack thought it best to run for cover. He figured his scene made enough noise to keep him safe for tonight. No way the barman would try anything now, not with all those witnesses. So he sprinted away, blasting past the petrified onlookers, flailing out of control.

Jack retreated to the safety of his room, checking the sealed caps of every mini-bar bottle before he opened them. It was then that he found the chocolate mints on the pillow, his devastated suitcase, and the note on his desk. He bolted the door then, glued to the peephole for what must have been an hour. This couldn't have anything to do with the drugs, could it? After steadying his nerves some, he'd made the call to Clint.

Things following the conversation were

fuzzy. Jack remembered smoking a few cigarettes, remembered titivating the hairs of his expanding gut with the aid of a straight razor, remembered drunk-dialing Merrick, who'd luckily not been home or refused to answer the phone; after that, nothing but blackness.

    In the morning, there was a note under the door. The hotel management deeply regretted the incidents of the previous night, and they hoped Jack had managed a pleasant stay, despite the unpleasantries. The young barman had been severely disciplined and summarily reprimanded, the message assured—score one against the catamites…!

    Additionally, as a token of their commitment to superior customer service, hotel management graciously hoped Jack would accept their offer to make his stay complementary. He was further welcomed, if he so desired, to stay as long as he liked in the suite (within reason, naturally (the note actually said that!)). And as a final gesture of good will, the management encouraged him to take one of the hotel's monogrammed terrycloth bathrobes with him when he did, at his earliest convenience, decide to depart.

    It was hard to know if the whole thing was a joke. Maybe Clint was playing a trick on him for last night, to teach him some sort of lesson. Whatever it was, Jack didn't want to hang around to find out. He threw the withered tuxedo he'd been wearing for the past few days down the garbage shoot, packed three robes into his suitcase, put on the fourth, and then lit out for the airport. Hot gulf winds blew warm in the convertible comfort of the Mustang.

    The car screamed down the boulevard, rumbling like a bitch in heat. Jack kept staring into the rearview to see if anyone was following him, if the bartender was on his tail. The main problem with this particular plan, of course, was that Jack had been so bombed yesterday that he couldn't quite remember what the kid's face actually looked like. So, rather than attempt to paste that puzzle back together, he took an Adderall instead, washed it down with one of the mini bottles he'd stuffed into the pocket of his robe, and sped out in to the late morning sun.

The Tejano Two-Step

By the time his plane landed on the Fort Worth side of DFW—"Where the West Begins—Jack felt refreshed. No one he'd met on the flight over had seemed to care that he was wearing nothing but a bathrobe, least of all the security guards, who got an unobstructed pull at his junk. Now he was in Texas, where no one cared about anything.

A bald man named Raoul met Jack at the gate and escorted him to the rare rental boat Clint had arranged: a vintage, 1974 Cadillac Fleetwood Talisman. Pimp white, the leather trim interior and shag flooring were part of an exclusive 2-car edition called the "Pat Nixon." Initial factory plans had been for a larger scale production of the model, Raoul explained, but the wide gate of political impeachment water decidedly got in the way. The only other model in existence was parked in Yorba Linda, outside "Tricky's Lie-berry."

The Caddie's original sun visor foldout professed that: *Like all talismans, this vehicle will exert powerful control on the senses, causing utter delirium at the wheel.* Jack ensured that was so, popping three pills as he took possession of the keys. He felt like Hunter S., cutting a high swath through the great American landscape.

What could be finer than being on assignment and having absolutely no clue what you were doing?

The Caddie only got 0.17 miles to the gallon, but luckily it had a built-in 300+ gallon tank. Jack's first fill-up cost $939 and got him barely 50 miles down the road. But who cared? It was Richter's dime, anyway. The Texas portion of the fact-finding trip wouldn't be long, but very expensive—almost 17 grand. Yet, as anyone will tell you, especially at Cadillac Corp., you can't put a price tag on quality.

Clint had identified six ex-strategic spots for Jack to see on his drive, all of which, again, would turn out to be orange-and-brown "Home(s) of the (W)Hoop-per." The quick sketch, for those highlighting their maps, first followed the main I-45 artery down to Houston. Stops were peppered along the Interstate, starting with a location on West Mockingbird Lane, by the Love Field, then at N. Kaufman in Ennis, and on the North Loop by the Lone Star Executive. From Houston, Jack followed the Katy Freeway, I-10, with two stops on the east side of Alamo City at Randolph AFB and on George Beach Blvd at Fort Sam Houston (as the Man says, it don't get more explicit than that).

The sixth and final address to verify was in Abilene, but again Clint insisted upon a set route. From San Antone (Countdown City), Jack was to take the I-10 to a town reassuringly called

Comfort, head north on US 87 to Brady ("The ♥ of Texas"), then take US 283 to Coleman and US 84 to arrive in Abilene. Jack's last get-to point was in Bldg. 7322 of, you guessed it, Dyess Air Force Base.

How in the heck, you may well ask, was Jack, our loveable lout, able to verify the BK locations at guarded military installations? Quite easily, as it happens: Clint had presciently provided a necessary ID badge, the designation "Civilian Military Advisor: External Liaison" stenciled over a passport photo of Jack's face. The card was poorly laminated, poorly printed, and poorly made altogether, but flashing the kindergarten pass immediately got Jack through the gates. So, welcome to the Texas leg of the country's covert military-industrial complex—tight as a sinking ship, she was...

According to Clint's notes, the first two sites had—like thousands across the country—purportedly been funded by some of the "public" liquidation scheme of I.G. Farben assets following Nazism's downfall. Of course, as everybody knows, the company was never truly liquidated. The slush money to build bases, outposts, and observations stations was but a bucket drop in the coffers of controlling interest groups and ex-Farbenites DuPont, Standard Oil, and Dow Chemical. Unfortunately, both the civilian and military projects, originally meant as corporate tax write-offs, were plagued by mismanagement and greed. The vagaries of the many parties, quickly crowded in the post-war bed, soon funneled the majority of the funnel money down the drain.

    The two half-finished Texas buildings, therefore, were eventually ceded to a Justice Department taskforce charged with overseeing the defection of scientists and politicians during the Korean War Initiative. The bases later became overflow holding chamber facilities for fugitives and "suspected" terrorists during the long decades of the Cold War. Senate appropriation money did help fund a partial interior refit of both the crumbling Dallas and Ennis units, in striking Rococo flourishes. In a surprising twist, the exterior redesigns were supervised by none other than Carlos "the Jackal," known for his amazing architectural freelance work (mainly in Art Nouveau style) for the CIA in the late seventies and early eighties. By the fall of the Berlin Wall, both units (like 117 others around the country) were discontinued and abandoned. After which, initial corporate parties eventually resumed their controlling interest with the explicit intent of restoring former, quondam glories. They were now Burger Kings.

    Jack's third target location in Houston, Richter's notes claimed, was the original Texas headquarters of the Echelon Initiative. Echelon referred to the Signals Intelligence (SIGINT) network operated by the National Security

Agency. The satellite post was one of seven interconnected locations in the coterminous US (+2 NSA-supervised venues in Canada) that worked in conjunction with bases in Scotland (Hebrides), Guam, the Cook Islands (Rarotonga), Uruguay, South Afrikkka (from 1948-'94), Saint Kitts (Basseterre), and Papua New Guinea. The primary purpose of the network was to record and archive personal telephonic conversations. As a good starting point, for example, men and women were charged with red-flagging people using words like "Bad," "USA," and/or "Evil" in the same sentence. This daily accumulation, classification, and sifting of data was a behemoth boondoggle and cash cow, which succeeded in creating a fabulous amount of cross-border work for decades.

The number of criminals caught by the Echelon counter-terrorist method was astounding (statistics still currently classified). Of course, as the surveillance and counter-surveillance tasks grew to include fiber-optic lines, wireless signals, and ethereal espionage, the operation itself went—for lack of a better word—virtual. Echelon then expanded to capture every single bitty-byte of data ever said, texted, or socially networked across communication lines. Once the surveillance system itself was cyberspace-streamlined, everything was outsourced to MegaComputer Databases in Bombay (now Mumbai), and all human workers were eliminated as they, and their brick-and-mortar bases, became altogether expendable—talk about modernizing yourself out of a job.

Anyway, onward Jack's "assignment," rolled. Farther down the Texas Trail, he came to the golden military base triangle of Lackland, Randolph, and Sam H.—formalized under the Joint Base San Antonio (JBSA) administrative umbrella—which brought the nightmares of red tape, clerical delays, and triplicate overhaul to new heights. Joint Basing, as it was colloquially called in modern parlance, was the 21st Century alternative to the individual covert ops bases once so popular in the era of Cold War tactics. Bigger really was better now and just think of the closet space fit for skeleton stuffing!

But back in the day, Clint's intel suggested, smaller simply meant more important. The Burger King that now stood under the shadow of Randolph AFB had once been the ex-filtration and laundering building for Bubba Bananas, a subsidiary of the infamous United Fruit Company. From this tiny Texas shack, the heavyweights of Neo-Colonialism washed to a bloodless trace their involvement in foreign affairs. Here, using a military front for volunteer personnel recruitment (during periods of compulsory conscription), countless sums were counted, cleaned, and re-circulated into fiduciary use under the "Banana Republic" banner.

In association with Alfonso Nuñez

(Columbia) and Paco Robles (Mexico), Lt. Col. Jacinto Martín, the son of migrant Peruvian farmers, spearheaded the entire operation. Martín sold out his ethno-heritage for God and Country, employing variously sanctioned strong-arm tactics, such as: breaking-up fledgling unions, bribing foreign dignitaries, fixing "elections," encouraging all-purpose fear mongering, massacring unruly mobs in public city squares, establishing puppet régimes and dictatorial enclaves with a wink and a smile, burning crops financed by European powers, illegally extraditing political figures who'd become "too big for their britches," funding numerous guerrilla factions to overthrow the governments they'd help put into power in the first place, and importing vast quantities of pure white coca and opiates into the United States to be distributed into minority neighborhoods as low-grade street crank.

    By the time he made it to the building at Dyess AFB, Jack was hardly paying attention to the conspiratorial nonsense any more. He just wanted to get wrecked and forget; but he pushed himself, heaving, to finish the assigned task, as if lifting a great Sisyphean boulder above his head in a last-ditch throw for indentured freedom.

    Supposedly, the Dyess BK had been the Texas liaison point and detention block for the so-called School of Assassins, known as Black Hawk Downs. Dressed-up as an auxiliary barracks for the "Beige Berets"—a Colored Army Special Forces Unit (so special, in fact, that they didn't exist)—the spot was primarily a multi-purpose indoctrination hub and reeducation center for degenerates. It handled the "Amer-immersion" of deported diplomats, the socio-sexual realignment of loafer lads, the political inculcation of conscientious objectors (most notably Commies, Mormons, and Nation of Islam supporters), as well as the basic training of sociopaths, homicidal maniacs, deviants, and violent crime offenders as paramilitary "Kites" (operatives who could be cut loose at a moment's notice) for delicate-duty combat purposes overseas.

  Once the dimensions of the site were properly documented, as per Clint's precise specifications, Jack settled down in the fast-food surround and took the hunger plunge. With four sloppy kid's meals on a tray, slobbered in Sweet 'n' Sour sauce, he quietly sat watching the jets land. His inspissated (not what you think) strawberry milkshake tasted refreshing. The thick frappé tasted even better after he'd dumped half a pint of Tequila into it.

  One of the schlepping zit-zombies had begun sweeping the floor with a moptop, contouring several burger thrones in streaks, whistling while he worked. When the revenant trans-fat maggot got close enough to Jack, he said in falsetto: "Pretty groovy Lancers, huh?"

"I don't know anything about planes, kid."

"Really? Why you on the base?"

"To blow it up," he answered, without thinking. But, before Jack could apologize for his indiscretion (and avoid being questioned or arrested for impersonating somebody with mid-level security clearance), the boy started laughing in a strange, patriotic way.

"Hahaha, I get it. You must be Ranger Regiment or Night Stalker, undercover. Am I right? You boyz always crack me up, sir!" The kid threw-up what looked like a salute, and then continued mopping.

That evening, in his $4,600/a night Honeymoon Suite at the Five-Star *Muy Bueno Eleganté*, Jack got desperately drunk. Yes, predictable.

Had he been able to surpass the nothingness, gurgling deep in the pit of his large intestine, maybe Jack would have better appreciated the "road trip" atmosphere of the journey; had he been able to surpass the nothingness, maybe then he could have enjoyed every bite of burger, onion ring, and deep-fried dessert as he pored over the covert history of the nation; had he been able to surpass the nothingness, maybe he could even have cherished every big-budget-film-tie-in toy he accumulated or made friends with Sir Shakes-a-Lot, Count Chickenfingurs, and the Duke of Doubt in the

Magical Burger Kingdoms spread across the land.

But unfortunately, the desperate pain in Jack's stomach was the void of the vast unseen, a vortex of wayward *weltschmerz*. His willed self-destruction was a continued, senseless act to battle the incoherent boredom of meaninglessness. At every positive turn lay a negative. Horace Greely's great directive of exploration—Go West, Young Man!—lingered like a mocking, lassitudinous refrain in the back of his mind. No matter how well Jack began to succeed, or how clear the path seemed, he inevitably managed to steer everything to ruin. Such overwhelming uncertainty always led to alcohol, at least for Jack, and once mixed with pills, his alcotrip hit more than a few road bumps:

Three days disappeared in a flash. Rather than pretend to take himself in hand, he flew into a storm of uncontrolled Nembutal and mini-fridge abuse, his uneaten room service dishes stacked high to the ceiling. Impromptu sessions of skinny-dipping in the downstairs pool, groggy excursions through the hallways, and scantily-clad interpretive dances for Japanese tourists were mitigated by indefinite blackout periods in the rooms of his suite, while a Sabu the Elephant boy "Mahout Movie Marathon" forever played in a loop on the blaring flat screen.

Meanwhile, Clint's schedule was going out of whack and falling dangerously behind its lapidary slate. Jack kept repeatedly blowing-off his charter to Winslow, Arizona, incurring massive fines; but he didn't care. The "fine sight to see" would have to wait until he managed to emerge from this black hole, somehow.

The phone suddenly started ringing, incessantly, until Jack finally thought to unplug the damn thing. How did Clint know so quickly that Jack had missed his plane(s)? Surely that bartender from Pensacola was still on his trail, and surely he'd informed Richter of the stalled process. Paranoia? Not quite. This mildly menacing communiqué appeared under the door, at some point:

All monies will be cancelled and withdrawn if "Mission" is not resumed pronto— Get your shit together, Mitford! CR IV.

Richter was furious. Even in his stupor, Jack could appreciate that. But, what was with the obsessive need to keep to this laughable schedule? The secret government structures and operations weren't going anywhere; in fact, they were long gone. They'd already been turned into burger-flipping dissemination points, it wasn't as if there was anything left to salvage, save, or fight for. Invisible Cold War operatives had done that work half a century ago, ensuring that one freedom continued to beget another, but was cataloguing said trajectory really that imperative? Who would benefit from it, historians?

Lest we forget, sure, but lest we forget why we wish to remember: everyday people had no interest in the potentially devious, gruesome, necessary, and inhumane deeds that have been perpetrated in order to secure independence, sustain sovereignty, and protect liberty—that sort of info was a real downer. The bottom line was, people didn't want to know *how* their burgers were made, or where they came from, they just wanted them. Well, fair enough.

And this latest bender of Jack's helped him put those kinds of thoughts out of his head, too. Yes, the whole endeavor was absurd and pointless—much like life in general—yet, he had no real choice but to press on. Merrick already had his nuts in a vice, and with Clint's dangling Old Money allowance in stasis inside his bank account and not his pocket, Jack could barely afford a candy bar.

He was a modern era slave on a mission, and his manumission from that situation was floating somewhere in an elusive emancipatory ether. So, Jack grudgingly pulled himself out of his three-day tailspin, his room a disaster of broken glass, soiled sheets, crossword puzzles, carpet burns, and accumulated ashes.

Ripe as he'd become, his pores oozing 80proof, Jack stumbled under the shower to dry-out in ablutions. "No more drink," he muttered as his new mantra, prophylaxis against the high-pressure drops of water stinging like pins. He took eight aspirin to numb his headache, as he toweled off, and two yellow jackets to ease his pain.

Jack's hands were shaking as he threw out the robe he'd been wearing since Florida. He blew a few grand of his "walkin' around money" on souvenir appliquéd garments from the downstairs boutique, as well as on another hotel robe (a lovely paisley pastel *yukata*), which he had room service send-up in a vacuseal. The 5-figure checkout tab was a blur of unintelligible numbers, which Jack signed for in a relieved swirl.

Crawling into the Caddie, the leather plush burned at his back. The engine made a whir as it started, coughing in the hot sun. A half-pint of Tequila was stuck under the accelerator, and Jack slinked down to reach it. His head was pounding, and in a flush he downed the putrid, boiling contents before smashing the bottle against a lamppost as he squealed away. The car rental agency fined him $13,400/day in late fees on the one-and-only "Pat," a guzzling gal of glory. It was Abilene's final, stiff-fingered good-bye.

Ditat Deus

Still stinking of booze, Jack made the seven thirty private charter to Winslow. His first order of business, as soon as he landed, was a visit to the gents. After throwing up whatever was in his stomach, he then proceeded to pass out with his arms around the bowl. Some tourist in white sneakers eventually kicked at Jack's feet to wake him up, basically checking to make sure he wasn't dead.

Once he'd cleaned off his chin, Jack wanted to get going as fast as he could. Unfortunately, Clint had jotted down quick, bullet-point notes about the history of the airport that needed to be read-over first:

- *Designed by Schutzstaffel double-agent operative, Chuck Lindberg, based on finger painting schematics drawn by Heinrich Himmler and Julius Schreck.*

- *Paid for by the good graces of Howard Hughes {codenamed Moustache Man} with the explicit proviso that he be able to store unlimited quantities of his "Curative" urine supplies in the bunker basement.*

> *Used as a World War II launch for B-17 Flying Fortress and B-29 Super Fortress bomber missions overseas. Later used as a War Games facility for Operation Flying Monkey {See forthcoming notes on Seattle/Boeing and pay particular attention to Artemus "Skull & Bones" Gates, Godfather to Billy Boy himself}.*

(PS~ If you have time, Jack, I strongly recommend a trip out to the Diablo Crater. The thingamajig is something like 4,000ft in diameter, and a doodad of raw magnitude. Government paid a couple of well-regarded scientific quacks to claim it was a meteor hit some 50,000yrs old, when it was in fact, you guessed it, one of the first UFO landing sites—before the brain-dead coneheads learned to be discreet! On the South-Southwest corner of the crater rim you'll find a hillock of beige boulders. If you duck underneath a double-black entranceway of moon rock there, you'll end-up in an "unofficial" museum of alien rhinoplasty probes run by the National Park Service—fascinating stuff!!!)

    Not a chance in hell Jack was going out of his way for more of Richter's nonsense. He'd stick to the plan and get the drive over with as soon as possible. The last thing he was looking for was to get his Kicks on Route 66(6).

    Inasmuch as Jack had managed to smooth

things over with Clint concerning his most recent irresponsible and inexplicable behavior (and been largely exonerated by the old man), the begrudging son of a bitch had none the less downgraded this next rental to a SmartCar^2. Hands down, it was clever water torture on Richter's part. With a miraculous redesign half the size of the original, the "automobile"—if such, the thing may rightfully be deemed—looked like a cereal box on wheels.

    Jack felt utterly wretched, and ill. Gelignite grenades were exploding in his skull, leaving a faint napalm fog. Stewing in his DT juices, with eyeballs sweating and intestines churning from stink, his rolling coffin would be one tight, trembling ride. Unsurprisingly, he puked again on his way out to the parking lot, and once more inside the claustrophobia of the SmartCar^2, which now reeked like Chef Boyardee's ass.

    The entire day was set in a thick fog. One more Nembutal only barely succeeded in calming his nerves for the irksome trip. Thankfully, the Arizona circuit was a straight cut west towards Flagstaff on the I-40, then a southern shoot down the I-17, and back to the multi-state I-10 southeast. Burger Kings were once again on the menu, each one a bazooka blast away from aeronautical military might.

    Jack didn't even bother reading Clint's comments, he just concentrated on taking the different site measurements. Given the *de rigueur* deep-fried wafts, he also barfed at each BK location, unable to settle his stomach for very long. The grueling three-stop slog was as follows: From Winslow (Lindberg Regional) to Mesa (Falcon Field), a bedroom 'burb of Phoenix, and then on to the loveliest little militarized inner-community of Tucson you ever did see (Davis-Monthan AFB, managed by the fine men and women of the 355th Fighter Wing and the 563rd Rescue Group, *One Base, One Wing, One Boss*).

    It was a miracle, or maybe just dumb luck, that Jack survived the drive to Tucson at all. He couldn't have made it without his pills, that's for sure, or the fourteen successive trips to various bathrooms along the way. But now that his two main orifices had expelled every last possible morsel, Jack began feeling halfway decent again. His fourth and final Arizona destination was in Wilcox, a hundred miles east of Tucson, which he planned to squeeze in tomorrow before his flight from Cochise County to San Diego. By now you've probably already guessed the Copper State's itinerary letter, yes?

    Insipid Tucson flashed in the twilight traffic. It was the end of day, and commuter faces were slumped over steering wheels. The bored bodies may have seemed dead in their cars, but they still looked better than Jack did. In the midst of that apathetic thrall, he checked into a Motel 6 for $ 31.^{95}$, which was Clint's continued fractious idea of a punishing downgrade: from 5-star digs to a stucco shithole by the airport.

Jack couldn't care less. The room was tidy, and the whir of planes produced a calming effect on his fragile state. But take great heed, fellow travelers! The one, single drawback to the Motel 6 Empire was its inconsiderate lack of mini bars. On any other evening, Jack would probably have taken this flaw as a sobering sign. As it was, he'd stupidly scheduled to meet mother Muggins this evening, and there was no way in hell he was facing that without proper, lubricated fortifications.

Jack was thus forced, through no fault of his own, on a libation quest. Fifteen years ago he'd cultivated this sort of crapulous behavior with the mystique of a troubled, brooding young author. Now he was just like the rest of the talentless drunks and junkies hanging around the liquor deli, and well past his prime. Oh, the harsh realities of age.

Back in the room, it took three solid belts of Mezcal to get Jack conversationally coherent again, and three more for him to pick up the phone. Muggins was amiable enough as she gave spotty directions. The restaurant wasn't far from her house, which was in a place called Oro Valley. He was glad to be meeting her in a neutral space. His relief largely sprang from being spared a tour of the house, expository descriptions of various accumulated knickknacks, and introductions to the latest in the long line of his ex-mother's husbands.

Jack changed out of his bathrobe, which stank of vomit and diarrhea, and into a matching set of sweats printed with *Abilene is for Lovers* in pink rhinestones and purple hues. After running his head under the tap in the tub, he prepared for the evening with a double dose of Adderall to focus his mind and a few more belts of the Mezcal to even the glow: "*Arriba, abajo, a la derecha, izquierda y pa'dentro*," as the bottle says, or "Up, Down, Right, Left, and into the depths it goes!" By the time Jack drove to the restaurant, it felt like he was wearing a puff cloud for a hat.

Though the evening was cool, they were seated out on the patio—one of the last bastions for Arizona ashtrays. Throughout the initial dinner pleasantries (not at all pleasant), the ordering, the hors-d'oeuvres, and first bottle of wine, Muggins monopolized the conversation with information about her most recent foray into grass roots activism with her multi-million-dollar neo-hippie neighbors, mostly jobless trophy wives and stay-at-home mothers without children. As she proudly admitted, the impetus was self-serving because she used the lives of the dejected bobs, bowls, and sweeps she came into contact with as raw fodder for her writing.

Muggins lit a cigarillo, barely covering

her mouth as she choked up a gutter-hack phlegm ball. "Yeah, so this writing genre is a whole new thing I've invented. I call it 'Verbatim Literature,' which is meant as a kinda foil to whatchoocallit…? Found Art. Plus, I'm totally off the hook creatively. None of these dopes could spell plagiarism, let alone tell ya what it means. It's great. All I gotta do is listen to these modern-day sewing circle crybabies and poof! I got me a plot and dialogue, word for word. Jumpin' Jehosephat, can't believe no one told me about this before!"

It was this same brand of unmerciful opportunism and ruthlessness that got her into print in the first place. When *Patagonia Piano*, Jack's breakthrough novel, was first published, Muggins muscled her way into a meeting with his agent and his editor—pretty much behind his back. The move wasn't meant as a show of motherly praise, but as a pitch for her own work:

"You'll make cash, ya understand? The shriveled suburban bitches will eat this trash up, I swear. No jive, I'm the new 'n' improved Jacqueline Susann! I say let's do the American housewife a goddamn favor and save 'em from all that stuck-up Erica Jong and Jilly Cooper bullshit! I'm giving you publishing twits absolute pearls here!"

Her calculated arm wrestle worked. In the seventeen-year stretch since refusing to take no for an answer, Muggins had published 34 novelettes (parts of three distinct Medieval Romance Sagas), five full-length novels, and a hugely popular self-help book for couples.[15] Muggins still used Jack's old agent, Myrna Lowe, who'd dropped him the instant his follow-up, *The Arcades Projectile*, showed poor reviews in the *NYRB,* the *TLS*, and the *LRB*.

"Myrna still asks about you, you know?"

"Yeah? Well, if she really wanted to speak to me, I guess she could call me. We do live in the same city after all—"

"Actually, she's rarely there anymore."

"Oh?"

"Betch'ur ass she moved. The sales on my last book alone made her enough dough so she could buy that Hudson River property out by Roosevelt's old Hyde Park flophouse—did you know he had the clap something like eight or nine times? Crazy. Anyway, no, Myrna spends most of her time out that a way now. She always did like you, you know—?"

"Not enough to keep me on, obviously—"

"With that meltdown you had, who can

---

[15] How a four-time divorcée became any kind of marital authority was beyond Jack, especially when she prefaced the hogwash swill with *It's safe to assume that all dating manuals are horseshit... couples who make it look easy annoy the bejeezus out of me and should be shot for the benefit of all mankind!*

blame her? Yikes! You can't just crash people's literary Central Park West parties, strip down naked, threaten to defecate on everybody there, and not expect some sort of social backlash."

"That's not *exactly* how things went down—"

"And the worst part was you weren't even being original. Pollack pulled that same lamebrain stunt at PiPi Guggenheim's a half century before you ever tried the bodily function trick—"

"It's not like I hurt anyone."

"No one except yourself. I mean, writers are supposed to be out of control, everyone knows that, but you really went too far, Jack."

"Here I thought that it was the quality of the work that mattered most—"

"You really are bonkers. And you wonder why you end up broke, divorced, and writing slop for other people? Soon you'll be a swaddled, forty-year-old papoose begging for someone to change your diaper."

"Maturity's overrated. Besides, according to major polls 40 is the new 20—"

"You trust that sort of malarkey? It's made-up by a bunch a' old men who've failed at life, it's a fact. Your biggest problem, Jack, is that you've never known how to read other people for personal gain. That's what's hurt your career most."

"Well, selling yourself short has never

been your drawback—"

"Damn right. The demure don't deserve to be popular. They're boring!"

"Where is that waiter? We should really jump on another bottle of wine."

"Anyway, enough about you and your problems. I'm sure you read all about those awards I recently got in Chile, Argentina, France, Portugal, Australia, Japan, Iceland (!), Egypt, Greece, and South Africa."

"Not really."

"Stop lying. Everybody saw that. The armchair critics keep saying I've written the sequel to *Infinite Jest*, whatever that means." Jack thought about explaining, then abandoned the effort altogether in the drone of her continued congratulatory ramblings. "It's been a whirlwind, quite frankly. As a matter of fact, I'm kinda glad to be staying put for a while, but that won't last. I have to go up to the White House in the New Year to give that goddamn acceptance speech. It's a wonder I have any time to actually write!"

"Split infinitive."

"What?"

"To *actually* write—"

"Oh, right, well… I love split infinitives; I think they give the language real verve. My career is based on split infinitives! Screw *Strunk & White*!"

"Where is that waiter, already?"

"One thing I will absolutely have to do

while I'm up in Chocolate City, though, is light-up one of these 'gars in the Oval with the Prez himself. The media says he quit, but I don't believe 'em for a lick. Not like I voted for the big-eared Hawaiian prick, but the least we can do is bury the hatchet by means of the ole smokem peace pipe tack."

"Sounds like quite a trip you got planned—"

"That's if I don't have to spend all my time doing stupid readings at the Folger Library for those PEN/Faulkner fucks."

"What? I didn't think this year's winners had been chosen yet?"

"They haven't, not officially. But I've got a man on the inside who gives me the scoop. Yep, I'm winning it this year. The cash is only something like 15 grand, but I have a Vera WingWang dress all picked out for the Oscars and the prize money should cover about a quarter of it. I don't need the shekels, a' course, but… oh here we go, finally!"

The main course arrived. Muggins ordered more Pinot Grigio, stubbed out her cigarillo, and shooed the waiter away in a quick wrist motion.

The meal itself was forgettable, a failed fusion attempt to blend some Asian delicacies with Southwest Sloppy Joes and Sierra Vista corndogs. Muggins continued to talk about herself, her projects, her travels, and her upcoming awards. Jack contributed "Uh-huhs" and "Hmms" whenever necessary, lit cigarettes to stay calm, and focused his attention on washing down his every bite with wine. There was a rhythm to the beat.

Once she was done eating, Muggins looked at her watch and snapped her fingers for the waiter.

"Yes, madam?"

"Well, can't you see I'm done? *Débarassez!*"

"I'm sorry?"

"Don't you speak French, bozo?"

"This is not a French restaurant, madam."

"What, is a little culture really too much to ask in this shitass state?"

Jack took the opportunity to slip out to the men's room, though gave serious thought to making a break for it altogether. Cardboard cut outs of Hopi women and Havasupai elders adorned the corridors. Contrived Arizona pride beamed a sheer light for the tourist gawk.

In the stall, Jack crushed an Adderall into a fine powder and bumped it all with the key to his SmartCar^2. The sides of his face were pulsing in hot flashes when he got back to the table, but his mind was clear.

"Herb should be here any minute now," Muggins said, lighting another cigarillo as she checked her watch. "I ordered us double Cognacs while we wait."

"Herb!?"

"Yes, Herb. My husband. You two haven't met, and that *was* the main purpose of tonight's little *tête-à-tête*... I thought I made that clear over the phone—?"

"No."

"You really should learn to listen more attentively, son."

Jack rubbed his face into the palms of his hands, trying to erase bits of the reality falling in around him. He lit his sixth cigarette of the evening. "I still don't understand."

"Don't understand what?"

"Why he didn't join us for dinner? I agreed to one meet, *one* simple dinner, that's it! And now this, this nightmare is going to drag on forever!"

"Calm down—"

"Couldn't he be here earlier?"

"No, he couldn't."

"No?"

"No."

"Why not?"

"His jet was late leaving Oahu. Besides, he's a dedicated veggie and an aspiring vegan. The whiff of meat makes him positively ill. Too bad, too, 'cause his family owns the second largest cattle farm in Montana—not that it matters. Ah well, at least his nausea for animal by-products only affects his carniphile collation habits and not his wardrobe choices. I've never seen a man look so handsome in full-length fur and alligator shoes—"

"So he's a coat rack, that it?"

"Herb's a producer. He's in the top three, according to *The Hollywood Reporter*, which pretty much means we move between our Coronado property here and the one in the Palisades a lot more than I'd like. Don't get me wrong, both homes have their advantages. But at least here we don't get hassled as much. Our 22,000 square feet Sonoran Chalet is stunning. Perched high atop our 58 serene acres, we get clear views all the way out to Pusch Ridge and the Tucson Mountain Range—"

"Jeezus, what *is* the deal with this fucking waiter? Could he be any slower?"

"Anyway, I'm telling you this to show you just how easygoing Herb is. I think that comes from his previous career." Muggins lit another cigarillo off the half-finished one she was still smoking. "He used to be one of the top academic feminists in the country, was guest lecturer and visiting faculty member at every Ivy League campus except Penn, taught at UC Santa Barbara, Texas A&M, and even at places for blacks like Howard."

"Top academic feminists? What the hell is that?"

"You don't have to be a woman to be a feminist, scholars have long understood this kind of stuff."

"Oh? And how would you know? You never even graduated high school—"

"Yet just look at me now!" The Cognacs arrived and another round was immediately ordered. Jack had ants crawling all through his skull but still managed to hold up his glass in a semi-comic, shaky toast that caused Muggins to snuffle, unimpressed by her son's antics. They had to wait to order dessert, however, thanks to Herb—Mr. Betty Friedan. Tardiness in others was so impolite.

Sometime after chugalugging half her snifter, Muggins bounded up from her chair, heaping slobbery affectionate kisses on a man whose gut curled over his belt in a swoop. In his mind, Jack had pictured Herb as a withered, glabrous gonad cretin who slouched, farted, and stuttered when he talked. But, except for his belly and a nose slightly bulbed by rhinophyma, the man put Cary Grant's chiseled-jawed looks to shame.

"I'm Herb. You must be Jack."

"I am." The two men shook hands and all three then sat down, cozy. "Do you mind if we order dessert now, Herb, I've been busily puking all day and I'm still a bit peckish after the miniature portions they serve up here—"

"Not at all, you two go ahead. Muggsie knows I never eat sweets after 8 o'clock."

Furious, Jack motioned for the waiter, who brought the second round of Cognacs. They ordered the restaurant's signature dessert, and Jack washed his frustrations down in a two-gulp swallow. Herb and Muggins flirted for a few seconds, in that obsequious way old couples do, their liver spots and raised veins caressing in sweet touches.

"So Jack," Herb said, when he eventually broke off from the sweetened embrace. "How's your trip been? Except for the puking today, I mean. You're sick?"

"No."

"O—okay."

"I'm getting by."

"And this trip is business or pleasure? We weren't sure."

"Neither, really. I've mostly been chasing down go-nowhere leads."

"I'm sorry?"

"It's a research-type deal for a memoir I'm supposed to be doing for this whackjob I met at a party up in the Hamptons."

"Is he famous? We probably know him."

"N'ah, just rich."

"That's a start. What's his name?"

"Clint Richter. He's a gazillionaire kook with his fingers in too many mud pies."

"Sure, we know Clint."

"You do?"

"He's an old… acquaintance. What's the old warhorse have you doing?"

Suspicions, all in a row, once again began

rearing their ugly little heads. What the hell was this, another one of Richter's set-ups? Were Herb and Muggins in on "it," whatever *it* was? Jack would try to play this off, be cucumber cool as he waded through the quixotic quicksand:

"Um, well, I've got to drive out to Wilcox tomorrow, then fly to California, Washington State after that, and then back to New York for good, I hope. Haven't made it that far ahead of myself on the itinerary yet, if you want to know the truth of it."

"I don't understand," Muggins interrupted, "why are you going to Wilcox? There's nothing in Wilcox."

"I'll bet you anything there's at least a Burger King there."

"A *what*?"

"A Burger King."

"Urgh! PETA really hasn't done enough to stop those majestic monsters! Their food is so vile, and expensive."

"I know, I've been eating it non-stop since Florida."

"Why?"

"Multi-tasking, you could say."

"The last time I ate at one of their places," Herb added, "they were doing the 'Where's Herb?' campaign back in the mid-eighties. Yeeeeeee-uuukkkkk! I got a free meal for saying 'I'm not the Herb you're looking for,' but it unleashed a violent peristaltic explosion inside me... making it the last bit of moo-meat I ever ate."

"Anyway," Muggins chimed in, "why go all the way out to Wilcox? If you wanted to meet Ted "The Million Dollar Man" DiBiase, you should have said something earlier—"

"Who, the wrestler?"

"Um-hmn, he used to be mayor there, even though no one told him about it and he doesn't even live there—"

"What?"

"I know. He did five consecutive terms in office, if you can believe it—"

"How?"

"No one else wanted the job. Besides, he grew up there, and he's probably the most famous person to set foot in that dump except for Tanya Tucker. He was good for local business, I guess. Point is, we know him. We'll get DiBi on the phone for you, if you want? Save you a trip?"

"I thought he died?"

"He did? Gosh, if that's true, I should probably get him out of my rolodex—"

"Actually, maybe I'm thinking of somebody else..."

"Well, if a paper crown is all you're after, then, there are Burger Kings all over Tucson, so—"

"I know. In fact, I've been to one already. Off Qui—Quijota Boulevard, is that how you say it?"

"Out on the Davis-Monthan Base?" Herb was talking again, in that sweet getting-to-know-you voice. He was a phony, just like Muggins, which explained why they fell in love at first sight. "Have you heard of Ed Burtynsky?"

"Nope."

"Oh, Jack, you've gotta check out this guy's work."

"Yeah? Who is he?"

"He's probably the most important and famous photog to come out of Can-Uh-Duh. He did some absolutely mesmerizing shots of the World's Largest Aircraft Graveyard™ out at DMB. He's stayed at our place a bunch in the past, and we usually see him up at our weekend retreat in Banff every August. Gretzky was there last year too, if you believe it—we video Skype all the time now… but sorry I interrupted you, Jack, what's so special about that Wilcox BK—?"

"Well, let's see, I have it in my notes." Jack fumbled through his small bag to find Clint's notebook. "Okay, it says here: *Class B interrogation hut, codename: 'The Hacienda.' Facility used primarily as a training center for captured fugitives and illegals of the brown diaspora that had crossed through the Baja California border points. Base target initiative: Train force of so-called guerrilla mutes for deployment in non-Latin American operations. Reasoning: In case of capture, men will be unable to utter a single word before they are either a)*

Tortured to death or b) Rescued/Killed by our forces prior to a translator being located by local captors. Recommended implementation sites: Asia (preferable) or Northern Africa."

"What is that, a joke?"

"Nope. Well, yeah, it is, but it's more of a long story. Let's see what the puppeteer's written for station Wilcox… '*The Wilcox Outpost has been an observation and monitoring station for paranormal activity, ever since the end of the Indian Wars. Built on the burial ground of Chief Cochise and his cohorts, the post monitored and recorded unusual spiritual occurrences. Hard linked to the grid at Fort Huachuca, subliminal monitoring systems were wired directly into the public cover unit of MARS (Military Auxiliary Radio System). Usually manned by two insubordinate cadets, whose duty-time was equally split out as tourist guides up at Fort Rucker, the outpost surveyed "bizarre" frequencies and 4th dimension portal openings. In operation for 111 years, however, not one unusual activity was ever recorded in the entire history of the base. Given such poor performance records, military/governmental funding was eventually pulled and diverted to a study of the nesting patterns of the Sonoran Burrowing Owl.*'"

"That's because the dopes didn't know where to look," Herb said, producing a strange, uneasy grimace on his wife's over-rouged face.

"What was that—?"

"I… uh, sorry, I was talking about the owls."

Muggins jumped in at this point, presumably to save Herb. "This is the kind of stuff Clint's got you going around looking for then?"

"I know, batty right? Like I said, it's a pillar-to-post hoax. But the money's decent, so I've stopped trying to understand." Jack paused with a taste of Cognac to cool his throat. "What about you, Herb, Muggins tells me you're a film producer. How's that?"

"I work exclusively on colossal-scope motion pictures, and only with A-list stars. Right now we've almost got that Neo-DaVinci genius, the Fresh Prince of Bel-Air's kid, signed for a recently greenlit blockbuster bit a' fluff called—"

"Okay, enough honey." Muggins said, transparently bored. "I think it's about time we got to the point—"

"Point?" Jack answered, lighting another cigarette. "What point?"

"Well, as you know," Muggins continued, brushing Herb's furry forearm. "We're both involved in 'the Industry'—"

"*Industry*? You're a," Jack paused, coughed hard, cleared his throat, and then swallowed his pride, "writer."

"True, Jack, but several studios are now hoping to option my work."

"Oh? I didn't know that. G—good for you."

"One studio in particular," Herb added, "is even proposing a five-picture deal for the Medieval Sagas, the whole stretch!"

"That's right—all shot down in Sheepland where that bearded fatso filmed those Hobbit movies. Anyway, that's neither here nor there right now. What's important is that both Herb and I have become firm believers in the teachings of Master Hubbard."

"Who?"

"You've heard of Dianetics, I'm sure."

"Is that the intensive, low carb diet?"

"No. It's a metaphysical belief platform from which to know, deepen, and heal the mind as well as the body—concomitantly."

"Are you talking about Scientology stuff?"

"Yes."

"That coo-coo spaceship crappola cooked up by Laugh-Y-ette Ronaldo Hubbard?"

Herb and Muggins looked at each other, despondent. Not only was the weight of the world on them, but that of the entire universe. Thus, undaunted, Herb began his intergalactic sales pitch:

"I probably don't have to tell you that The Hallowed Church of S—as we insiders call it—is a legitimate and powerful force in the American mainstream. Indictments, embezzlement charges, fraud, and manslaughter convictions just keep sliding off our backs. We've infiltrated federal governments in over forty-five countries, including Canada and the US, and we've managed to insinuate ourselves into the highest ranks of office and industry. The very fact that the C of S has had tax-exempt status in the past proves that we're the real deal. In fact, I'll let you in on a little trade secret: all that phooey propaganda disseminated to the public at large is done by our very own powerful Sea Org, as a means of keeping the true beings and believers protected from harm."

"Waiter!" Jack partly screamed, pointing at his snifter. "I'm going to need another one of these, stat! And no dessert for me after all—"

"But, sir, it's ready." The waiter put two plates down on the table. The desserts, unique specialties of the establishment, were best described as Twinkies origamied into lotus leaves, smothered in cactus cream and guava juice. Jack hoped that the combination of alcohol, pills, sugar, and cosmic stimulation would blow his head clear off his neck.

"Jack," Herb persisted, in his soothingly sappy soft voice. "I know this may seem odd to you, but believe us: it isn't."

"That's right," Muggins averred, "there's always been a conspiracy against the True Teachings of the Divine Donor of the Word, especially by the naysaying Journals of the those New England quacks. Those medical cabbalists don't want the *right* people to know the truth."

"The right people? Who are they?"

"The Chosen Ones, those with enough vision. Only the inner cadre, those with a strong *thetan*—or soul, if you will—can overcome the small-mind bigotry of this earth."

Jack, to shut himself up, tried stuffing as much of the dessert (which was surprisingly delicious) down his throat. His mouthful made him look like Dizzy Gillespie. He felt like slapping his cheeks together, barfing bits of yellow and white partially hydrogenated sponge cake all over Herb and Muggins and their thousand-dollar get-ups. He felt like gouging out his eardrums. He felt like dashing towards the nearest hillside, his hair on fire, palms over ears, naked and screeching at the top of his lungs. "Umm…?"

"We understand that this is a lot to take in. The intricacies of the particular structure of the Chosen Order would take too long to detail now, and detailing that structure is—naturally—forbidden. Suffice it to say that We, in the celebrity community, are keepers of the flame."

"But even within that celebrity community," Muggins quickly clarified, "there are varying degrees of responsibility based on Terrean success."

"Well that goes without saying," was all Jack could muster without chuckling.

"You see, at a recent Preclear's weekend retreat up in Navajo County, Herb and I were made senior auditors and overseers of the Kinship

Fraternity Association of North America—"

"Oh, congratulations—"

"Actually, the 'North American' part is kinda redundant because there aren't any Associations anywhere else in the world—"

"Why's that?"

"Because all the Chosen Ones live here. We're Beings thousands and thousands of years old, Jack, you think we'd be dumb enough to settle in some Third World stankhole or some teeny-tiny European country where they don't even speak English?"

"Honey, we agreed not to say too much."

"No you're right," Muggins agreed, wiping Twinkie cream from her lips. "Our primary concern now is inclusiveness, extending a hand of kinship to our less fortunate East Coast celebrities. I'm talking mostly about the playwrights and board-treaders who usually have their noses stuck in Shakespeare, Ibsen, Mohlly-Air or Noël Coward—"

"We're promoting equal rights, we want to ensure that our fellow followers have the appropriate tools necessary to achieve their spiritually-led hermeneutical quests for inner being: in other words, themselves. This requires a specific, appropriately calibrated tool to effectuate the process."

"Which is?"

"I'm glad you asked that, Jack." Herb almost rubbed his hands in glee as he advanced.

"They are important devices called Electropsychometers, which are crucial and have long been used, but they have often been inaccurate. The refined model that we're proposing is very discreet and easily inserted into the rectum, where it is kept in place for five days at a time by a small, non-threatening electromagnetic charge. Once a month the data provided should be used to gauge the accurate levels of symbiosis between state of mind and the subject's bodily incarnation. This, in conjunction with abreaction therapy, will ensure a harmonious interaction of the conscious to the unconscious and vice versa."

You couldn't make this shit up (well, you could), and Jack wanted to know more. It was similar to, if not exactly like, being unable to look away from a full-speed-ahead, mangled train wreck. "Okay. Soooo…?"

"So, the voltmeter within the Electropsychometers can only be recharged by a special device. This device is almost one of a kind—therefore, very rare—and can only be handled by an appropriately trained mind. We have one for use by all the involved celebs on the West Coast, but we currently don't have a storage, distribution, and monitoring center for the East—specifically, New York City."

"I'm sorry," Jack interrupted, "I'm a little gone right now—buzzed off my fucking ass, actually—so I'm not quite sure I follow what you two are saying."

"What we're saying is that we want to market our refined Electropsychometers on the East Coast soon—in small propagation patterns at first, but we anticipate a wide blow-out effect once word of mouth takes off—and we need someone trustworthy, someone like you, to ensure that all this is handled correctly."

"Wait a second, let me get this straight. That's what all this has been about, getting me involved with some sort of inter-dimensional Ponzi pyramid scheme?"

"It's not at all like a pyramid scheme! At all! We're—we're making a gesture here, a leap of faith in… uughh." It was clear that Jack's words had wormed themselves under Herb's skin; or, to be more accurate, under the flesh-like substance that contained the light-being's earthly incarnation. Herb regained his poise before continuing. "If anything, Jack, the paradigm we're proposing has much more of a parallelogramish shape, composed of two inner triangular forms. And these two inner triangles are made from the beginning and the end, the primordial Ouroboros of Intergalactic Life: the ABC triangle and the XYZ triangle. The first is the Absorption Belief Communication triangle, while the second is the Xenon Yapha Zernon triangle. All six points are synthesized into the 4-points of the Opus Paragon Ontogeny Parallelogram to form the interlocking map for

Inner Terrestrial Peace and Extra-Terrestrial Understanding—"

"All right, sweetheart. All right." Muggins once again stopped her husband, who now seemed patently eager to share the secrets of the Sacred Church of Big-Eyed Menders. "One thing should be made abundantly clear before we go any further, son. Just so there are no misunderstandings here, we are *not* asking ya to join, as such—"

"Oh, thank Christ." Jack exclaimed, probably with a bit too much vehemence.

"Umm… ya see, while there is a Legacy component to the Continuum, and y'are my legitimate son (at least I think y'are), only one family member can be formally welcomed in—and I've already asked your sister to join—"

"That's the best news I've heard all night." All three sort of sighed in relief, but for intrinsically different reasons. "One thing I don't understand… well, I'd rephrase that sentence but it would take too long." Jack took a sip, to pause, and restarted: if Shelley's going to be a conehead like you guys, can't you just get her to store and recharge your… your intergalactic isogon thingies?"

"She lives in Chicago, Jack. *Chicago.*" Muggins was using that tone, oh that tone. "I mean, not even humans in their right minds choose to live there. And we're much more… doesn't matter, no, the distribution and monitoring must be based in New York."

"Here's the deal, Jack, we've already got an invigilator, a trusted man named Cal, who's a properly aligned Body and Mind, and he's been anointed by the club to distribute and recharge the Electropsychometers. What we're asking—your role in all this—would be minimal, cursory really. We basically need a secure place to store our valuable commodities."

"Oh that's what you're…? Easy, get yourselves a storage locker."

The pan-galactic beings both scoffed, in unison, as if *that* were the craziest thing said all night. "You can't be serious!"

"I—! *I* can't be serious?? Herb, you seem like a decent enough guy—apart from your illogical beliefs, romantic attractions, and unforgivable habit for tardiness—but may I stop you right there and say *What. The. Fuck*?" Jack put his cigarette out in the remnants of his Twinkie delicacy, which melted black and gold. He turned to face Muggins: "This woman here—your wife, my supposed mother—and I haven't really said anything meaningful to each other since my father died at Lockerbie, well over twenty years ago, and certainly not since she stole my agent—"

"I never sto—"

"Shut up! Since you stole my agent and made a career for yourself. Is that how the Chosen Ones of your cosmic clan make it, by bilking their rightful rights from others? Muggins, I haven't seen you, I mean literally *seen* you in something like eight years, and these steaming piles are the best you can come up with?"

"Look, Jack, don't blame me because you're disappointed with your life—"

"I'm *not* disappointed with my life, not at all."

"You're drunk!"

"Of course I'm drunk, and stoned too I might add, but that doesn't make me wrong—or crazy like you two loonies! I'm doing exactly what I want with my life. That's the thing you've never been able to understand. It's not about acquisition, or fame. Not everything has turned out perfectly for me, that's true, but I'm happy enough—"

"Happy… enough?"

"Yes, *happy enough*. I don't need more than that. And here you two lure me to this ludicrous restaurant, pump hot air at me all night, and now you ask me to be some kind of go-to guy for your weird, fucked up cult? You have got to be kidding me!"

"But we trust you."

"Trust me! You don't even know me! Not for twenty goddamn years!"

"Well one thing is certainly clear from your performance tonight," Muggins couldn't help add, "y'obviously ain't prepared for the sort of enlightening, spiritual journey a' the kind Herb and I have undertaken and triumphed with. Our fame, wealth, and general likeability assures that we—"

"Aaarh, Jesus! Shut up already. I've had enough! I can't take one more second of this mystagogic stupidity anymore." Jack stood up from the table, suddenly. So sudden were his movements, in fact, and so readily inebriated did he feel, that Jack crashed into a table of giggling bachelorettes behind them. "Sorry ladies," he said apologetically as he swam a brief backstroke on their soft, healthy breasts. His balance was way off and his feet weighed a ton as the girls pushed him back (mostly) upright.

Herb was on his feet now, too, trying on his best diplomatic posture. "What, you're leaving? But we're just having a polite conversation here, and we hadn't even got around to the part where we told you that the Collective is prepared to offer fifteen thousand dollars a month as retainer—"

"What?"

"You heard me—"

Jack would be lying to himself if he didn't admit that, if only for a second, he did consider the cosmogonal cashola. "Ugh, well… thanks, but I already have a job—"

"For that—that lying, cheating, backstabbing Richter? He may be rich, but he's bad news. We weren't going to say anything about this to you, Jack, but you're working for a very, very dangerous—"

"Believe me, I'd take his whackjob theories over you two nutbars any old day of the week!" The chair he'd been leaning on for the past thirty seconds danced away from him, the deck somersaulting in swirls around Jack's flailing equilibrium. Time, self-preservation time, was of the essence. "And not for nothing, but if you two don't like him, must mean he's truly on the up and up. Now if you'll excuse me, I think you both know exactly where you can shove all those spiritual thermometers of yours—Sigh-Yo-NaRa!" Jack stormed away, bumped into a cactus hard, and almost got lost trying to find his way out off the stupid patio. Where was he again, Arizona?

Once inside the restaurant, he stood still for a second, by the restrooms, in an absolutely futile effort to retrace the entrance map in his mind. He was a frozen deer in the headlights, pupils a-blazing. Luckily, a kindly hostess sensed his drunken, deranged delirium and veered him in the right direction, ensuring that the power and drama of his stormed exit remained intact.

After having escorted Jack to his vehicular, buckled him in to the driver seat, and put the keys in the ignition for him, the hostess ordered Jack to "Get home safe, Bubba," before slamming the car door. It was a true display of Arizonian hospitality, a rare blue flame wisp of devoted decency. At least he'd successfully skipped out on the tab.

The SmartCar^2 reeked of adult diapers and crème brûlée. Sensory overload made Jack vomit a small portion of his dessert back into his mouth, which wasn't as tasteful the second time around. But once he'd rolled down the window and got the wheels moving, the world regained some semblance of its recognizable tangibility. He sped off in a rubber-burning peel, narrowly avoiding several head-on crashes with the lampposts of the parking lot.

Back at the Motel 6, Jack tried to remember driving himself home. He couldn't. All he remembered was following the voice of the GPS on the dash, that curdling computerized twang. At least the thing and the contraption surrounding it had been completely vaporized when Jack "parked," a violent occurrence that had promptly force-ejected him from the window the instant he'd crashed into the cement abutment behind his room. He was fine, not a scratch on him as they say, though the car itself had indeed imploded. As small as it had appeared before (1/16th the size of any normal road vehicle), the motorized machine was now no more than a crushed plastic-and-metal Rubik cube. He'd deal with this nonsense in the morning.

Inside the room, Jack no longer felt stumble around drunk. The fender bender with the cement block had really given him a jolt, like a thousand espresso shots. He was starting to feel something approximating sober lucidity. The night was still young, and his flight wasn't until tomorrow evening. He fished around for the bottle of Mezcal, which he'd left to cool in the toilet while he was away.

Facing the mirror, in only his underpants, Jack stood slamming shots and doing muscle poses until the liquid was gone—a matter of minutes. After that it was time to unwind, and for a paltry 50¢, the Magic Fingers of the bed shook the mattress in erotic vibrations. That quivering was the last thing he remembered, obliterated.

Jack was up at the crack of day, sharp as a tack. The Mezcal had somehow managed to raze all that came before it, and Jack's body actually felt good. This morning freshness especially helped him with the legal hassles of dealing with the wreck outside. The whole process turned out to be a breeze, though, given that Clint had wisely foreseen such sozzled eventualities. He'd pre-arranged for the *No Harm, No Foul* insurance on the vehicle. Because of that waiver, the company had provided a replacement SmartCar^2 outside Jack's door by 8 a.m., thanks to a *GloboPoint* transmitter beacon.

"Think of it like one a' them black boxes for airplanes," the fresh-faced boy who delivered the car explained, as he handed Jack the new set of keys. "Let's us keep track a' things, copy?"

"10-4," Jack answered, for no apparent reason.

"But don't worry, these fecken things are dime-a-dozen." Afterwards, the kid handed Jack a huge stack of blank legal papers, threw the old wrecked SmartCar^2 cube into the motel dumpster, and left.

Nothing surprising happened to Jack in Wilcox. He rode the straight rail out to the old boxcar town, a settlement now nothing but a shade. After taking the appropriate location site measurements, he sat gobbling his greasy king's breakfast in the Sulphur Valley air of the Dos Cabezas range. What atrocities had gone on here, in a land once ruled by the Chiricahua Apache? The fast food hut and parking lot were mute in the vast biotic stench of nature. The past had been paved over and fitted with a neon sign, linking this present to thousands of infinitely identical points in a constellation of modern light.

Fatmen & Lilbuoy

In California, the expected changed. Jack flew into Palomar Airport in Carlsbad, spent the night at a nearby fleabag resort (the 4 Seasons), and finally got some well-needed abstinent rest. In the morning, the valet service drove Jack all the way down to San Ysidro, for his KIA—a rental location site close enough to whiff the spray-painted, mange Zebra *bourros* of TJ, but too close to the Micky D's massacre of '84.

In the high school field across the lot, broad-backed girls in plaid skirts wielded field hockey sticks and screeched like wild boars.

Thanks to the attendant, Jack arranged to leave the car at the regional airport all the way up in Stockton—for a nominal charge of five seventy-five a mile (roughly $3,500 bucks with Clint's anticipated detours)—and took possession of the keys.

It was one of those gorgeous mornings when healthy, financially stable people exclaimed: "It's a great day to be alive!" And almost clearheaded, Jack could feel something approximating that, too.

His first California stop, and first California shock, came in National City (on a wide street called 500 Miles of Cars Way, no joke! But that wasn't the shocker). He did the classic double take when he arrived, looking desperately for the monkey-shit brown BK colors much like one would for a missing child. As it was, Jack stood frozen, transfixed by the crimson and gold arrow of the In-N-Out Burger franchise (In-N-Oooot©, in Alberta and Saskatchewan), standing firm at the address Clint had provided. What the fuck was going on?

"Excuse me," Jack asked several pedestrians under the soft, November sun. "Isn't there a Burger King around here?" His desperation made him look like a drooling, electro-shock bedlamite. After a while, he simply stopped asking, resigned.

What could this mean? Someone or something had pulled a slogan switcheroo, on the sly, from BeeKay's "Have it Your Way" to INOB's "Quality You Can Taste." Jack had entered a new land of fast food, without a net.

Inside the twilight zone of the In-N-Out, utterly oppressed by the unfamiliar primary colors of the surroundings, Jack sidled up to an employee. The kid at the counter had no idea if this had been a Burger King in the past.

"Is there a manager around," Jack asked, terrified. He glanced up to the *Not-So-Secret Menu*. "I—I—I'd, I'd really like to speak to the manager, please."

"What for? Ain't no Burger Kings 'round here, a'ight?" The snot-nosed little brat adjusted his paper hat and added: "Look, doo'de, you gonna order or wha'?"

"I don't know *what* to order. Is there anything you can recommend?"

"Recommen'? They're burr-grrrs, man! Whatchoowant from me?"

"What's the 4x4® combo meal about?"

"Four patties, four cheese."

"All-beef and mozza?"

"N'ah, dawg: 50% Beef/50% SoyWhatever™. Cheese is yo' option of Velveeta or processed slices. For a small fee, you can add more patties and cheese to the san'mich—"

"What's the all-time record?"

"101, G."

"Urgh, gross! Just give me the #2." At his table, munching with apprehension, Jack went over Clint's notes.

This was indeed the right place. Known as the "Baja Babe Bunker," the ex-facility appears to have been *the* cathouse for military high-ups and dignitaries on layovers to the South Pacific: *Code-clearance of "Baby Whisper" and higher needed by all personnel authorized to enjoy the services of the BBB, colloquially known as one bitch of a BnB. Effective immediately following bombing of 7 December 1941, through to signing of Korean ceasefire on 27 July 1953, the Bunker was under the direct command of LTG Roland Spears and managed by Miss Celia Estelita. The Bunker's great bar, voluptuous Mexicana hostesses, and discreet location made this facility a real hit with the elite. Its unofficial official capacity serviced hundreds, and even allowed for occasional USO entertainment such as Glenn Miller, Mitzi Mayfair, Guy Lombardo, Count Basie, Spike Jones, Amos & Andy, Duke Ellington, Dinah Shore, the Dorsey Brothers, Jascha Heifetz, and Bob Hope.*

The Bunker went dark under Eisenhower's presidency, only to make a brief reappearance as a cigar lounge during the Bahía de Cochinos *(Bay of Pigs) incident. Also during this time, the Bunker served as a greaseball planning center and illicit clubhouse for the ZR/RIFLE plots of Operation 40, a joint CIA/Mob taskforce that primarily targeted Pinko revolutionaries like Che and his butt-buddy Fidel. The Bunker space was later redesigned to emulate the Playboy Mansion "Grotto," during the Vietnamese military action, and was even given Hef's personal seal of approval during those heady days of hedonism during Governor Reagan's Raunchy Republican Hayride. The BBB was a bastion of bi-partisan pleasure, with big-timers Clarence "Pubic hair in the Coke" Thomas and Billy "Won't you be my Congressional Aid" Clintoon {sic} only a few of the notables to make good use of the historic site. That is, before the bubble burst and the politically-correct-powers-that-be drained all the fun out of life and let the place fall into disrepair—restoring the prurient perverts to order...*

    Jack's stomach wavered, gurgling from the foreign food. Outside the In-N-Out, his eyes welled up like a newly sliced melon. On the manicured patio, he lit a cigarette and washed down a few Nembutals with his root beer. He'd planned to try a bit of sobriety, but this latest curve ball threw him for a real loop. So, with one of Ernesto Robertson's prescription sheets in his back pocket, he strolled over to the drugstore for a refill. While he waited for the pharmacists to get their shit together, Jack walked over to Hector's House of Spirits and bought a quart of Wild Turkey.

    Back in the KIA, with fresh new vial of pleasure pills in hand, he poured half the bottle of bourbon into his wax cup. The rental car was actually a fantastic front, he now realized. Why? Because only socially-conscious, environmentally-friendly, morally-upstanding folks drove KIAs. Nobody would ever suspect a KIA driver of doing anything bad, much less irresponsibly reprehensible, behind the wheel of one. The KIA brand was actually a societally-sanctioned free pass to get retarded on booze, tranqs, and dope while cruising the strips and main drags of Anytown, USA. After all, KIA stood for "Kee-Yuh," the Lakota word for Wise One, not a homonym for Killed in Action. Jack was safe inside the bubble.

From here on in, it was going to be a long haul. The closeness of this first ex-covert-site-turned-burger-joint was the great tease of the Californian itinerary, which required hundreds and hundreds of useless driving miles for five lousy spots—all of which turned out to be In-N-Outs, by the way.

Back to your maps, you eager highlighters, because here were the locations of the other four Golden Arrows: Bakersfield was the center pivot point, then down to Barstow (Colonial Drive), and back up to Bakersfield for a night of rest. Next morning it was up to Clovis, on the other side of Fresno, then back down to Bakersfield again. From there Jack hopped on I-5 North to his last scheduled stop in Stockton, where Clint promised to have a Learjet waiting for him at the Metropolitan Airport.[16]

Except for the bodacious babes in bikinis (on billboards), the change of chain burger joints (which immediately acquired a different sort of familiarity), there was nothing very exciting about the Golden State excursion. Why, you may ask? Wasn't it obvious? Think of historic Bixby

---

[16] Oh-ohh! Omigawd! Yes, yes, our maps spell it too, that horrible, vulgar, and repugnant word! Unfortunately, we can't dwell on this sick joke right now; we'll have to come back to it, only once Jack's made the discovery for himself. So, for now, back to our man:

Bridge, Ocean Beach, San Simeon, Point Lobos State Reserve, Manteca, Garrapata, Hurricane Point, San Luis Obispo, and the very indescribable magnificence of the entire Big Sur coast. What sort of idiot drives the inner-Interstate highway going to goddamn fast-food pits, a stone's throw from Joshua Tree, Sequoia, Death Valley, Yosemite, Pinnacles, and the Mighty Mojave, and stayed the course? Jack did, the ever-pragmatic and penny-poor puppet.

    The interior of California had little of the cachet of its coastal cousin. This middle place was the refuge of the bland, crowded, and ordinary. Highway towns stretched in endless clumps, populated with indistinguishable gas stations, restaurant chains, malls, and big box stores. You couldn't make up this sort of landscape. The suburban dream had progressively morphed into this, a nightmare of repetition and paranoia.

    Speaking of which: throughout his now foggy trip across Arizona, Jack hadn't once felt under surveillance watch like he had back in Florida or Texas. Maybe that was the crippling katzenjammer he rode. Whatever it was, though, and whatever sense of security he'd reacquired, began to falter now in California.

    His KIA wasn't the fastest vehicle on the road (redlining it at 60mph), which effectively relegated Jack to life in the slow lane. Keeping him constant company there was a sea of VW

Microbuses, Bugs, and Things, old Ladas, and Volvo station wagons, making it practically impossible to tell if he was being tailed or not.

As a matter of precaution and in order to blend in, Jack bought a beach bum get-up at a rest stop on the 58, just before Barstow. All they had was a stick-on moustache and a long blond wig, which looked utterly ridiculous on him, but at least it gave him some cover. He slipped into some flip-flops, too, which now that he was back to wearing a bathrobe instead of shirts or pants, allowed him to fit in perfectly.

It was late by the time Jack made it to Stockton. The lights illuminated the ink-black canopy above, drowning out the night. Bloated from the change of burger diet, and sick from the weeks of road drinking, he parked outside the regional airport and decided to crash in the car. First, though, he'd drop Clint a line to show him that he'd managed to clean up his act a little by staying relatively sober.

There was a payphone outside the deserted hangar building, its receiver cooled from the evening mist. The operator's voice was nasally familiar as she dialed Clint's place. It was a fluke that the old man himself answered, rather than one of his usual servants: "Mr. Richter, sir, I have a collect call from a former Governor Schwarzenegger, will you accept the charges?"

"No way!"

"I'm sorry, sir, would you repeat…?"

"I said, No! Absolutely not! Tell the ex-Governator that I still can't forgive him for the friggin' Shriver affair. How could he ever let that shit go public—?"

"Clint it's me," Jack tried to say, but the operator had already cut him off. The line was dead, just like his stupid joke. Just as well.

Jack went back to the car for some change. He threw his disguise to the floor of the passenger side; a harried, haggard look reflected back at him from the rearview. With the money stuck into the seams of the seats, he bought pop from a vending machine, popped four Nembutals, and floated to sleep. In the morning, a banging fist against his door woke him up. It was a woman's touch:

"Fuuuuck," Jack muttered, rolling down the window. The morning air was crisp with manure and sod. It was an early-day moment when the sky has the bloom of a rose.

"Werd Berd!"

"What?"

"'Mornin', boss!"

"Uh… good morning." His neck was rigor hard, having slept at a 90-degree all night. The woman's face was pale, speckled with tiny brown freckles. Her melody eyes were shaped in Asia almond. She had the cheeks of a boxer and the delicate ears of a suitcase.

"You Jack Mitford?"

"Y—yeah."

"I'm Hanna Lejaja."

"Who?"

"Hanna Lejaja."

"Okay."

"I'm your pilot. Clint arranged it—"

"Right. Yeah."

"I'm supposed to bump you up north in m'Cessna—"

"Cessna? He said Lear."

"Don't believe a word that dirty crook says, unless he's being sincere. You ready to flap your wings, pardner?"

"Wh—what time is it?"

"Six-thirty."

"Jesus!"

"Yup, it's getting' late—time t'a get a' crackin'! That's my girl over there, the pink and blue plane with 'Sissy' painted on the side—"

"Sissy?"

"I'm a sucker for Sissy Spacek. You like her work?"

"*Norma Rae*, is it?"

"No, that's Sally Field."

"Oh. Shit, ummm… *Coal Miner's Daughter*—?"

"We'll get along jus' fine, Jack. Now, blow your top and get a move on. Hope you packed light!" He watched as she waddled away towards her plane, the top hang of her flight suit tied around her waist. Jack grabbed the small bag in the passenger seat, the one with the pills, hotel robes, notes, and sunglasses. The car keys he threw on the driver's seat and left the rest behind.

"Here, this should help." Hanna handed Jack a large steaming mug of black coffee as he climbed into the plane. He thought he might kiss her.

"Thank you… so much."

"No sweat. I don't have any cream or sugar. As that old KKK saying goes, I like my coffee black like I like my men—"

"Black's fine."

"Help yourself if you want more, I have a built-in espresso machine back there."

"Really?"

"Only way to fly."

"Are we taking off now?"

"Wheels up, yep. Why?"

"I was going to have a cigarette before we—aw, it's no big deal, don't worry about it."

"Go ahead and smoke in here, if you like."

"You smoke?"

"Nah, but I don't mind. That second-hand smoke stuff is just a bullshit lie as far as I'm concerned. Look, there's even an ashtray in the door there."

"Great. Thanks." He shook a coffin nail free from his soft-pack and lit-up.

"You look like you could use one. Rough night?"

"Rough month."

"That why you wearing a bathrobe?"

"No." Jack reached back into his bag, pulling out the first vial he could find.

"What are those, aspirin?"

"Adderall."

"I like you already."

"You want, uh—?"

"You bet."

"Sure? What I mean is: should you be flying this thing in… well, in an altered state?"

"Aw, you're more likely to die in a car wreck than a plane crash. And anyway, as you know, Adderall concentrates your brain, gives it cognitive snap, crackle, pop! Besides, Sissy practically flies herself and nobody's gonna say jackshit to us up there. Ain't no pigs with wings that I ever heard of…"

"Yeah, but…"

"But nothing, Jack! Just relax, man, this is my sky." Hanna took a double-dose of the "A" and grabbed her green, David Clark headset. She then put on a pair of dark-framed aviators that made her Asian features look severe. The sun was just coming up on the horizon as they lifted off into a blanket of stratus clouds—the perfect autumn aurora.

They took the long way around, once Hanna heard about Jack's boring California zigzag so far. She flew towards Monterey and Santa Cruz, purposely winging in the wrong direction. The agile craft banked off imposing mountainous switchbacks and deep meadows littered with cup of gold poppies and cactus flowers. Viridian valleys pushed forth in massive green swaths populated by settlements, inter-cut by wires, and connected through a vast network of intricate road systems. An entire microcosm landscape built itself up below the plane before its frenetic fall into the Pacific.

    They skirted the constant coast along San Mateo, swooping down through the splendor of Half Moon Bay, before droning up towards San Francisco and Marin County.

    "This place is called Stinson Beach," Hanna said after what seemed like a long silence between them. The whir of the propeller buzzed at a high, persistent hum. "See that house down there? That used to be Jerry Garcia's place—"

    "Yeah?"

    "You like the Dead?"

    "Not really."

    "What's wrong with you, man?"

    "I—?"

    "Never mind." The plane dipped towards a set of bluffs, marked by jagged red rocks. Hanna talked about various local harbor seals and pointed out some colorful vegetation like sea thrifts, lingering paintbrush, and beach strawberries. "Say, you like drinking wine don'tcha, Jack?"

    "I like drinking just about anything."

    "Outstanding. Say, you game for a little detour?"

"Absolutely."

"Great! Do me a favor, can you grab that big brown carton back there?"

"Sure." Jack struggled with the weight of the box, his ass wiggling while he nudged it loose. The curly cable of his headphones swayed in the moment. "Huh, this stuff's really heavy!"

"Tell me about it! Here, just prop it up between the seats. Go ahead, open the lid."

"What is it?"

"Water balloons."

"Water balloons?"

"Yeah, but I filled 'em with cat piss, diarrhea, and puke."

"Jesus! Why?"

"To drop on this place we're going to fly over here in a sec. It's called Rubicon Estate. That ugly rat-faced cunt Coppola owns it, so I never miss an opportunity to bomb the shit outta that shithole—"

"Why's that?"

"'Cause he's a talentless fuckwad and he deserves it, that's why! Now get ready, I'm making a double pass." Hanna dove the nose of the plane toward the main building of the property, ornate Japanese plum trees leading the charge.

The Rubicon château rose up from the green wood like a sore thumb. Its pergola was draped in vines, blazing reds and browns. Four or five men stood around drinking coffee in the early morning mist, their heads craned toward the sky. When the plane doors were pushed open, a great couloir of wind rushed through the cockpit and violently shook the insides. Hanna started yelping and screeching—a crazed, out-of-control baboon—grabbing madly at the multi-colored balloons. She tossed them out by the mitt-full: "Bombs away!"

"Holy Jesus!"

"I know, right?" All the men on the ground were nailed on the first pass, which sent them scurrying for cover like scared, mad children. Balloons of feline excrement exploded on the lampposts, benches, grass, statues, and stone stairs of the romantic garden patio. Manage your sphincters, boys…

"Whooooooooo-HHHhhooooooooooooo!" Hanna and Jack screamed in a bizarre, arrhythmic unison. Where was Wagner, that wretched wrathful Valkyrie, when you really needed him?

On Hanna's jouncing second pass, a bearded man stood firm by the front fountain. He held his big-bellied ground amidst the exploded dead projectiles of brown, beige, and butterscotch.

"Is that who I think it is?"

"Gettin' slapped in the face at Coppola's place… blast the fat fuck!" They threw what they could (mostly missing him) and dumped the rest of the box into a long reflective show pool nearby. "GeeeeZuss that was fun! I don't know about you, Jack-O, but I could use a drink. Eight o'clock in the morning ain't too early for ya, is it?"

"God no!"

"Good, we'll stop in at one of the best wineries in all of Northern Cali. It's not that far, just in the hub of the Russian River Valley, before Lake Sonoma." Hanna avoided flying over highways, pointing instead to obscure natural landmarks below. The lean winter was on its way, a still holding pattern in the distance.

"You know a whole lot about this region, Hanna. Were you born here?"

"Kinda. Plus, I learned to fly up around here, when I was at Stanford."

"You went to Stanford, for what?"

"I was a Wallace Stegner Fellow there back in the nineties—"

"Man, you write, too!"

The winery they were headed towards had a long dirt driveway running up sharp to its main buildings. Fields of lavender kissed the road, and Hanna steered the plane directly down the center of its beaten trench. Thick clouds of dust billowed freely into the air. It was a bumpy-smooth landing.

The buildings ahead were a mash of styles, mixing Spanish Mission architecture with Bauhaus flourishes and rustic Wild West décor—somehow it was an effortless smear. There was a small parking lot off to the far side of the front property, and Hanna wheeled her way into a spot in a mangled sort of parallel park. An ineffable elation pervaded the cockpit. Jack's arms felt like feathers as he took off his headset and hung it on its hook. His body was going through a joy of sensations.

"How was that," Hanna smiled, "not too bumpy?"

"I—I can't describe how I feel. It's, it's amazing!"

"I know, right?"

"I've never felt this way before."

"It's a combination of the altitude and the opioid effects, a wicked buzz!"

"I'll say."

"Next time, try Ambien, Sonata, Xanax, Lunesta, or any of those other rich-bitch pills. I used to fly with this Mexican-made methaqualone—you know, 'ludes—but the stuff's too hypnotic for me and its muscle relaxant qualities just tear my insides to shreds. I kid you not, I once dropped a deuce in my flight suit here and didn't even realize 'til I landed."

"Really? These things sometimes keep me constipated for days, which is such a time saver. And, I actually think they've made my dick a little bigger, too."

"Who ever said drugs were all bad, huh?" As they opened the doors and stepped out, a young man came rumbling down from the main estate house. His face was flushed red, but he didn't wait to catch his breath before he started barking at Hanna:

"What in the hell d'you think you're doing?"

"Comin' to get some vino, Jabroni. Whadd'you think?"

"I mean the plane?!"

"Oh, that. Don't worry, no one will fuck with her here. She'll be safe—"

"I—that's not what I meant."

"Well? Spit it out then, shitstick…"

"Wh—What's the big idea?"

"What, mumbles? Speak up!"

"The plane! The plane!"

"Take it easy, Pepe. You sound like that midget from *Fantasy Island*!"

"I could call the cops, you know?"

"Wha-haha, easy there, tiger. No need to call the fuzz."

"Explain yourself then! What's with the goddamned plane?"

"What's your problem, smartmouth? We have a plane, not a car. Get over it!"

"Get—! Do you even know where you are? This estate isn't open to the general public! We're available by appointment only!"

"Gosh, you sure do gots a humungoid pickle up yer azz, ain't yaw? Now don't get your panties in a twist, I know Phyllis and Edwardo. It's all right."

"No it isn't! You—you can't just, just—"

"Just chill, ya goof. You're making a complete fool of yourself with this whole scene, when what you should be doing is getting us some Chardonnay—"

"At this hour?"

"What, you're part of the morality police, too? Can it, shortstack!" The kid was speechless. He looked like an eel frying in oil and brine. "What sayest thou, Jack-O, crisp bottle a' white to start?"

"Uhh, sounds good."

"Awesome. My good man, we'll take a double magnum of the Chardonnay—a bottle of the late harvest, not the Estate Reserve—and bring out some savory meats while you're at it, hmm? Some goat's Gouda, shortbreads, tartar, and calf's tongue should do to start, as well as some jalapeño and red hot chili peppers—the food, not the band."

The kid stood stunned, immobile. Hanna, on the other hand, seemed in her natural environment as she began leading the way up the path. She swam in the invigorating air, naturally, speaking in a soothing tone to drown the whole floating world: "You see, Jack, they age the wine in French oak casks here and don't believe in malolactic fermentation, which I think is great because it's for wussies. The balance they achieve has an astounding, incredible involution. Christ the complexity! Just fuckin' mind-blowing! I'll take my chances with acidity any old day of the week if that means—"

"Excuse me, miss!"

"Hmn? Oh, you're still here?"

"I'm sorry, but I'm afraid I can't possibly allow you to stay. You simply can't be on the vineyard grounds unannounced, there are rules against—"

"Unannounced! *UN*-announced? Listen, shithead, I've been polite with you until now, but you've really got to stop with the poncy philippic—"

"The what—?"

"I've been coming here since you were beating your tiny excuse for a pecker to the Sears catalogue, okay? So you better get, and get now, if you'd like to keep your pathetic excuse for a job."

"I'm—"

"Is Hugh around?"

"Y—yes."

"Great. Tell him Hanna's here. I'm his niece."

"Oh." Jack and Hanna were immediately escorted to the panoramic terrace, where they were waited on hand and foot. While sitting next to a perched parasol, they drank fantastic big wine for breakfast under the warm, third-season sun. It was heavenly.

Vintage Valhalla

Symmetrical rows stretched from the front grounds out to the nearby hillsides, wild mustard creeping between the vines. Though it was an arid, sparse landscape, there was a unique lushness to the surround. Hunched migrants carefully tended the grape trails, their voices resonating through the valley in lyric song. Moist, gravelly soil was at their feet. Everything seemed tanned, slow roasted to perfection. The atmosphere made it easy to feel at home.

Hugh eventually came out late morning, wearing a duster and sun-visor, beaming proudly over Hanna as he opened a chilled bottle of what he called a brut "Blanc de Noirs." He was loud but genuine, gray-haired yet virile, a man best described as rugged, rather than old. His hands were the strong hands of a workingman. Hanna had earlier described him as a "true voluptuary," and Jack could now see why. It was plainly evident from his presence and speech that he owned all the surrounding lands, which he innately strove to share with the world.

"M'darling girl, such a pleasure to see you, as always! How long has it been?"

"Well over a year, at least…"

"You know you gave Cedric quite a start—"

"Who?"

"The young man who first greeted you—"

"Cedric, that's the weeny twerp's name?"

"Come now, be kind. He's the son of the Gonzales family down the way—you remember them? Been with us six months now. It's true: at times, he *can* be a useless twerp, as you say, but he does work hard."

"He sure as shit yells hard enough, I'll give him that much."

"By the way, are you flying up or down this time?"

"Left from Stockton this morning."

"Ah, well, in that case: did you, perchance, pay a visit to the Vague Vintner, our propriety poseur friend to the south?"

"Yup, sure did."

"You give that corked cad the Angel's Share?"

"The whole nine—"

"Attagirl!"

"*Merci, merci.*" Their glasses came together in a self-satisfied clink. Who knew what motivations they shared? Sunlight sparkled through the clear liquid of their goblets, shimmering in faint ripples. They all three sipped at the dripping, alembicated beauty of the gods. What a time to be alive.

"So, Jack, how long have you known my Hanna here?" Hugh gripped the bottleneck with force, pouring more nectar freely. "You must really be a special kind of sort if she brought you up here—"

"Well, actually, we only just met. Someone else arranged everything."

"C'mon, don't kid a kidder, Jackie boy. It's plain as day—"

"What is?"

"You two are in love—"

"Pppffffft!" Jack spit the entire contents of his mouth all over Hugh's shirt. "Oh, shit! Sorry, sorry, sorry. Shit! Hugh, I'm—"

"Please, Jack, it's fine."

"Forgive me."

"Happens all the time." After three more bottles, flanks of venison and medallions of roast pork on a bed of blackened Périgord truffles, Hugh took them on a tour of the caves.

"Do you know much about Californian wines, Jack?"

"No, not at all. The only thing I really know about the area is Ernest & Julio Gallo and that Mondavi guy—"

"Euurk! Well, it's never too late. My Hanna here is a true connoisseur and a font of enological knowledge, though she's also too modest to admit it. She grew up with the Maestro bouncing her on his knee."

"The Maestro?"

"André Tchelistcheff. If California is Mount Olympus, he was Zeus. We are but mere mortals reeling in the wake of his legacy, the doyen of the domains. Ask this one, she knows."

"It's true." For the first time since this morning, Jack stared at Hanna. She was radiant, and not altogether unpretty. She owned her slender sleek figure, her angles appropriate in all the right places. The genetic cross-patterns were blended to perfection in the tight harmonies of her face. Asian bloodlines embraced Caucasoid ones, and they rolled along together merrily.

"The California dirt is under her nails, the smell of vines is in her nose. How she stomachs that awful Washington State swamp water, I'll never know!"

"Stop it, Uncle Hugh." Down in the cask room they met Jordan, a bald rake with a big nose who was introduced with great flourish. Jordan was Hugh's partner, and clearly more pleasure than business. Both he and Hugh were bloated with privilege, giving their tanned skin a goutish red hue.

The four pleasantly ambled around the grounds together, crystalline goblets in hand. Jack and Hanna were introduced to some of the Hispanic workers around the property, who all seemed delighted to be working at the winery.

Later, the four visited the adobe barracks, held over from Gold Rush times, which now served as a showcase office and private entertaining lounge. Jordan produced some illegal Cohibas from a walk-in humidor, and they sat in the fading afternoon sun drinking more gorgeous wine and puffing out exquisite smoke.

It was getting dark by the time an opportunity presented itself for Hanna and Jack to leave. Figuratively speaking, they were standing atop a murky, slippery slope. He couldn't vouch for her, but Jack was well past gassed.

"Why not just stay the night," Hugh said, petting Hanna's hair. "The *Cuvée Cabin* is ready for you, as usual. You two can stay up there."

"No, we can't."

"Why not?"

"I promised Jim I'd have 'Sissy' back by tonight."

"Oh, he's still in the picture?"

"He's my husband, Uncle Hugh, of course he's still in the picture."

"I know. I guess I just hoped—"

"What?"

"That you'd outgrown him—"

"Why?"

"I dunno, I thought maybe you'd overcome your… chocolate phase."

"Aw, really? You're still on the whole black thing?"

"What, black thing! You know better than anyone how I feel about black people. I fought for Civil Rights—"

"Yeah, on the Berkeley campus."

"Hey, don't be like that. I still care about the cause. I—we—have got tons of African American friends down in San Francisco. Tell them, Jordan."

"It's true."

"See?"

"So what?"

"I just don't want you to settle, Hanna, that's all."

"Who's settling? I love Jim, and that has nothing to do with the color of his skin! Besides, he's not really black, he's a mongrel like me."

"Semantics! Black, mulatto, quadroon, who cares?"

"You do, obviously! You can be incredibly narrow-minded sometimes, Uncle Hugh, you know that?"

"I know. But what else is Jim, really, apart from stupid?"

"Is this when you pull out your rulebook for undesirables? You feel like learning a bit more about Eugenics, Jack?"

"What, sorry?"

"Hugh here can tell you all about race betterment, streamline breeding, and the growing endowments in the US for that sort of shit—"

"All right, enough!"

"No, go ahead, Uncle Hugh. Enlighten Jack on the gobs of grants the Rockefeller Foundation gave 'Beppo' Mengele after he graduated from the dorms of Auschwitz, Treblinka, and Sobibor. Tell him about how the Manhattan Institute has since concentrated its efforts to fund leading researchers of the so-called

Cognitive Elite, which seems to include very few non-white, non-Anglo-Saxon, non-Protestant cats, if you know what I'm sayin'? C'mon, let's go dig out your signed copy of the *Turner Diaries*—"

"Okay, okay. Let's all just settle down." Jordan was doing his best to calm the escalated situation, standing tall in his best efforts of appeasement. Jack had absolutely no idea what was going on. "Here, let's have another little bit of—"

"I don't want any more goddamn wine!" Hanna stood up and pointed at Hugh. "I want you to apologize this instant—"

"Don't point at me, little girl!"

"I'm warning you—"

"Oww, threats now? That's rich!"

"I don't get you sometimes, Uncle Hugh. Are you bipolar or what? You're a faggot, for chrissakes!"

"Thank you very much—"

"I mean, is this the way you acted when my dad met my mom? Did you tell your brother then not to marry a dirty fuckin' zipperhead?"

"Whoa!" Jordan looked lost in the middle of the room, helpless. "That's—that's completely uncalled for, Hanna—"

"No, no. She's right, Jordan. She's absolutely right. What am *I* saying? I sound like a bigot. A big, dumb, ignorant—"

"Gay—"

"*Gay*... hypocrite. I'm sorry, darling girl. I don't know what I'd do if you hadn't been born. Forgive me? Please?"

"All right."

"Settled?" Jordan was hesitant, worried about breaking the peace. It was a den of nutcases. The tension dissolved into some pleasantries and, eventually, silence. Hanna and Hugh made up, but the evening was over. What a relief.

Hanna had, wisely, decided not to fly north. Instead, she and Jack went to the especially reserved Cuvée Cabin for the night. Ostentatiously refurbished, the building did everything to call attention to itself, both inside and out. "Gee, this is quite a place."

"Isn't it?" Hanna was busily searching the cupboards for glasses and cocktail mix, like a decided pro. She could give a wino a run for his beggared money. "Supposedly, this hut is where General Vallejo and Pancho Villa got sloshed one night and hatched their dastardly plan—"

"For—?"

"For taking over the world, numbnuts! Guess Montezuma won that revenge."

"Guess so." Jack felt too tired to bother asking what she was talking about. History could be a real bore at the best of times, and right now, he was riding a decent buzz. Amidst the several flat-paneled televisions, chrome appliances, 18-piece living-room set, and massive modern art pieces, it didn't take a genius to figure out there was only one bed in the place. Still, maybe a bed was hiding under all the patterned chintz, so he started pulling at cushions.

"Hey, get the fuck away from that!"

"What?"

"What are you looking for?"

"A spare bed."

"Why?"

"I'm tired. Unlike you, I'm not used to being up at six-thirty in the morning."

"The bed is up the ladder, on the loft level. See?"

"Yeah, I see. I just figured you'd probably want that."

"I do."

"... Hence my looking for the hide-a-bed." Jack backed away slowly as Hanna started sidling over from the kitchen.

"I'll tell you what I wouldn't mind hiding, Jackie boy—"

"What?"

"How 'bout showing me that WMD you got bulging down there?" Jack wasn't sure if he was supposed to laugh at the corny rehash or take it seriously. Even this drunk he felt awkward, of that he was sure—if nothing else. "Well aren't you going to say anything?"

"What I'm supposed to say."

"You like girls, don'tcha?"

"Absolutely."

"So, you got anything against a friendly roll in the hay?"

"No, it's just that—"

"What?"

"Well, I don't know, what about all that stuff earlier?"

"What, with Uncle Hugh?"

"Yeah."

"Ah, don't worry about that. We do that bit for show, it's like a Vaudeville act."

"Huh?"

"Hugh's the least racist guy you'd ever want to meet. He loves Jim, my husband, they're actually fishing buddies—"

"?"

"I think, if he could, Uncle Hugh would *be* black."

"What was with those Berkeley cracks, then?"

"Just jokes, like I said. But Hugh was there all right, with Mario Savio, Bettina Aptheker, Jackie ("Whoopie") Goldberg, Steve Weissman, and that whole Free Speech Gang (FSG). And bet your ass he was at Kent State, too, dodging friendly fire from the National Guard. Nope, Uncle Hugh's the real deal—New Left all the way. He even marched with Martin Luther King and was a Freedom Rider down in Birmingham, Montgomery, Selma, Mobile, and Little Rock. And you've seen how well the help here respond to him. He's a true supporter of the

Sí, se puede movement, you know that whole César Chávez thing?"

"I…?"

"He even used to be a lobbyist up in D.C. against the federal and private support of the 'Raceology' type research I mentioned. Our little 'act,' if you wanna call it that, comes from the fact that he firmly believes in sedition, free speech disguised as inflammatory statements made to shock or disgust. It's a unique approach, I'll give him that much. I think he got that flair for raw activism when he was with the Digger collective in the Haight, back in the day."

"I'm—I'm totally lost here."

"Don't worry about it, Jack. I'm sure he'll tell you all about it in the morning. Hugh's always had a thing for radical performance that makes you think, but he usually gives you a night to sleep on it. For now, what d'you say we climb up that ladder and get to the hokey-pokey? I'm way past tipsy and horny as shit…"

"You can't be serious. What about this Jim guy?"

"What about him?"

"You're married."

"You're not one of those closet prudes are you, Jack? That huge stash of pharmies and all-hour drinking schedule made me think you were a lot hipper than that."

"No, I'm not a prude. It's just, I thought you said you two were in love so—"

"We *are* in love, we're just open about it that's all. Look, can we stop talking and just do it already? I feel like I'm in some interminable Swedish movie."

The sex was great and lasted for several hours. Hanna kissed like a demon at the gates of Hell, and she oozed a genuine passion. From his end: Jack did his best to keep up, putting in a more than passable, perfervid performance. They drank bottles of chilled white wine during the extravaganza, which kept their palates moistly perfect. There was a great intimacy that Jack hadn't expected. Thanks to the calisthenics, they christened just about every inch of the cabin and ended up passing out on the cushions of the sofa after all. So much for expectations, goes the saying, and so much for sleep.

A Camelot Approach

In the morning, smug with semen, Hanna had a salacious glow. She was completely naked, the sylphlike lines of her hips swaying in the open-concept kitchenette. They couldn't have slept for more than a few hours, but she looked rejuvenated. Jack felt like a rented mule.

"Jack, there you are. Coffee or wine to start the morning?"

"Ugh! Coffee, please." The smell of roast beans soon filled the air. It was a delight in the thick hangover haze.

"How you feelin'?"

"Awful."

"Good. At least your mind won't be gettin' ideas on more hanky-panky then." That was untrue, but he was in much too much pain to correct her. "Besides, we should be getting a move on pretty soon here. Uncle Hugh'll have some fancy breakfast send-off for us, I'm sure."

"Yeesch, I hope not! There's absolutely no way I can eat. I'm wrecked."

"You better, or he'll take it personally."

"I don't care! I'll puke all over him this time if I try choking anything down right now. It'll be a deluge compared to last night's itty-bitty spit-up incident—"

"I'm sure you're exaggerating—"

"Wanna bet?" The bean brew was done, and Hanna brought both steaming mugs over to the bed. Her thin trail of pubic hair was a fuzzy auburn in the light. The sofa shifted as she sat next to him.

"Here, try this. It should fix you right up. They call it Cowboy Coffee, which is just a fancy name for coffee with grits at the bottom."

"Thanks." He took a quick sip and lit a cigarette. Nothing could beat that combination. The road to recovery appeared in the distance.

"Listen, Jack-O, I feel it's only right to tell ya something—"

"Okay—"

"Just a heads-up, but I've pretty much had every STI and venereal disease in the book, so—"

"What!" He spilled a dollop of coffee on his groin and nearly scorched his penis.

"It's cool, don't worry! Nothing permanent, mostly just the good ones—"

"What? What good ones?"

"You know, the curables—"

"Wh—why didn't you feel the need to tell me any of this STD business *before* we slobbered all over each other?"

"Chill out, dude. It's no big deal. The shit's been cleared out, eradicated. Anti-bios, man. I'm clean. At least I'm pretty sure I am because I haven't had a breakout in ages—"

"You're unbelievable!"

"Thanks. I guess I just felt like you should

know. There's always been something in me, whenever I have sex with someone—man or woman—that makes me want to be utterly honest. That's why what Jim and I have is pretty magical."

"I'm absolutely thrilled for you two—"

"Don't be like that. I'm just trying to be upfront."

"Gee, great—a little late for that, isn't it?"

"Oh, also, while I *am* being honest. I may as well tell you: I'm the one who's been tailing you since Florida."

"Huh!?"

"Uh-huh, on the money since you landed the Mustang drive from Miami. Dade County, wasn't that where the pigs tried to pin all that shit on the Lizard King for pulling out his one-eyed monster? The real doors to perception, man, talk about a great publicity stunt with Manzarek and Krieger pulling full moons during Light My Fire!"

"Hang on a minute, you're the one Richter put on me?"

"Don't get me wrong, the man's as nutty as a Thai peanut salad, but it's hard to fault the fucker for trying to keep an eye on you, Jack: Mr. Drunken, pill-popping reprobate! Can you say a dick, Dick, dickted? You rilly went off the fuckin' deep-end there for a while, buddy, zoned out of your mind. You should have seen your face too, every time you pulled up to another Burger

King! Every time you were just a little more defeated, and every time you took just a little more medicine or a little more booze to cope. It was like clockwork, until your meltdown in Pensacola and then the one in Abilene. And boy, didn't those In-N-Outs throw you for one hell of a loop! I'll say one thing for ya, you've been entertaining as a five-point rodeo!"

"I can't believe you've been following me this whole time—"

"Think of me as your guardian angel."

"Is that what they're calling syphilis-laden mercenaries these days?"

"Hey, bub! That's below the belt!"

"Very funny—"

"I mean it! Did you hear me say *syphilis*?"

"Who knows what kind of—?"

"*Did* you hear me use the word syphilis or not?"

"No."

"There. Now take that back!"

"I'm sorry, I take it back." Jack took a few puffs on his cigarette, calming his nerves quietly. "I knew someone was following me, I just knew it! I could feel this presence sometimes, you know?"

"Nobody said I was the world's best spy. You had me dead to rights a couple a' times there, too. I usually got out of it by making out with random strangers, though."

"Conspiracy Clint! That shitbird's had it

in for me since day one!"

"Are you kidding? He's got a real soft spot for you, talks about you like he would his own son—if he had one, that is. Clint maybe be a world-class confidence man, but at least he's frank and genuine—"

"He's a con, a crazy-ass nutbag!"

"I won't argue with you there, but make no mistake: his fortune makes him eccentric, not crazy. If you want to know the truth of it, he doesn't know what to do with all that fuckin' dough! Fact is, there're only so many charitable organizations you can give to before the IRS crawls right up your hoo-hoo. They've got a hard line when it comes to what they call 'conspicuous compassion,' let me tell you. He has to give in other less fortunate countries like Canada, Italy, and France just to keep his books straight. Too bad for Clint that nasty mental-case disease keeps him holed-up in the Hamptons or else he'd be doing nothing but traveling at the same time. Hope *that* phobia doesn't run in the family, or I'm screwed."

"Now what are you saying, you two are related?"

"He's m'uncle. I thought y'knew that—"

"No."

"Yep. He's Hugh's brother, too, but they don't speak. Not since 1970, something about an unpaid bar tab and an argument over the Chicago 7 really being the Chicago 8. Whatever you do, don't mention Bobby Seale to either of them, unless you wanna get your head bitten off."

"I'm—I'm speechless… again. What the hell is it with Clint and his whacko family tree?"

"We're a special breed a' folks, that's for sure."

"You can say that again."

She did, as Jack stood up and tried to find an ashtray. He found a nearby plate and tapped its side with his cigarette. Standing straight, he felt the rush of the previous night lunge at his brain. The pain nearly knocked him off his feet.

"So listen, Jack-O, no hard feelings about the tail, huh? I wanted to tell you when we left Stockton yesterday, but then I got stoned. Plus, we started having so much fun together and I kinda wanted to fuck you by that point. I didn't know how you'd react to the news, so I guess I chickened out. These past few weeks on the road, shadowing you like that, I was horny—sue me. I don't even remember the last time I went so long without a poke."

"You tried to kill me!"

"No I didn't!"

"Yes you did!"

"You're paranoid, dude. In fact, I've never met anyone so paranoid and at the same time so delusional about their own acute paranoia. You're seeing shit everywhere—in every nook and cranny, under the rugs, behind the paintings—and you think everybody else is deluded?"

"Can you blame me? Did you read the notes Clint had on any of those places? He'd have you believe that the Vienna Boys' Choir is an army of midget commandos trained to carry-out political assassinations—"

"Are they?"

"No! The guy's a total headcase—"

"No doubt. But alcohol and pills haven't exactly been helping you out much in the reality department recently, Jack, that's for sure."

"Look who's talking?"

"Hey, I ain't no saint. I'm just sayin'—"

"Jesus, just thinking about this shit hurts my head."

"Speaking of, you got any more a' them gaga pills?"

"Good idea, I should probably take a few—"

"I meant for me, Co-cheese! Don't start being stingy now, especially not after the kinky shit you pulled on my ass last night. Where d'you come up with that stuff?"

"The Internet." Jack dropped his stub into one of the empty wine bottles. He fished three vials out from under the still pristine robes in his bag, turning around in full, undaunted glory. "Which kind do you want, Nembutals or Adderall? I also have some Demerol left, if you want that instead?"

"You running a pharmacy biz on the side,

champ?" As Jack demurred, Hanna took the opportunity to tickle at his junk, playfully. "You know, you're in pretty damn good shape for a drunken smoker living on happy meals and pushing forty—"

"Hanna!"

"Sorry. You got a problem with compliments?"

"Which one do you want?"

"Ah, jus' give me a few Addys, I gotta fly soon and I want to stay level-headed."

Hugh and Jordan came to the door about an hour later. By then, traces of the coital hurricane had been obliterated from the place, and Jack managed to feel something approximating normalcy. The four ate crêpes with strawberries out on the terrace of the main building, while Cedric—that toadying little cretin—waited on them like a perfect bootlicking servant to the Raj.

Bottles of champagne littered the table. It was an embarrassment of riches, bathed in fresh splendor. "This golden ambrosia is sent to us from Bollinger," Hugh said in his morning-person voice, "they're our sister estate in France. This *Ultra Très Spéciale Cuvée des Élites et Non des Minables* is a secret Grand Cru. They only bottle between ten and thirty-five a year."

"Mmn, too bad. It's very good."

"Isn't it? Gives the mimosas a particular lift." Hugh stared at Jack, who looked mildly presentable behind the panache of his dark shades and a filched winery robe. Hanna, somehow, managed to look great—glowing, even. "So listen, darling, did you tell Jack about our little improv skit last night?"

"Yes."

"Oh, good. I apologize for that, Jack. We have a tendency to get carried away with the guerrilla theatre we act out for people. I hope you'll forgive us."

"What's to forgive?"

"I'm glad you're being such a good sport about things. I dreaded the idea of you leaving here thinking I was actually some sort of neo-Nazi good ole boy, constantly railing against Yids and jungle bunnies, burning Howard Zinn books, my walls plastered with pictures of Klaus Barbie—"

"Who's Klaus Barbie?"

"The Butcher of Lyon, head of the Gestapo in occupied France. That monster massacred and deported tens of thousands—one of the worst mankind ever produced. They named a doll after him. Anyhoo, I hope you'll excuse our little attempt at Theatre of Cruelty—I blame Julian Beck for showing me the way; still, t'was but a small lie, a fiblet on our part to while away the time. No doubt, it's what we do best."

It was just before noon when the plane was ready to go. One of the migrants on the property had refueled the tank this morning. Now, a whole line of the brown-skinned winery workers stood at attention as Hanna said her goodbyes to Hugh and Jordan. It felt like the ceremonial departure of an important foreign dignitary.

Jack watched, standing by the fuel barrels, smoking pensively. "Grab those cases of Pinot over there," Hanna said to him when she finished her solemn farewells, "and throw them on the back seat, will ya, Jack-O?" She jumped into the plane and began her pre-flight inspections.

Jack carried the three heavy boxes of wine with glee, knowing what was in store. He waved one last time to Jordan and Hugh, as well as to the two-dozen men and women standing stiffly behind. He felt relief as he hopped up into the plane.

"How long's the trip," he asked, fiddling with his headset.

"It'll take us 4-5 hours at least to get up there, depending on the winds. What say we see just how much damage we can do to those crates on the way up north—you cool with that, Tonto?"

"Giddy up!"

"No. What I mean is: you gonna be able to keep up?"

They blitzed back down the same road runway where they'd landed, soaring into the great blue expanse halfway down the drive. The flight took about the time Hanna predicted, gliding high above the unkempt coastal landscape. A bottle an hour is what they managed, toasting every natural wonder with grand gestures. The weather was with them, as was good fortune.

They flew along the Siskiyou Mountains, gaining speed from headwinds, and stayed east of the Klamath until Coos Bay. Hanna wanted Jack to see Oregon's famed sand dunes and threaded up the coast past the sea lion caves to Yachats. From the salal and huckleberry of the shoreline, they passed over Devil's Punchbowl, up through Cape Lookout, Rockaway Beach, Chinook, and the head of the Columbia River, where the coastline started becoming foggy and rough with offshore winds.

At Taholah, on the edge of the Quinault Indian Reservation, they banked northeast over the vast National Park of western Washington. The Olympic Peninsula leg of the flight was truly spectacular.

Though mountain flowers like the avalanche lily and queen's cup were well out of bloom, Hurricane Ridge and its glacial range companions did not disappoint. The pristine azure sky also did its part, allowing for a striking view clear across the straits from Port Townsend, all the way out to the majestic monolith of Mount Baker's wintry white peak. The scenery truly was too overwhelming to describe.

Hanna was wearing her aviators, which were like mirrors. She was in complete control up here, master of the air. "So Jack-O, how d'you feel about takin' it easy for the next few days?"

"I'm open to suggestions?" He said, lighting a cigarette and popping the top to his vial. "Hey, do you want any more of th—?"

"Yup." They both took a single yellow soldier each, washed down with gulp of the bottle. Onward, they raged. "Like I said, I'm more than happy to drop you off in the Tacoma-Seattle area. But Jim and I have a cottage house out on Orcas Island—"

"Where's that?"

"The San Juans. It's Shangri-La for the chi-chi set, only about ten or fifteen nautical miles from Anacortes. You'd be more than welcome to crash with us for a bit, might even do you some good to chill out for a few days—catch your breath, you know?"

"Sure, I'd love to. But Clint'll probably be furious if I don't wrap things up soon, this trip's been costing him a fortune in time and money."

"So what? Let the geezer get steamed!"

"I thought you were on his side?"

"Side? We're all on the same side here, Jack-O. What I'm sayin' is that the old coot could use a coronary at his age, might even do *him* some good. Besides, he burns money in his fireplace when he runs out of wood, it's not like he cares about the peanuts he pays us."

"Well…"

"Come on, you're already a week over

schedule. What's a few more days?"

"I know, but Clint still has a bunch more planned for me—"

"Don't worry, I'm sure there'll be plenty of time for you to do what you need to do in Seatown later. Whadd'you say?"

"Okay." They landed at the small airport in Eastsound village, where island life was far from a bustle. Hanna parked the plane in a hangar and they jumped into an unlocked Land Rover waiting in a nearby field.

"Is this thing yours?"

"Maybe, they all look the same to me." At the bottom of Prune Alley and Main Street they picked up a few preserves from an upscale general store. Local artisan crafts hung down from the rafters, while soothing semi-plangent ocean sounds played low. Hanna waved at a few people and made small talk with the owner. Outside, the early evening air was cool, fragrant with the crisp death of the Indian summer.

"They seemed like friendly people."

"Big bunch a' snobs, actually. But hey, they're our neighbors, so whadd'ya gonna do?" They started down the vertiginous roads in Hanna's rusted Rover, doors and windows open to the wind. Jack pointed to the enormous blue-and-red skull, with a lightning bolt through it, painted on the ceiling.

"What's that?"

"A Steal Your Face."

"A *what*?"

"Grateful Dead, man."

"Oh, right."

"I really have to get you listening to the boys, this is unacceptable."

"Sure, whatever."

"Or are you more a Spandau Ballet kind of a guy?"

"Mmnn." Jack's grunted response was non-committal and purposely meant to shield his ignorance. Beyond the Impressionist arabesques of people like Erik Satie, Federico Mompou, Gabriel Fauré, and Karol Szymanowski, Jack's musical knowledge was superficial at best, and his tastes unfailingly popular. If anything, he was a child of the radio, of top-40 hit parade. Perhaps that was embarrassing. He didn't particularly care, though, seeing as music played such an insignificant part of his daily life. Podcasts were his real passion, music was just background. "So, how far is this house of yours?"

"Not far. Nothing on the island is far. I really think you'll dig our little place; it's just outside the small settlement of Olga, on the East Sound.

"Who's Olga," Jack asked, as they rolled through town.

"Some toothless Gerry hag. A local strip-club owner got it named after his mommy, back in the 1890s. There's always been a hefty contingent of xenophobes and anti-Semites around the island. Some people even think it was a tertiary destination for cliques of Fourth Reich colony settlers, Gestapo goon squad dropouts, Martin Bormann devotees, Hollow Earth theorists, and ODESSA network operatives after '45."

"I keep feeling like an ignorant ogre here, but what's ODESSA?"

"*O*rganization *d*er *E*hemaligen *SS-A*ngehörigen. It's an organization of former SS members who split from the Fatherland with the help of the Franciscans. That's true religious zeal and kraut *Gründlichkeit* for ya! *Gott strafe U-S-A!* Jim and I keep a mezuzah at our front door just to let them—and the rest of the Christian Front cunts—know where we stand."

"What's the deal with those mezuzah things?"

"Seriously? It, uh, well… it helps ward off evil spirits, kinda like Lummi totem poles. We have some of those up at the house, too. You'll see."

"And what do people keep in them, anyway?"

"Snacks."

"Really?"

"Yeah, it's like the whole Christian milk and cookies deal at Christmas, 'cept this is for the other bearded one."

"Come on, that's not true—"

"N'ah, you're right. Our mezuzah's like

all other muzuzot: secret incantations to the big guy: "*Hear, O Israel, the Lord our God, the Lord is One pig,*" from Shema Yisrael. Those Torah tough guys eat that shit up. Can be a real hit with the atheists, too."

"Are you and Jim Jewish? Or is that rude of me to ask?"

"Rude? Why would it be rude?"

"Some people take that stuff seriously."

"I know. They're the ones I especially like fucking with."

Hanna's cottage complex was, to boil it right down, breathtaking. The property was a secluded spot, not far from Obstruction Pass, with views out to Mount Constitution and the surrounding prominences of Moran State Park. Old growth lushness pervaded the steep hillsides.

A pink hue wafted over the mackerel clouds of the sky as they slinked up the long, wooded driveway.

"Jeez, I love the feeling of coming home!" Hanna was beaming. The narrow drive then opened into a cathedral clearing, where a temple-like cedar log manor sat perched atop an escarpment.

"Holy moley!"

"I know, right?" She slowed the Rover down to a crawl, pointing out landscape features. "These nomadic hippies built the original five-story tree house, and a bunch of fully functional yurts, as a commune back in the early seventies.

They eventually joined the People's Temple Cult, though, and split for Jonestown—big mistake! This reclusive tycoon later bought the land and buildings; he spent nearly two decades renovating the property. I think he originally intended it to be a private Valhalla to rival the massive turn-of-the-century resort at Rosario, just down the road from here. Talk about an obsessive compulsive, kee-rye-stttt! But kudos to the old fart, though, there are some truly awesome guest cabins around—they all have humungoid satellite teevees, outdoor hot tubs, the whole nine yards. Stay as long as you like, 'kay?"

"I've never seen anything quite like it before—"

"That's 'cause there is nothing like it. And get this: the entire compound is completely off the grid, exclusively run off solar power. Bitchin', huh?"

"Wow, this place must have cost an absolute fortune—"

"You have no idea. But it was all paid for by jam money, so I hardly ever think about that. The property taxes are what really get my goat!"

"'Jam money,' what's that?"

"I got a huge settlement from Smuckers and Knott's Berry Farm in a multi-tier, class action suit. I'm not allowed to talk about it, actually. There's a whatchoomacallit, gag order on me. Suffice it to say, though, we're talking rodents, baby diapers, and lots and lots a' fecal matter. Jim was in on it too, that's how we originally met."

"Oh, he's a lawyer?"

"Hell no! Jim was a Boy Scout, back in the day, and the trip leaders used to feed 'em gobs of the jam when they went camping. Some scientists analyzed the chemical composition and supposedly ingesting gigantoid quantities of that stuff, like those pimply brats were forced to do, can numb and paralyze you—kinda the same way Rohypnol does. Luckily, there aren't any statute of limitations on past childhood abuse cases. The jam giants were scared shitless of the panic a very public lawsuit might cause, so they caved super easily. I guess they let the Catholic Church and their Servants of the Paraclete handle most of those molestation cases nowadays—"

"Wise move, yeah."

"I didn't know this before the suit but apparently Baden-Powell—you know that barmy Brit who founded the Scouts—was a big time closet pedo. He even had the world's largest scrapbook collection of naked boy pictures at the time of his death—"

"Seriously?"

"Uh-huh, they keep it on display up at the Library of Congress now." Hanna parked under an awning, behind a row of a dozen or more other cars. "By the way, help yourself to any of these jalopies while you're here, the keys are usually in the ignition. We also have three golf carts back there, fully kitted with knobby off-road tires, if you feel like zipping around the trails on the property or bombing down the road towards Obstruction Island. There's plenty to explore."

"Thanks."

"Oh look, there's Jim." A crouched, unassuming man sat on the porch. He stood up, immediately, holding what looked like a cigar in his hand. Jack couldn't say what he'd been expecting, but this man was far from it. He wore I-am-the-walrus spectacles, had a sparse black-man beard, little hair, and narrow Modigliani-type features. As they climbed out of the car, he stepped towards the drive to greet them.

"Well, hello, stranger."

"Hey, babes." Jim wasn't wearing any shoes and the "cigar" he was holding was in fact a huge spliff, or what's long been called a "Philly Blunt." Hanna and Jim started groping each other like a couple of school kids, their hands unabashedly pulling at each other's private parts—an elegant display for the classic voyeur.

"Ugh!" Hanna uttered, when the pair finally broke free. "Gawd, you make her so damn wet!"

"Let's go inside, I want your dripping little miss right now!"

"Babe, wait! Introductions first—"

"Owww, yea, you're right, sorry." The two turned, clearing their throats, ready for a prom picture shot.

"Jack Mitford, meet Jim Koreato, my husband."

"Hi, Jack. Howzit goin'?"

"It's going just fine, thanks."

They shook hands. Jack immediately noticed the words written in heavy black ink on Jim's right forearm, *Death Before Dishonor*. The skin around the lettering was slightly paler than the rest, almost a scaly beige. Earlier, Hanna had called Jim "mongrel pure-breed," a mix of Sioux, Dutch Mennonite, and blueblood Jamaican. Up close, he looked not unlike a baked potato left a tad too long in the fire and had what could only be described as a donkey face: a sour, lemon-biting donkey face.[17]

"I hope you don't mind, Jack, but I'd like to spend the next day and a half ravaging my woman here—"

"I understand."

"I bet you do, seeing as you're the last man to have your cock inside her. Prob'ly should bust your head open for that one!"

"Euuuhm…?" Jack was instantly petrified. He wanted to run—wouldn't you? But instead he stood tall—the boozy, drugged-out adulterer frozen stiff, waiting for the punch that

---

[17] All right, that's not true. He was a better-looking version of Tyrone Power and, understandably, Jack was more than a little desirous…

would knock him down for some sort of count. Even Jack could agree that he had it coming; still, it was hard for him not to turn his face away and wince, braced like a coward in the moment. Then, the dénouement:

"Don't worry, Jack-O, Jim's a pacifist. He's just fuckin' with ya—"

"Absolutely." Jim echoed, almost unbelievably. "H and I have a completely open marriage, it's totally caj!"

"*Caj*?"

"Casual, yeah—"

"Totally caj… huh, okay. Great!" From then on, Jack's fear mostly vanished. Before Jim and Hanna went off to do the Margaret Mead bondage thing, they pointed him down towards his guest cabin.

Jim's "Don't worry, there's everything you need down there" Jack took as a polite reassurance, but it was actually true. Jim had had the fridge stocked, the bed decked with tulip petals, and he'd even made sure a small map of the nearby islands had been drawn-up; that way, from the magnificent view of his porch—a hundred feet off the ground, and on stilts—Jack would know what he was looking at. No question about it whatsoever, the cabin was a floating, earthly paradise.

That night, after driving his bag of robes and notes down to the cabin in one of the golf carts, Jack sat in his outdoor Jacuzzi watching the sun dip low. It was a roseate twilight. There was a golden sparkle to the water from the Sinclair and Vendovi Islands, clear out to Spanish Bay and the mainland. The aequorin in the ocean waters produced a miraculous, bioluminescent light topped with percolating spume. Jack drank cold beer and ate the delicious meal that had been left for him in the industrial steel oven. For the first time since getting hooked on his trip up to Canada, he didn't even think of Nembutals or Adderalls or Demerols. He was simply peaceful, sober(ish), and content. Whoever would have guessed?

Silenus Silenced

The television was still on when Jack woke up, around one o'clock the following day. WAC, the Woody Allen Channel, was playing his pitiful Parisian name-dropping flick, arguably the brightest star in the firmament of the man's forgivably bad last-two-decades period. Jack switched off the idiot box, tuned the radio to NPR, and smoked a glorious trail of musky cigarettes while drinking a morning beer. What a day to be alive!

After cracking his second wobbly pop, Jack took the opportunity to call Clint. He hadn't talked to Richter since Arizona, which didn't really matter he now knew. Hanna had surely been keeping the old codger apprised of "their" progress.

The phone in the cabin was part of a high-tech communication center that linked to a mess of surrounding gadgets. It took Jack a few minutes of fiddling around to get a dial tone, and another few to place the actual call.

"Uh-hgh?" A voice answered, non-committal in pitch. "Wha' choo want?"

"Is—is this the Richter resid—"

"Who be askin'?"

"Umm, this… this is Jack. Jack Mitford."

"Middlefud? Aint n'er hur'd u'h d'em."

"No—no—*Mit*-ford. Mitford."

"A'ight, I'll see iff'n da bozz wan' take d'uh call." The line was dead for quite a while before Clint's voice came on:

"Hello?"

"Hiya, Clint."

"Who's this?"

"It's Jack—"

"Jack! Christ, it's been so long so I hardly recognized your voice. You still work for me?"

"Haha, very funny. By the way, who was that before?"

"Oh, him. That's Oooga-Booga. He's new. The boy's a complete retard, thick as a brick or a quart of frozen molasses, but he's Swanny's cousin so I cut him some slack. They're like family to me—"

"Speaking of which, I'm calling you from Jim and Hanna's retreat—"

"You up at Orcas? Fantastic! Do they have you set-up in one of those guest cabins?"

"That's right."

"Tell me, d'you see a lever attached to a table console there?"

"Uhh, yeah, as a matter of fact I do. How did—?"

"I had that whole place modernized and rewired as a kind of present a few years back. It was supposed to be a miracle of futuristic proportions, before Skype and those Mac jerkwads 'revolutionized' everything. Anyway, just pull that lever towards you and watch the magic happen."

Jack followed the instructions and almost instantly the wall screen came on, projecting a split-image of his face and Clint's. The projection was intrusive and disconcerting, but it was too late to turn back now. Clint's matinee idol looks were refreshed, manful, and vigorous. Next to Jack, he was the picture of health—traitorous youth be damned!

"And here I was, just warming up to the idea of portable phones."

"Ahh, you're a closet Luddite, Jack."

"Maybe you're right."

"You don't look too bad. Considering—"

"Considering what?"

"You still popping those pills like candy?"

"Who told you about that?"

"You did. Don't you remember?"

"No."

"That's cause those things aren't meant to be eaten like Vitamin C, son! They're supposed to be for helping you sleep, taking the edge off, and shit like that. You start mixing 'em in with your cocktails and pretty soon you can't think straight."

Jack reached over to the bed for his cigarettes. His image was off the screen, meanwhile. He took the opportunity to pour the rest of his beer bottle into a coffee mug for the cameras. A cloud of smoke trailed around his head as he came back into focus.

"Listen, Jack, I did have a more elaborate plan for you, but looks like we'll have to cut all this runnin' around a bit short—at least for now."

"Oh?"

"The trip's dragged on longer than I scheduled for, seeing as I stupidly forgot to factor in all your impromptu bender time. So, we're gonna have to call it a day after the Seattle-area sites. I'm having Pappy fax over the final itinerary for your investigations now. It's just four quick location stops."

"You mean that's it, I'm done after this?"

"Depends what you mean by that, but yeah. Say, have you been highlighting the map of the points I've had you visit so far?"

"No."

"You're joking?"

"No."

"You—you should really get on that, Jack. There's sort of an embedded message in there—"

"All right, all right, I'll have a look this afternoon."

"There's something I should say about the message, first, just in case you get the wrong idea. Now, before I explain, I'd like you to know that—"

"I *can* figure some things out for myself, okay? Get off my back!"

"Fine, forget it then! Christ, you're testy

for a guy who's been livin' large lately."

"Living large? That's rich!"

"Haven't I kept my mouth shut about the princely retainer I'm forking out, or the busted-up hotel rooms, the outrageous fines, and all the astronomical bills I've gladly paid for you?"

"I thought that's what you'd hired me for—"

"No, I hired you for research purposes, instead I've ended up funding your own personal gonzo trip fueled by amphetamines and 90 Proof beverages. Not that I'm opposed to that sort of thing, mind you. In fact," Clint poured himself a single malt glass, neat. "It's already cocktail hour here in the east. Are you all right, Jack? You look… concerned."

"I'm just curious about what kind of conglomerate you'll have me 'spy' on this time. Let me guess, I'm going to investigate the roots of Starbucks, how no-foam *venti* lattes are the newest form of brainwashing, mind control, and the best way for the FBI to keep track of the world population."

"What? You are *way* too paranoid, Jack. You should learn to chill-out once in a while. Sometimes a rose is just a rose, you know?" Clint lit a cigar just as Jack stubbed out his cigarette. "Mmm, listen, while we're on the subject: you're gonna need to be back here by next weekend at the latest. H-hour's here—"

"Huh?"

"Am I going too fast? I'm having a pre-book launch for this thing and I really need you to be here—"

"A *book* launch? What are you talking about? The thing isn't done. Fuck, it isn't even started!"

"What d'you mean? I already submitted it, ages ago; we're going to press in a few days. You think I've been lollygagging around these past few weeks while you've been out gallivanting your ass around the country?"

"Galli!—are you out of your fucking mind? I'm busting my neck for you out here, going to the places *you* told me to go to—with Hanna following me every step of the way, I might add—taking ridiculous notes and dimensions on a bunch of goddamned burger joints—"

"Shit, she told you?"

"Yes, she told me. What, were you saving that little gem?"

"Call it added insurance."

"So much for trust, huh?"

"Listen, you can't blame an old man for being circumspect, wanting to keep an eye on you. You can be unreliable—which *is* entertaining, to say the least—but…"

"I don't need a babysitter. I've done everything you asked—"

"I know, and I respect that. But you're not always the best communicator, Jack, or the best at keeping in touch. That's why I got my niece on the job. Hanna let me know what you were up to so she could assure me that you were sticking to the plan and so I could share in some of the fun. Bicephalous, baby: two heads are better than one, put it that way."

"Oh, bullshit!"

"Anyway, you were never supposed to know—for your own sake. Things like that can really serve to emasculate a man. Hanna's a good girl, I love my niece to death, but she's always had trouble understanding things like that. I hope she made it up to you in other ways. You sleep with her?"

"What? None of your goddamn business!"

"First my daughter, now my niece? Boy, you're really trying to insinuate yourself into the family, eh buckaroo—?"

"Hey, fuck you, man!"

"A joke, Jack! Come on, lighten up. Where's your sense of humor?"

"You are one screwed-up puppy, that's for damn sure."

"You still didn't answer my question but, anyway, we can talk about all that when you make it back for the launch—"

"What *launch*!?" Jack was exacerbated, and visibly so. He chugged half of the beer in his coffee cup and lit another cigarette. "Look, no one has a book launch for a book that hasn't been finished!"

"Nonsense, happens all the time."

"Clint, you haven't got a book!"

"'Course I do, always did—you wouldn't believe all the things you can get accomplished as a shut-in. The raw data was already there, I just took your initial advice from Jude's party that first time we met. I focused on my playboy days, my high society contacts, and big business deals. You were right, that's the kind of book that sells."

"So what the fuck have I been doing all this time?"

"Background research. I never said it was for the book I was currently working on, did I? Oh gee, if I did… I apologize. No, what you're doing is for later, if I ever decide to publish the muckraking, covert-theory stuff. Edwards says the whole conspiracy subject is too passé and controversial, which I would have thought contradictory terms, but apparently not in the publishing world. He's here if you want to say 'Hi,' we're working on some dust jacket ideas right now." Richter turned his back to the phone camera and began yelling down the corridor. "Hey! Edwards! Yo, Edwards! Yooo-hooo! You there? I swear the fucker's deaf."

"What are you saying, Florian's going along with all this baloney?"

"He's in charge of the publishing house, ain't he? Which, incidentally, I just bought out for a joke. Guess that really makes you my son now, huh? Anyway, as soon as I became CEO we halted everything the press had on the go to push this puppy through—can you believe what a handful of cash can accomplish in a few short weeks? I think I'm gonna jump on this whole ePublishing tip, too. Know anything about that stuff?"

"No. Look… I don't… uh… I just don't know what you're talking about, so—"

"What's there to *not* understand? Like I said: I took your original advice on this first memoir and I want to give you full editorial credit, capisch? It seemed fair, the least I could do under the circumstances. That's why I want your lily-white ass back here for the shindig. Stella Beardsley is being gracious enough to offer up her dump for the event. Her banquet hall is about three times the size of my place and it's just down the road. She could fit half of New York in that shack of hers—well, the important half anyway. You know her?"

"Should I?"

"She's married to Dewar Beardsley—"

"You mean Dewar Beardsley, the oil and whiskey multi-national? That's one person? I thought Dewar and Beardsley were two different people."

"Oh no, no. One man, Jack. Sir D. He's from some English shithole in the Home Counties. The stereotype fits: Eton, Oxford, and all the other wrong places. You'll see, he's a raging poufftart, xenophobe, and clumsy oaf. His countrymen call him a twat, but I just think he's a dick. Still, I guess he's mostly harmless. Mn, by the way, speaking of homes, I had Angelina Trundle Meider redecorate yours for you."

"Who? What?"

"The Meider Galleria, on East 76th. Heard of them? They're one of the best—well, *the* best, if you ask me—interior decorators in the City, maybe even in the whole of our fabulous country."

"You had them decorate my apartment?"

"It was empty. I wanted to surprise you, but I guess I couldn't wait."

"I—I don't know what to say…"

"A simple thank you is fine—"

"Thank you?"

"You're welcome."

"No! I meant: *thank* you, are you kidding me? You, you violate my privacy—"

"Privacy! There wasn't a single stick a' furniture in the dump, your ex made sure of that—"

"How did you even know about—?"

"Sorry, Jack, I'd really like to keep shooting the breeze with you, but I've got a call on the other line. That's probably another shithead calling to congratulate me. Seems like half the calls I get now are from fans—"

"Wait a second, I'm not finished with yo—"

"Look, you feel like tearing a strip, I get

it. But what good would that do? Let's just pretend that you blew your stack, that I turfed off a bunch a' *mea culpas*, and leave it at that. You'll still have a kickass apartment either way. So whadd'you say?"

"Bu—"

"Trust me, Jack, you'll love the new place. This designer chick nailed your style down to a 'T.' At least I think she did, the pictures she sent me were kind of distorted. But for one point four mil she better have done it right, huh!"

"How much?"

"Out with the old, in with the new. Don't worry about the cash—call it my way of apologizing for the way I overreacted to your bender in Abilene. Kosher?"

"Wait a second, you spent $1.4 million… dollars? On my place?"

"Forget about it, Jack, spending's good for the economy. Aren't we still supposedly in an economic depression? Honestly, who can keep up these days? Oh, also, don't bother booking flights back. I've got a retro-model Concorde that's been sitting at King County Airport for ages. I'll have 'em ready the old girl and set the fly-date east in six days. Sound reasonable?"

"No."

"Good. And rest up, kid—"

"No rest for the wicked, they say—"

"And even less so for the weak, but I want you ship-shape for this event. You can act as my shield against the literati scumsuckers. Meanwhile, have fun in the Pacific Northwest. Toodles!"

As soon as Clint hung-up, the screen went black. Jack waddled to the kitchen cupboards and looked for anything to drink—varnish might even do. He found several bottles of something called Poire Williams, as well as an Austrian herb liqueur in the pantry, and unscrewed the tops off them. The sickly-sweet nothingness of the first rivaled the bitter ooze the second, which dribbled down his throat in a medicinal trickle. The tastes of both were revolting. He barely managed a few gobbles of each before hurtling the bottles across the balcony, into the tall trees.[18]

The fax machine immediately began whirring, spitting out a list sheet for the four remaining spots Jack was meant to visit. Clint's handwritten message read: *The name of the game here is engineering, from chemical to aeronautical. Detailed notes to follow. You'll see, the trip's a quick horseshoe shape. Good luck! CR IV*

---

[18] It's important to iterate here, kids, that anger, stress, or simple ecological ignorance does not make it all right to ruin our pristine environments. Please, whatever happens out there, *Don't be a litter bug*! A message brought to you by the National Park Service.

    1) <u>Hood Canal Bridge/Port Gamble</u>
    2) <u>"Galloping Gertie" and Gig Harbor</u>
    3) <u>Boeing Museum of Flight (between King County & Sea-Tac International Airports)</u>
    4) <u>Everett: The Future of Flight and Boeing Assembly Plant</u>
    PS~ Don't forget to look at your map!

    Jack went to his bag for the map. From underneath the plush of hotel robes, he dug out his notes and itinerary list. He laid everything out on a wide desk by the balcony. First, Jack placed dots on every spot Clint had sent him to. Then, with one of the felt pens from the drawer, he started highlighting the tetra-state route. Florida's route was an "F," the Texas letter was a "U," Arizona's was "C," and California was a "K." And now, with this new Seattle add-on, he had another "U"…

    That was the last straw. Fuck me? Fuck me! Jack screamed to the room before he went utterly berserk. He raged for what must have been a good ten minutes or more—yanking, breaking, pulling, smashing, twisting, clawing, busting, and dismantling whatever was in sight. Rage consumed and drove him, unrestrained.

    Finally, he ripped the telephone, fax, and screen out of the wall, tossing them off the deck and down into the knurled bushes far below. In the ensuing epic broken mess of his primordial fit he collapsed, defeated. There he cried, in that hacking style without tears, for the way things were: pointless. The gesture was nonsense, but it was needed.

In the wake of his outburst, Jack sat smoking in the still rubble. The cracked vial by his feet he only noticed by accident. Serendipity. There was enough swill in the bottle of his drained beer to swallow three yellow-jacket babies, which calmed him almost immediately. He couldn't tell how much time went by while he sat there, disbelieving, but he managed to smoke four more cigarettes in the post-rage glow.

It was at about this time that the vacuseal message came spurting into the room. The entire compound, Jack later found out, was connected by an intricate system of buried plastic tubes that carried communiqués back and forth to the main house. It was the Old World equivalent of texting. Such a mode of contact was much less intrusive than the telephone and required no actual direct communication.

The message read as follows:

Jim and I are done with our most recent Kama Sutra trip.
Feel like a big feed with us tonight?
Show up whenever.
7, ideally
H.

Jack sobered up in the hot tub for the next

few hours, nakedly watching the day fade. The destruction he'd caused was too overwhelming to consider and was best left ignored. Clint's message and instructions were also best ignored. Jack tore up the fax pages, stuffing them down the garbage disposal. He'd finally come to discover his principles in this needless, runaround ordeal. What was money when he had his self-respect to consider?

Near Neorxnawang

In the fading twilight, Jack shuffled through the mess of glass, plastic, metal, and wood to get to the closet. What a complete disaster. All his precious hotel souvenir robes were now rags on the floor. Of the complementary cabin clothes, very few were left intact. Given the options, however, he settled on an English foxhunting outfit complete with riding boots, top hat, and ascot.

It was just past seven when his golf cart wheeled up to the main house. He popped one more yellow pill, just to keep knocking that edge off, and rang the doorbell.

"Jack, you made it." Hanna hugged him as he walked inside. The main hall was decorated in mahogany and leather. Enormous silver-gilt trophies adorned the front foyer, next to the mounted heads of bear, deer, and moose. "Jim and I are getting sloshed on a fifty-year-old Laphroaig. Wanna join?"

"Sure."

"Great. You'll love it, too. This shit was released on the 50th anniversary of Queen Elizabeth's coronation, and they only made a total of about two hundred bottles, or something like that. We're getting rid of this cheap stuff before we start in on her most recent Diamond

Jubilee batch."

"Mmn, how is it?"

"Burns like a motherfucker, just like her face! It's phenomenal! C'mon, let's pour you a glass."

Hanna led the way into the open-form living space. The hunting-chalet theme continued throughout. Jim was sitting by a prodigious stone fire pit, next to some burnt majolica ornaments, centered in the middle of the elephantine expanse of cedar beams. Sofas, tiger-skin carpets, and Zulu warrior artefacts littered the place. Somehow the overwhelming room was inviting, without a hint of the overborne.

"Cheers," Jim exclaimed, as Jack walked in. "So glad you could make it, bro!"

"My pleasure."

"No, the pleasure really is ours!" Hanna motioned over to a heavily padded armchair, and she handed Jack a crystal glass as he sat down. "Ice?"

"Neat, thanks."

"Man after my own heart," Jim said, with a strange look that Jack had no idea how to interpret. As Hanna poured a generous four fingers into his glass, he felt compelled to tell them about the afternoon's incident.

"How bad is it," Hanna asked, once Jack had relayed the salient details.

"I'd say the entire main part of the cabin is destroyed. Thrashed, really."

"Fuuuck, that bad? Must have been some chat with old Clinty."

"Of course, I—I—I'm more than happy to pay for the damages."

"Nonsense, we wouldn't hear of it, right babe?" Hanna was practically sitting on Jim's lap, stroking his hairy sack.

"No, that's right. We wouldn't hear of it, Jack."

"It'll give us a chance to remodel—"

"Yeah. And you know what? This is perfect, actually. We have a custodial staff that comes in twice a week to clean everything and to do maintenance around the grounds. I'll make sure they see to everything, even the stuff you threw off the balcony. There's poison oak down in those woods, you'd be blotchy for weeks—"

"Great idea, babe! We'll have the Molly Maids clean it all up! No big deal, Jack."

"I'll even insist they buy replacement things somewhere on the island, which'll encourage the local businesses."

"See," Jim said flippantly, "this is turning out to be a real blessing in disguise!"

"Huh! I don't know what to say. Thanks, you two, for being so understanding about everything. It's such a load off my mind. I can't tell you how sick I've been over it since this happened. I didn't know how to tell you—"

"Not another word about it, Jack."

"Hear! Hear!" Hanna added, raising her

glass.

"Well, here's to you both."

"*Sláinte!*"

With the formalities out of the way, Jack could finally concentrate on his drink. As the incredible smoothness burned down his throat, he looked over the elegant arrangements of the room. Hundreds of primitive-culture knickknacks were solemnly strewn about the tables and shelves in what was meant to seem like a slapdash manner.

On the walls, inter-dispersed between the tokens to human hunting glories, were the poorly finger-painted portraits of past presidents. Of the few kindergarten approximations he could make out, with the aid of some nameplates, Jack saw: Teddy "Rosy Cheeks" Roosevelt, Rutherford "Be a Man" Hayes, William H(andlebar) Taft, Herb "HotDog" Hoover, "Cool" Cal Coolidge, "Icky" Ike, and Warren Gamaliel Hard(on)ing.

Cautiously entering the bi-partisan debate, Jack said: "I see you two have some real politico beauties hanging up there—"

"The décor is meant as ironic," Hanna was quick to answer, "but I'm sure you already guessed that. I mean how could we not keep this? It's perfect. The guy we bought the property from—I think I was telling you—was this totally committed shut-in and honest to goodness tycoon. He had hundreds of factories around Asia, Mexico, and Canada. These paintings are from the winners of a yearly talent contest he had for the kids working in his sweatshops. Every summer the winners and their entire immediate family, which could be as many as twenty people, each got a two-week, half-expenses paid vacation to the Magic Kingdom. Isn't that sweet? What'd he make his fortune in again, babe?"

"Astroturf."

"That's right. Anyway, this man—Dominick Bell-Marsden is his name—was a pretty major philanthropist, but he was totally estranged from his family and had no friends. For the last ten years of his life a private service from the mainland delivered his groceries, newspapers, auction-bought cases of booze, books, and prescription pills every few weeks by floatplane. The supplies were always left at the head of the drive, and no one ever saw Bell-Marsden—not even the live-in staff. If you go look it up in the *Farmer's Almanac*, to this day he's still only #2 to Howard Hughes. Bell-Marsden was such a recluse, it turns out, that it took his own staff nearly a week to realize the poor bugger was dead—"

"Died right in that chair as a matter of fact," Jim said, pointing to Jack's seat.

"Ewww, honey, don't say that! That's not true. He's pulling your leg, Jack."

"She's right. The old man actually died on the crapper upstairs, if you can believe that! He'd drawn himself a bath, made a pickles-and-onion snack, and wham-o, bastard croaks!"

"Jim's not joking, it was a bit embarrassing all around."

"How so?" Jack tried to look interested, despite the mesmerizing taste of the whisky in his throat.

"They found the poor dumbshit with his shriveled little cock in his hand, a copy of *Barely Legal* magazine next to him on the ground. Eighty-four-years old this geezer was and there he is spankin' it to pictures of some pubescent tail—"

"All right, all right, that's crass, babe. Enough about that." Hanna poured another splash into her glass. "I mean it's funny, sure, in a sad sort of way."

"Did us good in the end, though—"

"That's true. Bell-Marsden's family was too embarrassed to deal with things related to his death. The fuckers were cheap, and petty. None of them really cared about this place or what was in it, they just cared about the inheritance money. Once the lawyers settled that part, the family couldn't wait to offload this money pit and everything in it."

"Why?"

"Why?" Jim's voice took on a momentarily authorial tone, "I guess because it's too far, too cumbersome, too crazy in property taxes, and too much to maintain. Kinda like the Castle of Mey, up in Caithness, where the Queen

Mum hid out for so long." Jim half stood out of his chair, in a weird silent toast, which Jack didn't even bother attempting to go near. Seated again, Jim continued: "You should have seen the state of the grounds when we first bought it—disgraceful."

"In the end, we got the place for a song—a very exorbitant, make-you-go-bankrupt kind of song. But, we got lucky with the timing of our jam-settlement money, like I was telling you, Jack."

"We also got lucky on the wine cellar, my God! I think we recouped one-third of the asking on bottles alone! The idiots didn't even venture downstairs when they had the place appraised, can you imagine? There are innumerable crates of priceless port, whiskey, and wine down there. We're well stocked for at least the next five years!"

"Speaking of which, what shall we drink tonight, babe? It's a special occasion—"

"Very true. Would it be too cliché of me to suggest the Rothschild '45?"

"That's exactly what I was thinking. Three magnums should do us, huh?"

"For now."

"Great. Back in a flash." Jim and Jack sat silent for a while, sipping on the dredges of their whiskies. After a refill of both glasses, the atmosphere seemed easier between them.

"By the way, Jim, I notice you've got

Lincoln up there, amongst all those right-standing Republicans—"

"Well, actually, Lincoln *was* a Republican. Very few people know that. Of course, in those days, the party wasn't quite what it is now. Like H said, we pretty much left the design of this main room alone."

"What, as a sort of testament to this Bell-Marsden guy?"

"You could say that, sure. I don't know, there was just something about this room that was perfect; very feng shui you know?"

"And Republican."

"That too." Jim chuckled as he took out a small woman's vanity case from a sideboard. Opened, the box held a mirror on one side and white powder on the other. Jack politely refused the line he was offered, watching as Jim took two big blasts and quickly put the case back where he found it. "Hanna hates when I indulge in the nose candy, but this stuff is so clean. It's like snorting big puffy clouds off a baby's ass. Now… what was I saying? Oh yeah, well, I suppose even Republicans have a loveable side to them. In a way, Lincoln's one of the least inner-esting of the pictures hanging up there."

"Is that right?"

"Haven't we heard enough about the assassination plots and the likes of Edwin Stanton, the Knights of the Golden Circle, Doc Sam Mudd, John Surratt, Vice President Andrew

Johnson, George Atzerodt, or John Wilkes Booth? Blahblahbloodyblah! Gawd the endless conspiracy theories on it are nauseating—"

"Mmn, yeah, it's so old hat—"

"For my money, I'd much rather have a real shady delinquent like Harding, avowed Grand Wizard and godfather to the Filthy Few. Still, if I had to choose, my favorite of the gang is Hayes, commonly known in teetotaling circles as Lemonade RutherFraud—"

"Oh?"

"That clever, cross-eyed beardoh and his buddies from the korrupt Kuklos Klan were responsible for the end of Reconstruction. They rigged the elections of '76 and shoved those 40 acres and a mule right down the throats of carpetbaggers and jigaboos alike. The rest just choked on it. I'm part black and even I have to admire the gusto of those racist crooks. Just one link in a chain of crushed American dreams. My Aunt Maya used to tell me all these stories when I was little. She was a reactionary, but she's cool. She was pretty big in the Symbionese Liberation Army, back in '73/'74."

"The Patty Hearst gang?"

"It wasn't *Hearst's* gang, man! That bitch was just a joiner. My aunt and Field Marshall DeFreeze founded that shit. They were tight, for a time, and even read Sam Greenlee's *The Spook Who S(h)at by the Door* to each other in their underwear. The way Maya tells it, the whole experience sounds like a great, crazy time, but she got out before things got violent, co-ed, and integrated. She left Berkeley for good during the Carter administration and owns a flower pot shop down in Wazoo City now."

"Listen, Jim, I didn't mean anything by what I said—"

"It's chill, Jack, no worries. Forget about it." They each went back to their snifters, swishing the thick liquid around.

"Uh, so, is that where you grew up, the Bay Area?"

"Nope. I was on an Indian rez in South Dakota until I was about eleven, then my moms and I were shipped off to live with my grandparents in Pennsylvania. It's not very inna-resting. Say, you hungry? I better have a quick nibble before this blow kills my hunger completely. Follow me."

They walked over to the kitchen. There was no exterior wall, just fifteen-foot glass panels that overlooked the entire wooded valley down to the water below. As the sun disappeared, the lights of the far off islands twinkled in sparse constellations. Sitting inside the food alcove felt like being part of a modern art masterpiece.

Jim took out a honking butcher knife from the hanging set. He had a crazed look in his eye, but maybe that was just the cocaine. After pulling a cured salami roll from the cold storage, he started chopping slices in a loud, violent manner.

There didn't seem to be anything cooking on the stove, which made the prospect of the elaborate meal Hanna mentioned seem very unlikely. Were they waiting for take-out?

Jack kept his mouth shut while he ambled around the room. On the far brick wall, he recognized the familiar Benday dots of Lichtenstein's panels. The large installation was an interconnected comic book triptych, pieces that had nothing to do with each other. It was the idea of the house itself.

"So," Jack said, once Jim finally put the knife down and started nibbling on the pieces of meat. "What's your line of work?"

"Is this supposed to be our male-bonding portion of the evening?"

"What? No. I'm just making conversation—"

"Uh-huh. You don't have to talk for my sake."

"Look, we don't have to if—"

"Guess you could say I'm sort of retired, if you're determined to get into it."

"Aren't you a little young for that?"

"Not really. I haven't worked since I was 25."

"That's a pretty decent gig."

"Yep. I mean I still do bits of this and that, sometimes, but mostly I indulge in self-gratification schemes. Maybe I would have called myself a sellout—back when I was a rebellious teenager—but I couldn't be happier to have sold my business when I did."

"What did you do?"

"Owned my own virtual singing telegram operation before the Quick & Dirty Gates conglomerate came along—"

"Is that right?"

"Uh-huh."

"Why did they buy it?"

"They couldn't understand what the business was all about, so rather than try, they bought me out. Made a pretty penny, too. Whiz kids are geniuses with numbers, not figures, know what I means?"

"Hmm, good for you." Jim eyed Jack, holding a stick of salami between his teeth. There was no way this was supposed to be a sexual advance, was it? If anything it seemed more like a territorial threat, or maybe nothing at all.

"Are you boys behaving yourselves?" Hanna was back with the wine, and Jack was relieved.

"Yup, bonding… sorta." Jim tore into the salami with the voraciousness of a rabid dog. "Hey H, Jack's dying to know more about us—"

"I am?"

"It's in your eyes, Jack."

"Oh? 'Cause my mouth didn't say a damn word."

"Why don't you tell him about your wedding song while I go take a quick crunch—"

Jim left the room, but not before taking Hanna in his arms and French kissing her for close to a minute and a half. It was a pissing contest, obviously, but Jim was the only one doing any meaningful micturating. Once Jim left the room the dust settled, and Jack resumed the discussion:

"Is he, like… out of his mind?"

"N'ah, he's just awkward around new people sometimes. But he does like you, he told me so."

"Yeah?"

"Yeah." He helped her prop the large bottles up on the high counter, their faded labels barely legible.

"So, what's this wedding song?"

"Mmn, right. It's kind of silly. Jim's favorite flick is *Rio Bravo*, you see?"

"The John Wayne one?"

"That's right. I can't stand the thing, but the Ricky Nelson ditty, with Dino Martini and Walter Brennan, gets me every time." Hanna, absent-mindedly, set to opening the first bottle while she talked. "I started singin' that tune to Jim and I found I just couldn't stop: 'Wish I was an apple, hangin' in a tree, and e'ry time my sweetheart passed, he'd take a bite of me… Get a long home, Jimmy Jimmy, get a long home, I'll marry you sometime…'"

"Listen," Jack said, lowering his voice. "Sorry to harp on this, but are you absolutely sure

Jim's okay with everything that went on between us?"

"Sure. Why?"

"I don't know, he was acting a bit whacko while you were gone."

"Did you let him do any blow?"

"*Let him*? Uh, he—he did a little, yeah."

"The first few toots always send him for a loop." Hanna said, fiddling with the cork. "Don'tcha worry 'bout Jimbo, really. He just loves fucking with strangers. It's, like, his favorite joke in the whole entire world. Whad'you expect, he's part Injun ain't ee?"

"Well, I—"

She managed to pop the cork and then let out a sigh. "His mom was a darkie, right, but his dad was one a' the GOONs—"

"GOONs, what's that?"

"Guardians Of the Oglala Nation. They had some big shoot out with a bunch a' Feds and the AIM boys—that's the American Indian Movement, along with that now famous Leonard Peltier cat—during a standoff at Wounded Knee in the early '70s. Supposed to be symbolic, I guess. Who the hell knows with these abbozs and their mystic shenanigans?!" Hanna took down three glasses from the overhang above the alcove and started pouring. "Anyway, those bindle bums eventually all landed in the hoosegow. The charges were trumped-up, kinda like Capone's IRS deallee-oh. Jimbo's pops did a nickel in the slammer for supposedly filching this old bat's '48 Studebaker. The whole gang went screwy as soon as they started getting Cajun andouilles stuck up their pimply patooties. Jim's mom didn't want him to be a part of that and she took him to live with her parents out east—"

"H and I are both prime undesirables," Jim said, creeping back into the open of the room. He put his arms around Hanna's waist and kissed her neck from behind. Storytime was over.

"Gee, that was quick—"

"Yezsum! Turns out I didn't have to squeeze one out after all." They each took a glass, sitting then at the high stools of the solid cedar counter. "I put on some music," Jim said, before a subdued cacophony of car horns and mechanized train squeals sounded from the stereo.

"Arh, what is this, babe?"

"This is from that Edgard Varèse Anthology you got me for my birthday. I thought you liked it?"

"Honestly? No."

"What about you, Jack?"

"I'm the last person you want making musical pronouncements. But sounds like a bunch of trash cans being smashed together, if you ask me."

"Varèse is very important in the canon of the 20th Century composition, almost as much as Vissarion Shebalin."

"I don't doubt it."

"Varèse was a ginormous influence on people like Patti Smith, Stockhausen, The Runaways, John Cage, and Pierre Boulez-*vous coucher avec moi ce soir*? Sorry, that's my composer humor spilling out."

"Don't apologize, I let it go right over my head."

"Well, if none of those are your bag, Jack, he also did a lot for Zappa—Zack Glickman himself! Should I throw some of that on instead?"

"Like I said, I don't know the first thing about music theory."

"Your education starts now, then! Big Bowl of Soul comin' right up—" Jim skipped off to change the tunes again.

"I'm with you, Jack. I like listening to music, not analyzing it. What d'you like?"

"It's pretty much all Chinese to me... uh, no offense, Hanna."

"Hmn?"

"Sorry... aren't you part Chinese?"

"Oh, right." They exchanged glances, stalling the easy flow. Jim came back beaming. The new sounds emanating from the stereo sounded approximately the same as before.

"You'll see that Seattle is rife with musical history," Jim said as he picked up his glass again. "Quincy Jones, Woody Guthrie, Sir Mix-a-Lot, Pearl Jam, Nirvana, Soundgarden, Ray Charles, and Kenny G. You can even head down to the MotherLoveBone Skate Park at

Seattle Center, which was designed by local boarders with a $50,000 gift from grunge guru Vedder and the boys. You might even see Eddie pop an Ollie!"

"Well, I know just as much about music as I do about Seattle."

"Which is?"

"Rain... coffee... the Seahawks—"

"Don't forget the eco-conscious vegan hypocrites—"

"Yeah, and the Mariners."

"I know one other Seattle thing," Jack added, clearing his throat. "Jimi Hendrix was from here, right?"

"Officially, yes."

"What do you mean, officially?"

"Oh, no, don't get him started on this, Jack, or you'll never hear the end of it."

"No, I'd like to know."

Jim put his palms on the table, as if settling in for an exhaustive yarn. "Well, the history books tell us that James Marshall Hendrix was born in 1942—the same year 6,000 Japs are shipped off to internment camps in Idaho, by the way—but that was just the front."

"Front? For what?

"They claim that Hendrix was drafted, pffffft! It was all a front on behalf of the government to keep the hippie yahoos from burning their draft cards. *Operation Purple Haze* was one way of enticing young people to believe that fighting in Vietnam was really groovy, to use the parlance of the time. 'Hendrix' was a codename for Lt. Colonel James Henderson, Army Special Forces, who was head of the Purple Haze. The operation was part of a larger umbrella initiative called *Project Mega Fame*, which involved other high-profile codenames like Holly, Valens, Bopper, Morrison, Joplin, Pigpen, Bonham, and Moon."

"You're as bad as Clint is—"

"Who d'you think turned me on to this? Think about it, Jack, a nation of rock-'n'-roll converts? What better way to plant thoughts into people's brains than by having subliminal messages directly embedded in the record grooves? Before that, mind-control experiments had been limited to the rinky-dink labs of initiatives like MKULTRA. The whole shebang was blown sky-high during the reign of the Woodstock generation and its mass ingestion of psychotropics on a national scale."

"Those are some… interesting thoughts, Jim."

"Don't patronize me, Jack. I didn't come up with this shit, and neither did Clint. It's all over the Internet. Check it out! Espionage rings have been a fact for centuries—you think that's news? The Octopus has tentacles across the globe, and techniques only improve with age. Seattle's Hendrix EMP (Elemental Monitoring Platform) is just another link in that long chain.

Those interactive exhibits are an easy means for collecting fingerprints and compiling data on sympathizers."

"Sympathizers?"

"Yeah. Dope-smoking hippies only breed more dope-smoking hippies, you see? So the lefty pinko freethinker who brings his kids to, say, the Rock & Roll Hall of Fame in Cleveland or the Hendrix shrine in Emerald City, is only dooming his children to an existence inside an infinitely evolving database-tree of flagged citizens."

"Masses lying in wait—?"

"Precisely. Worst part is, most of these covert operatives aren't even dead, they didn't OD or choke on hambones, they're collecting fat social security pay. Must be a laugh riot to live to witness such an intricate hoax play itself out. You know what they buried in that box instead of 'Hendrix,' up in Greenwood Cemetery? A fucken Les Paul! Just one last finger to the legion of fooled fans."

"Huh, that's one for the books."

"I'm warning you, Jack, as a friend. Just stay away from those places if you value your freedom."

"Jim?" Hanna interrupted, pouring the rest of the first magnum out equally into the three glasses. "Let's not talk politics tonight. Okay, please?"

"Who's talking politics?"

"Let's smoke a canon of sinsemilla

instead. Jack, you wanna puff some ganj?"

"Arrh, I'm not much for pot."

"We did have some hash, too, but beats me if there's any left. Jim, d'you know?" His face contorted, for a second, and he disappeared into the living room. When he reappeared he was carrying rolling papers and a pungent, black brick. "We have these friends up in the Gulf Islands—Canada side—and they drop off shipments whenever they're pleasure-boating by."

"Yeah," Jim added, enthusiastically. He began burning and crumbling chunks of hash, giggling madly. "They also grow these amazing, organic, knock-you-on-your-ass 'shrooms that'll send you on a magic, far-out trip. I think I might eat some for dessert. You in Jack-O?"

"Nm, not sure about that."

"What? Why? It's not like you have to work or anything—"

"Speaking of which," Hanna said, inhaling some of the smoke Jim was burning. "How long *are* you here for? Have you decided?"

"Mmm," Jack answered, taking another greedy sip. "This wine is utterly fantastic, by the way."

"Not bad, huh? We've become pretty used to it. It's practically our table wine. Hard to believe some people are actually willing to pay over $15,000 a bottle for it." Jack almost spit out the liquid in his cheeks. "Anyway, what were you saying?"

"Oh, uh, well, I—uh…"

"Take your time."

"No, it just comes back—uh—to the talk I had with Clint earlier."

"Right."

"He wants me back in New York in a week for this book launch he's having—"

"Book launch? But I thought you were the one taking notes for him on this deal? At least that's what he told me."

"That's what he told me, too! I guess he had another book idea up his sleeve this entire time."

"Sounds like him, for sure."

"I've been doing research for nothing this entire time, a restaurant guide on fast food burger joints!" Jack took another mouthful of wine, letting the journey settle in his mind.

"So what's Clint saying about Jet City?"

"He wants me to check-out four more Seattle spots, but it's even more pointless now."

"Why?"

"Why? Because the jig's up."

"What're you talking about?"

"I traced the routes he had me—*us*—follow on the map, Hanna. You know what they spell?"

"What?"

"F-U-C-K… U."

"Really?"

"Fuck *me*, can you believe that?"

"Hand it to old Clint," Jim said, "he's one of the last true muckamucks. And he sure as hell knows how to play a practical joke."

"But what's the point of that? The whole trip has been useless, utterly devoid of reason or meaning."

"Don't you get it, man? That *is* the meaning of the whole trip, and its great sheer beauty. No?"

Once they smoked the hash joint, time lost all meaning. As for the elaborate meal Jack had been expecting, turns out Hanna and Jim had an entire team of live-in chefs that prepared their every meal from a specially designed cabin nearby. The culinary crew arrived at some point in the evening, bearing lobster, Alaskan King Crab, and other benthic delicacies, which they presented and cleared in an appropriately invisible manner. Stoned and drunk, Jack gobbled his way through each gustatory course, the subtle tastes dancing across his tongue in a fabulous flutter washed of wine.

For the next three days, Hanna and Jim were stellar hosts. They took Jack to various coves and secret tree cathedrals around the island. They showed him sacred sites of the Coast Salish Indians, longhouse settlements at West Sound, and a moving memorial at Massacre Bay, where a raid by Haida warriors had once served to decimate the entire tribe of the island.

Together, they went kayaking from the pebbled shore of Obstruction Pass to the kelp tide pools at Buck Bay. After eating several "grams" of Jim's Canadian-connection magic mushrooms, the three waded nude through the warm shallow waters of Cascade Lake, inside Moran State Park. Between that and the luxuriant manzanita trail up to Mountain Lake, they stopped to marvel at the autumnal colors and whispering sounds of Hidden Falls.

At the very top of the Mount Constitution lookout, stretched an unhindered view of pastoral slopes, wooded peaks, scenic island silhouettes, and the oceanic flow of the Juan De Fuca Strait. Few were the earthly sights so breathtaking.

They spent what seemed like an entire day being waited on by the obsequious staff of the Rosario Resort—*the* commercial compound of the San Juans, emerging from the splendor of the Moran mansion and grounds. Massaged, fed, served, saluted, coddled, and pandered to, the debt of a small African nation could have been eradicated with the final bill Hanna settled:

"Just don't think about it," she said, joyfully. "You're on vacation!"

For three days the trio had been inseparable, sharing events that were woven into a thick tapestry by disjointed filament threads. No one combination of illicit substance or self-gratifying activity had served to make the experiences what they were, but without that precise intermingling of events the magnificence of the trip would have crumbled. The confluence was a sort of alchemy.

By secret sorcerous incantation, Jack was welcomed into a mythic land. This vast, protected secret was a Pacific Eden in which time, responsibilities, bank accounts, and expectations had no meaning—the fabled end of the rainbow, where wood nymphs and unicorns frolicked freely. A sort of homeopathic homeostasis. This secluded surround was a geographic wonder, a fable, a refuge of untainted lavishness. Here, Jack willingly let go and completely embraced the world of his surroundings, as if symbiotically. What a curious, intoxicating feeling. It felt like being young again.

Consentual Mainland Comeback

When Hanna's floatplane eventually glided over the still waters of Lake Union, Jack's mind was doing its utmost to emerge from an impenetrable, hedonistic fog. Why was he even bothering to go back East after being so utterly content? Where was the appeal of alimony, ex-wife troubles, floundering vocation, and inescapable servitude to a harebrained billionaire whackjob? Clint, Christ, Clint! He'd managed to forget all about him for three days, and now Richter's ephemeral control was back. Shit.

Part of Jack desperately wanted to keep feeling the way he had on Orcas, to keep bathing in that indelible source. But it was fleeting. Once safely on the dock, then, he let two pops of Demerol pull him back from that terrifying edge of truth. The mild sedative took his mind off things, appropriately numbing.

By the time he and Hanna had finished lunch at Ivar's—a gimmicky seafood dive on the water—Jack was chemically rebalanced and under the simple spell of the restaurant's hokey motto: *Keep Clam, Buddy*!

"So listen," Hanna said as she picked-up the check, "I'll drop you off at my place, give you the basic lowdown, but then I gotta split home. My head's pounding major Schönberg tones right now."

"Is that bad?"

"Yes, it's bad. I don't remember where this last week's gone. I think I'd like to sleep for about the next month or so."

"I understand. Completely. And thanks for not making me take the ferry—"

"Those things stink, like I said, and the service at this time of year is no better. Besides, the skippers are all drunks recruited from Exxon and BP slushpiles."

"Still, I appreciate you taking me all this way."

"No sweat, Jack-O." Nonchalantly, she gave his groin a light tap and his balls a squeeze. "Now, you're on your own for the sightsee—I can't stand that fucking tourist *scheiße*!—but you should feel free to catch views of Mount Rainier and the Needle up at Kerry View Point Park or else go slum it with the rest of the tourists down at Pike Place Market. You might even catch a low-flying fish to the face from Sockeye Sal, the big-toothed Tokyo gorilla. This town is clean and cute and chockfull a' surprises!"

It was a fabulous fall afternoon, filled with sun. The robust car jockey at the private harbor lot recognized Hanna immediately, and he greeted them with a goofy smile. "Miss Lejaja, so good to see you again!"

"You, too, Wally."

"Which wheeling vehicular are you

looking to drive today?"

"My'zwell bring out the barn burner—"

"The DeLorean?"

"Yeah. I'm just dropping off my friend here at the crash pad and then I gotta bounce back to the island."

"Yes, ma'am." Hanna's crash pad was in a place called Shady Oaks, near Washington Park. It was a refuge for wrinklesacks and dried prunes.

"What the hell is this," Jack asked, as they parked the futuristic retro-mobile in the underground parking garage of the complex.

"What?"

"This is some kind of joke, right?"

"What?"

"You live in an old folks' home?"

"Mmn-hmn, so?" They pushed opened the gull-wing doors, which rose up towards the ceiling in a whoosh. Even the concrete smelled of mothballs. "I love the peace and quiet of the place. Plus, any of the horny geriatric toads who might annoy you are usually in bed by 6pm—"

"But it's an old folks' home!"

"No, it's a 'Macro-Biotic Community for Active-Living Adults,' not that I go for labels. Anyway, most of the geezers are interesting, the meals are pretty good, and no one moves too fast. You feel like a rock star strutting down the halls. Just wait and see, these saggy-tit bags are gonna love you. Pick a' the litter, Kemosabe!"

Hanna's apartment looked like one of the old Beatnik lofts in the East Village. Slate tabletops and redbrick defined the décor in a layout unfit for the faint of heart. Ultramarine lounge chairs, Dorothea Lange portraits, and tight-weave carpets were scattered randomly throughout the Art Deco pervade. The ceilings must have been about thirty-feet high and the place stretched on for miles along an outer wall of gigantic glass panels. The panoramic views spanned the North, South, East, and West.

"That's Lake Washington," Hanna said as she sifted through some mail in the front vestibule. "Down there is the Arboretum, and that's the Lake View Cemetery. Isn't it weird how fogies always like being close to graveyards? Is that because they think they'll save on the transport fees of their funerals or something?"

"Hanna…?"

"Hmn?" When she looked up, the glare of the sun hit her square in the face. She was the flash of a screen, incandescent in light.

"This—this apartment is…"

"Gorgeous?"

"Well… yeah."

"See? Don't knock it 'til you try it, I always say. Figured it would ease your slink back east, help you reacclimatize. Feels like being in New York here, doesn't it? Except for the mountains and the oceans, I s'ppose."

"Are all the units like this?"

"You crazy? I had to buy the two apartments next to mine and the three above. We knocked down support beams and tore away ceilings and floors. I had all this faux brick laid across the walls, mahogany slats put down and this row of forty Japanese lights installed by the only antique dealer legally licensed to do so on the entire West Coast. What a nightmare! Then I had those pipes put in along the ceiling, which—FYI—are entirely non-functional and purely for decoration. I even paid Jeff Koons a couple hundred grand, I think it was, to come out here back in '99 to paint that mural of his dick over there." Across the close-up of the massive main member it read, in big black block letters, *Thanks WTO, it was a Riot!* "Nope: it sure wasn't easy, and it took a lot a' people a lot a' work to get this pad the way I wanted it, but it was totally worth it. Even though I only stay here once every few months."

"Really? That's it? I thought you and Jim came over to the mainland much more than that."

"Oh we do, we do, but we always stay at our lake house in Laurelhurst. This is *my* crash pad. To be honest, Jim's never even seen this place."

"Seriously?"

"Seriously."

"How come?"

"Sometimes I need a place to get away to, you know, to recharge. This is where I do that. I don't share this space with anyone. It's my personal sanctuary."

"Hmn, in that case I'm honored."

"Don't be. I mean, this is also where I usually bring my one-night stands. So what's a couple nights between acquaintances, right?" Jack had nothing to say, so he simply grunted in agreement. He turned back to face the windows for the defenestration of his resentment. He felt hurt, and somewhat used.

Hanna then dropped the mail on the front hall table and walked over with a resounding heel clump. The city sprawled below. "And don'tcha just love the view? I absolutely adore this neighborhood, feels like home. You should go for a jaunt around the area once I jet."

"When are you taking off?"

"What, already eager to get rid of me?"

"It was only a question."

"You're making progress, Jack, I'll give you that. Gullible but gutsy."

"Gee, thanks." She interlaced her arms across his shoulders, staring at him in a periphery.

"What's wrong?"

"Nothing."

"You sure?"

"Yeah. I'm just beat, that's all."

"Me, too." She spun Jack around, intently. "I should really blast back to Orcas before it gets too late. You feel like a quickie before I go?"

"You must be joking—"

"What?"

"*What*? You've been screwing Jim for the past however many days—in front of me sometimes even!—and I've actually come to like the guy quite a lot—"

"Your point?"

"First of all, aren't you sore?"

"Sure, but there's always room in the lovesoup for more pecker, Jack-O."

"Is that so?"

"Would a girl lie?"

"Undoubtedly." Jack was easy prey, but weren't all men? It was quick, as Hanna promised, the pair pumping away in unison against the windows while life proceeded apace at their feet. When Jack finished, Hanna shimmied her skirt back down and went to the kitchen to fluff her hair. Her movements were as simple as breathing.

"Here," Hanna said, tossing a set of keys to the table of the main living-room area. She looked completely unfazed, and detached.

"What's this, another car?"

"Nope. She's a silver-tank 1976 Norton 850 Mk3 Commando. Her name's Esther and she'll ride you to hell and back if you let her."

"Man, I haven't been on a bike in ages."

"Stay outta trouble, Buckeroo." She kissed his cheek, lightly, and walked out towards the front door. Jack followed, close behind. "By the way, cafeteria mealtimes are posted up on the fridge over there. If you were looking for the best coffee in town, I'd recommend *Vivace* in Capitol Hill. But if you're too cheapo for that, there should be some Fair Trade bean canisters in the storeroom, next to the gluten-free fagatoni, quinoa crisps, and algae loaf. *Mi casu, su casa,* okay?"

"Great."

"There's also a first-class dive nearby called The Cuff, if you're lookin' for some easy tail or good drinks. Take a cab there and stumble home."

"I think a bar's the last thing I need."

"Suit yerself, I'm just giving you the options."

"I appreciate that."

"You can leave the apartment keys at the desk downstairs when you boogie on outta here."

"No problem."

"Been a real pleasure, Jack."

"Likewise." They shook hands, like well-acquainted business associates.

"Hope you'll forgive my spying on you for Clint—"

"Already forgotten."

"Thanks, that's mighty white a' ya. And if you're ever back this way, you know where we live."

"Indeed."

"I'll look you up next time I'm in the Apple—"

"Do that."

"So long, Slick." Jack took a long shower as soon as Hanna left. Afterwards, while smoking several cigarettes in the expansive open space, he snooped through her kitchen drawers, bedroom closet, and display shelves. Hanna's show library was a standard mix of highbrow trash, self-help books, DIY manuals, and signed first-edition tomes. Evidence of his own literary work, ghost or otherwise, was nowhere to be found—no great surprise.

Flopped on the soft shag sofa like a ragdoll, Jack fell into the deep sleep of a helpless innocent. Interminably, the sun gave way to the moon. Time went by, uninterrupted. When he did eventually awaken in the calm vast, lost to the world, he realized the West Coast was finally done with him.

Home, Turfed

Jack's doorman, Manny, gave a heartfelt "*¡Hola!*" when he opened the limousine door. Against his better judgment, self-medicated abstraction numbed Jack's haze of the last twenty-four hours. He'd been busily playing an irresponsible game of Russian roulette with a big-ass bag of multicolored medications that he'd been given as an obligatory parting gift from the old folks' home. Turns out that, as a sort of game of their own, the residents pour a portion of their pills into a communal monthly pot. The towering fish bowl in the lobby acted as a massive mint jar of pharmaceutical wonders—from rheumatism reds to bladder-infection blues, and glaucoma greens. The custodians of these capsules hadn't let Jack leave without thrusting a huge stash into his hands, which only meant one thing for a fragile addict such as he: trouble.

    Within minutes of leaving Hanna's building, Jack couldn't feel his toes. Within hours, he'd forgotten his name. Having begun his own requiem for a dream, he'd shared his bag of tricks with any and all willing to partake, doubling his own dose in a continuous and topological gambit of snakes and ladders, until the mysterious beauties were all gone. Consequently, he could barely remember having lit out for the King County airport, could remember even less about partying his way through to Clint's Concorde (complete with cigar lounge, sultry stewardesses, and bowling alley aboard), and remembered practically nothing about actually getting to New York.

    Yet here he was, standing in front of his building at last, staring into the gaping gap of his doorman's cunning, prognathous jaw. After Manny's rhetorical "How baaz your treep, Meestur Meetfurd?" The two exchanged pleasantries, mostly about the weather, and waved at each other as they parted. Linear time was gone, a total washout.

    On the door to Jack's apartment upstairs was a monstrous purple bow. His key fit the lock, but the place inside was unrecognizable. He'd come home to an interior decorator's perverted wet dream. Gone was that comfort of nothingness that had been his, as were the dust bunnies and empty beer cans he'd left behind. Jack stood with his gonion—jaw, if you prefer—dropped, oppressed by design.

    There were numerous plans and blueprints sitting on the Gilbert Rohde campaign desk of the front hall, to his left. Jack knew the thing was a "Gilbert Rohde" and called a "Campaign Desk" because a small, dangling tag told him so. He would soon discover in fact, while wandering dazed through what used to be his apartment, that all the freshly arrived furnishings had handy identifiers on them for his architectural edification.

    For instance, Jack now owned several "Kem Weber" and "Warren McArthur" lounge chairs in the "salon" area; he was also the proud possessor of a peacock-style day bed, chaise longue, and settee set designed by someone called Thomas Pheasant; in what used to be his living room, Jack found bland V'Soske selvage rugs contrasted by bright Muriel Brandolini fabrics on the sofa throws and pillows; Diego Giacometti, for his part, had been gracious enough to design more than a few of the tables, which were curiously adorned with Christian Liaigre curios and a heap of trinkets called "Blobjects"; also, the trim new bedroom ensemble, emblazoned in monochrome, was a combined effort by Danish powerhouse Poul Kjaerholm and Billy Baldwin, a designer Jack could only assume was no relation to the mediocre thespian of the same name.

    The ceiling guilloche, flamboyant finials, and apartment flooring had also been entirely redone, an integral component to the "themes" of each given room. For example, a black-and-white checker pattern (in honor of Truman Capote's legendary Balls) tiled the outer hall and led toward the lush Brazilian cherry wood of the main living spaces, which "give the overwhelming sense of natural Rainforest bliss."

    The flagstone floors of the kitchen, in a style inspired by the "luxuriousness" of Marie-

Antoinette's Versailles, were meant as a complement to the tadelakt plaster, niello and red chenille of the walls—making it a perfect place to eat cake (Haha darling, designer joke!). Concurrently, the parquet of Jack's bedroom (in a posthumous design by Jean-François Daigre & Valerian Rybar) subtly echoed the rich serenity of the Serengeti, while Bilhuber's persistently purling "Water Closet Concept" of the bathroom evoked the legendary Lourdes.

Jesus, Mary and Joseph, what exhaustion! Each mood-room was the fitted epitome of a name-dropping extravaganza. Just think of all the people Jack now lived with, and in never-ending microclimates. Let's face it: simple living was simply passé.

Sitting in one of the high-backed armchairs (Jules Leleu) at the marble island in the kitchen (Philip Beesley), Jack lit a cigarette. Exhaling deeply while running his fingers through his hair, he noticed the stained-glass ceiling hanging above him. It was a Suzi Potter-Forbes, so the tag said. He dragged over a sculpture by Cornelia Kavanagh and used it as an ashtray. Under a magnum of Cristal Champagne, Jack found a handwritten personal note from Angelina Trundle Meider, the woman responsible for this decorative abomination. Before even picking it up, he swore to himself that if he ever met the woman, he'd punch her teeth in.

The solecistic, and syntactically abhorrent note read:

Welcome home to your new abode, Jacques!
~ although we've never met b-4, just poz you'll ♥ what we've accomplished together w/o u.
~ overall décor is very "En Vogue" right now, as our Parisian friends say, and is better known as Classic/Fusion/Contemporary Design or what I've dubbed NeoDadaShabbyClutter Chic: think Sister Parish & Albert Hadley meet Robert Rauschenberg meets Juan Montoya meets Karim Rashid, but in earth tones instead of bubble gum colors.
~ all the flair pieces just blend together & you're so privileged to be lucky e-nuff 2 exist in a living, breathing, Baroque masterpiece work of art!!! ☺
Think of this as a Life Laboratory, like Habitating inside Bernini's Ecstasy of St. Teresa!
~ U R now "officially" livin' the dream...
Bisous! A.T.M.

"Dumbass can't even spell!" Jack gabbed a nearby vase (Kerr Keller) and threw it at an arrogant set of photographs (Colby Caldwell) framed in mahogany. The smash exploded in forms and rhythms on the ground. That felt mildly better.

Next, he took the burning tip of his cigarette and held it to an astonishingly vulgar painting by Antonee Mannberß, vaginally derivative of Georgia O'Keefe's senile period. The canvas took some convincing, but soon it was engulfed in flames, scintillating shapes on the cold flagstone squares. This minor ruination felt exponentially better.

Jack broke, burned, slashed, and cut-up the most morbidly ostentatious "flair pieces" he could find and felt sated. The disaster of destruction he caused allowed for a touch of humanity to enter the clinical order that had befallen his surroundings. After which, he fell to the polished cherry wood of the living room in the cackle of an imbecile at the asylum. Good God, had Clint finally succeeded in driving him to insanity? Or had he achieved that brink all on his own?

When he woke up, Jack couldn't remember where he was. The room looked like any of the dozen hotels he'd stayed in during his multi-state trek through the void. He finally struggled to his feet and shuffled across the wreckage to the kitchen sink. After barfing, he looked through the nooks and crannies for signs of edibles. Immaculate as were the cupboards and pantry shelves (Nienkämper), not a speck of food was to be found. Didn't these designer bozos eat at home? The least this no-good Meider madame could have done is divert a few bills of her budget to some cereal or pasta. Were a few preserves too much to ask for?

The only thing around was the bottle of Louis Roederer, which Jack opened by smashing its neck against the side of a marble countertop. Thankfully, there were sculpted glasses (Elika) and bowls (Jeff Goodman) to drink from. Even warm, the sparkling wine tasted superb. What time was it?

From his airplane-shaped telephone on the counter, complete with propeller dial (NEC's Imagination Series "Alexander Graham Plane" model), Jack called *Caligula's Pizzeria*. They were open 24hrs, quick to deliver, and everything on their circadian menu was perfect for breakfast, lunch, or dinner. He ordered a Praetorian Pie, with extra anchovies, from some greaseball with an attitude. No doubt it would also come with extra spit, free of charge.

Jack's stomach suddenly rumbled. Finally! He rushed to the bathroom. How long had it been since his last constipated cascade?

Once he was done with the polished facilities (Estelle Rookå), Jack got back to the flowing champagne. Woozy was the way to go in this celebratory return to the unknown.

When the intercom buzzed, at least *it* sounded like it should. "Hello," Jack said into the grille, gulping from his crystal dish of Cristal.

"Meester Meet-furd?"

"What's up, Manny?"

"This is Hector, sir."

"Oh, sorry, man. What's going on?"

"There is a man here, señor."

"Already? Jeez, that was quick! Send him up!"

"But s—"

"It's all good, bro, I called 'em."

"*Si.*" Shit, did he even have any money? Except for his two vials, Jack's pockets were empty. Looking around the apartment was pointedly pointless, obviously. Maybe there was some change in his bag?

By the door, Jack starting riffling through the various hotel robes and souvenir sweaters he'd amassed, which Hanna had had sewn back together for him in the aftermath of his violent cabin debacle. Under his notes for Clint, he found a crumpled $20, torn into three sections, and hoped the delivery guy wouldn't hold it against him. As the bell rang, he stashed the remaining vials under one of the robes. The Italian delivery boy turned out to be one of Clint's *mulignans*:

"Pappy! What are you doing here?"

"Mist'uh Rick-tuh tole me t'come. Big sheen-dig dis after."

"That's today?"

"Yez'uh."

"What time is it?"

"Paz nine."

"In the morning?"

"Yez'uh."

"When's this thing start?" The manservant shrugged his shoulders and grunted. "I'm sorry, come in. I'm afraid it's a little messy, I broke a bunch of furniture a while ago." Clint's man stood outside the vestibule, unmoving.

"I—well—I'd offer you something, but there isn't anything in the entire place. I do have a pizza coming—"

"We bez be go'win aneehow."

"Why, what's the rush?"

"Mist'uh Rick-tuh say come git'chaw. So, I comes t'uh git'chaw."

"I see. And you always do what Mister Richter tells you to do?"

"Yez'uh, eey'eebuddy does."

"Nonsense. Come on in, and take a load off. Relax!"

"N'aw, s'uh. Mist'uh Rick-tuh says—"

"Mist'uh Rick-tuh sez, *Mist'uh Rick-tuh sez*. You sound like a goddamned broken record. Fuck, Pappy, learn to think for yourself once in a while!"

After he clubbed Jack over the head with an umbrella urn (Thöm McGövern), Pappy said "Speak for yersel', azzhoe."

Circling the Drain

When Jack came to, they were halfway to the Hamptons. He was wearing most of a tuxedo, minus jacket and bowtie, which were propped under his head as a makeshift pillow. What were they driving in… a stretched Maybach? He had a splitting headache.

"Jeeziz fucken sheeeiiiit!" Jack said, sitting up.

"Hello, s'uh."

"Did you knock me out?"

"Mist'uh Rick-tuh said I shuld, iff'n I needs to."

"But you didn't *need* to! I flew all the way back from fucking Seattle, didn't I?" Pappy shrugged again, keeping his eye on the road. "I just wanted to wait for my stinking pizza pie to get there, was that really too much to ask?"

"I'z dere, on da flo'h."

"What?"

"D'ey came while you wuz sleep'un."

"Ohh, first rate!" Despite the nasty pain pulsing through his head, Jack tore in at the grease-dripping food from the box on the floor. "You want some of this?"

"No, s'uh. Thanx."

"You sure?"

"Yez'uh."

"And by the way," Jack said after eating two more slices, "I wasn't 'sleeping,' you knocked me out cold, okay? You beat me unconscious."

"Uh-hn."

"You can bet your bottom dollar Clint's going to hear about this, along with a whole mess of other shit! I'm sick of being treated like a goddamned dog!"

"Uh-hn."

"I'm going to give that bastard a real talking to!"

"Uh-hn."

"I'm serious, I'm going to tear him a new one! I'm done with that manipulative looney tunes! I'll even bash *his* face in if I have to!"

"Uh-hn."

"Christ, aren't you just a sparkling conversationalist!" Pappy, despite having knocked him out, had nevertheless been thoughtful enough to bring Jack's travel bag. At least Jack had his valuable commodities to see him through this ordeal. It was hard for him to think of a time before the pills—which was just over a month ago—but right now sure as hell wasn't the day to go clean.

If Jack was going to set things straight with Richter, he'd need lucid concentration, making Adderall the choice of champions. From the built-in backseat mini-bar, Jack pulled out some single malt Scotch and washed his medicine down with burning peat. He put on his jacket, fiddling slightly with his bowtie as he lit a cigarette. There was a deep-pulsing throb at the bridge of his nose.

"Hey, Pappy?"
"Uh-hn."
"Thanks for bringing my overnight bag, I really appreciate that, man."
"Uh-hn."
"I still think you're a fucking jerk for knocking me out, though."

When they pulled up Richter's driveway, Clint was pacing the front lawn. A herculean black man stood watching from behind an outdoor, makeshift bar. Even though both men wore tuxedos, they looked like a pair of convicts. As the limousine pulled to a stop, Clint opened the car door. Jack's fist to his face was surely an unexpected surprise.

"Fuck, Mitford!" Clint squished around for a few seconds on the pebbles of the drive, before looking up. He pushed back his bedraggled hair and tongued his lips for blood. "You pack quite a punch, Jack-A-Moe. Help me up, would ya?"

"Are you all right?" Jack asked, extending his arm.

"Let's hope you knocked a bit a' sense into me. Can I offer you a drink? Join me for a slam of Mulligatawny?"

"What's that?"
"Jägermeister and sherry."

"Eurgh!"

"They're actually pretty good." After three quick shots of the stuff, Jack had to agree. Still, he was glad when they switched to pints of Irish Car Bombs afterwards, which he slowly watched curdle in his hand. Why did he feel so at ease out here in this ridiculous place, in the company of this ridiculous man?

"Mmn, good choice, Clint."

"Right? I used to drink these with Tomás Mac Giolla and Ruairí Ó Brádaigh whenever they came to New York on political fundraisers, before that whole Sinn Féin factional malarkey and Erin go Bragh shit set-in—dumbass Micks. Well, *na zdrowie*, Jack!"

"Don't you want to know why I hit you?"

"I assume I had it coming."

"Uhh, yeah, but—"

"Hey, Oooga-Booga," Clint said to the tall man behind the bar. "Why don'tcha go get the golf cart while we finish these, huh? Don't want to be late to my own funeral."

"Ye'sah."

"Have I seen him before?"

"No, he's new. Maybe you talked to him once."

"Oh yeah. Someone's cousin or nephew, right?"

"Yeah. He reminds me a lot of Sterling St. Jacques—"

"Who?"

"This beautiful male model giraffe who used to scene the clubs in the seventies. He might even be at the launch today; if he were still alive, that is."

"Listen, about this launch business—"

"By the way, thanks a heap for coming. It means a lot to me."

"You're welcome."

"And thanks so much for being such a sport with the flight crew—"

"What?"

"Yeah, they said they had an absolute blast with you coming back from Seattle. Kitty, Christine, and Meriel—the stewardesses—said they loved the strip bowling game! You were quite the charmer, apparently."

"I was?"

"None of them wanted to see you get off the plane. That's why the flight took so fuckin' long because the pilot just kept flying around in circles to keep the good times goin', and that's no easy feat in a Concorde! They want to know if you're free next week for a quick trip to Paris or Rome or something. I told them that you were on furlough from me for now, so you were probably free to—"

"Wait a second, wait a second! There are a lot of things that we need to set straight before this goes any further."

"Look, Jack, I don't disagree with you. But couldn't it just wait until this afternoon? As it is, reading in front of people already has me as nervous as a virgin sucking on her first cock. Why d'you think I'm fortifying myself so early?"

"You always drink this early."

"That's true, but not usually this heavily until after lunch. Now it's before launch, aha!" Jack shook his head instead of laughing. "What? No good? Christ, I really hate giving speeches! Beats me how adroit, articulate demagogues like "Nancy" Reagan, Goldwater, and George Wallace did it. It's one of the main reasons I decided *not* to run for president."

"You'd've made a perfect politician, Clint."

"That's swell of you to say." He patted Jack on the back, endearingly. "So, how d'you find Seattle? You dig up any dirt on the Boeing boys?"

"No."

"No?"

"That's right, no! I tore up your fax and pissed on it."

"You what?"

"You heard me. I wiped my ass with it."

"Wait. First you pissed on the papers and then you used them to wipe your ass?"

"No, I meant—"

"That's perverted, son."

"I meant figuratively, not literally."

"Too bad."

"The rest of the notes I took on the trip are

in my bag, in the car."

"Great. Swanny!"

"Yez'uh!"

"Make sure Jack's bag makes it to my study! Can you handle that simple task?"

"Yez'uh." Oooga-Booga wheeled up in a stretched golf cart designed to look like a Rolls-Royce Phantom V. The plastic sides and rims were done in psychedelic paints, and the tires were sand slicks. It was a flossy, coruscating ride.

"Whadd'you think, Jack?"

"Not bad—"

"Pimpin', I'd say. It was a gift from Yoko Ono, isn't she great? Hop on, Jack."

"What about my drink?"

"Bring it with you."

"In public?"

"Beardsley's palace is just a quick hop down the road and across the sandbar to the other side of Georgica Pond. Besides, cops around here do what we tell them to do."

Cars honked and people waved enthusiastically as they drove past the cart on the main drag. It was too windy to talk, which suited Jack just fine. Clint was an oblivious bastard, but this (ludicrous) launch obviously meant a great deal to him. Jack knew from his own past disasters how hard it was to read in public, he wasn't about to make that worse for the old man. Jack would make a scene after things were said and done.

A trail of cars and parking attendants littered the fore of the Beardsley grounds when the golf-cart limo pulled up. Oooga-Booga dropped Jack and Clint off by the imposing *porte cochère*, did a few donuts on the front lawn, and peeled off towards the boathouse to sample the hors-d'oeuvres.

Everything about the Beardsley house and its acres of private surroundings stank of old money. It was a preserve of traditions, traditions carried on through since the rocks of Plymouth started cracking skulls and taking names. Chauffeurs still held proper sway here, as did butlers, valets, cooks, parlo(u)rmaids, housekeepers, footmen, kitchen slaves, pool lackeys, and groundskeepers. Upstairs/Downstairs thrived, and all the glorious shit in between.

The festal event was already in full swing. Florian Edwards, Jack's onetime boss, editor, and friend, was spearheading the directions. He looked somewhat frazzled, stamped by the Richter effect. Still, for a guy who barely graduated high school, Florian was a cool, calm, and collected mastermind of PR. He swam with ease in the wealthy waters of ooze:

"Clint, Jack! There you are!"

"Are we late?"

"Yes."

"Good." Clint took three glasses from a passing silver tray and gave one to Jack.

"Edwards here is a teetotaler, so I'll drink his. Nasdrovia!"

"So, Jack, I hear from Clint that you've had quite a trip! Guess it beats the old days in the office trenches with me, editing some poor slop, huh? I look forward to hearing about it sometime soon. How are you?"

"Fine, Flor. How are you?"

"Scattered." There wasn't even a hint of remorse in his voice for selling Jack down the river, if that's indeed what had happened. Maybe business was just business, as the saying goes. "Umm, you two go follow the trail down and around the mansion while I set the wheels in motion for the sparkler intro. Then, I gotta go do some damage control on our gracious host, Dewar Beardsley. That guy's a genuine prick!"

Clint and Jack were directed towards the back of the house, which was too overwhelming an architectural design for a word as paltry as mansion. The resplendent construction of red brick, balconies, and gothic arches fell somewhere within the spectrum of inbred English Manor Hall and raucous Royal retreat. A forest of oak and maple trees bordered the sloping lawn in an autumnal red and gold arc. Fifteen-foot hedges lined the manicured flower gardens. The grandeur was undeniably sublime.

In the midst of this wide view of the Atlantic tidal pond, streamers, flags, and two-story-high pictures of Clint adorned the landscape. Socialites old and new littered the area in a sprawl. The buzz of their conversation sounded like far away, barking dogs. As usual the elite entourage wanted to see and be seen, and you could tell they were very eager to know exactly what sorts of lies Clint had written about them.

Amidst this drone of patter, the New York Philharmonic played softly from an egg-shaped bandstand by the water, where several dozen yachts were moored. Banner-sized posters of Clint's book cover, *The Caged Bird Speaks*, were also everywhere to be found.

"What d'you think of the title," Clint asked Jack, as they strolled towards the massed throng.

"Not bad. Angelou?"

"Yep. I asked Maya-cakes about using it and she thought it was a great idea. Probably figured the thing would boost her own sales on the bestseller lists, the opportunistic showoff! She'll be here, I'm sure. I'll introduce you."

The daytime fireworks Florian had promised suddenly exploded. Heads turned to witness Clint's grand arrival. On cue, the band began its Handel processional, in glowing royal notes. Doves were released into the air. A fleet of World War One daredevil planes trailed multi-colored smoke through the sky. The Mormon Tabernacle Choir began to sing. Time stopped. It was an ostentatious embarrassment of riches, as only the rich could afford to do.

The crowd parted in a Red Sea mimic as they arrived. Jack was presented around the sybarite swamp mire as the book's editor and occasional ghostwriter, even though he had absolutely no clue what was in the thing. "You must be so proud," was a common response, as well as the laudatory "Congratulations!" People invariably asked for Jack's card and then teeheed, tittering when he said he didn't have one: "Of course not, why would you!"

Because of the pills floating through his system, it was hard for Jack to know just how long the run of introductions lasted, or how many hands he shook. There were easily three or four hundred people milling around, and he'd met over half of them by the time Clint excused himself for a quick "piss in the bushes," accompanied by a nubile companion named Najma.

Jack actually needed a piss himself by then, and he strolled through the adoring crowd to find release. Inside the museum-majesty of the house, one of the caterers (dressed in the tunic of a Roman pageboy) gestured to a diagrammed floor plan of the fifteen ground-level bathroom options—a big, red YOU ARE HERE dot ably positioning him within the maze.

"Hello," a woman said to Jack when he came out of the facilities, zipping up. The sparkle of the Champagne fountain, in the central foyer, reflected the highlights of her silver-blond hair.

She was in her late fifties but looked good, and that wasn't merely because of the polished outfit she wore—Lady Guinevere, guarded.

"Hi," Jack answered, adjusting his jacket as he strolled over to her. His walk had added swagger, thanks to the Adderall he'd just snorted.

"Would you like a glass of this, it's Veuve Clicquot?"

"Sure." She scooped directly from the waterfall of mirth, handing him the flute. "Thanks. My name's Jack."

"Mitford?"

"Yes. Do I know you?"

"No. It's just that—ehm—Clint's mentioned you often. He likes you tremendously."

"Is that so?"

"I think he sees a lot of himself in you. His younger self, of course."

"I doubt that very much."

"You'd be surprised."

"Yes, I would." Jack finished his Champagne in one gulp and dipped into the swirling pool for more. "Can you believe this spread? It's probably owned by a couple of complete schmucks."

"I hope not, or else I'll have to rethink my entire self-image."

"Wait, don't tell me. You're Estelle Beardsley—"

"Call me Stella, all my friends do."

"I… well, I apologize for—"

"Putting your foot in your mouth?"

"Yes." They tapped their glasses together and all was forgotten. Stella seemed too preoccupied with engaging in innuendo to let insults stand in her way.

"Tell me, Jack, do you live in New York?"

"Supposedly."

"Near the Park?"

"No."

"Pity." She looked him up and down, imagining herself twenty-years younger. "Why do you say 'Supposedly'?"

"Seems I've been on the run for the last few months—"

"Hmm, intriguing. Do tell. Where have you just alighted from?"

"Seattle."

"Seattle, really? I get out there at least once a year."

"Why?"

"We own one of the professional sports teams there—I can't remember which one—and so we're forced to put in an appearance on Opening Day every year. While we're there, I book into a sensational colonic health-farm retreat for ten days—"

"Is that right?"

"Mmn. Their cappuccino clyster works wonders."

"I'm sorry?"

"My favorite's the Ecuadorian Enema, cleans me right out from tip-to-spout!" Jack coughed, slightly, sipping from his glass with a pasted simper. He looked around to find something more to say. "I see you staring at those two matching pieces above the foyer fireplace, Jack. Beautiful, aren't they?"

"They're all right."

"Mark Rothko. They're from what was known as his "Oresteia" Period. Absolutely awe-inspiring—"

"Not sure I'd go that far."

"When it comes to art, amongst many other things, my husband Dewar is utterly useless—bit of a limp noodle all around, you could say. The only thing he's any good at is climbing on the backs of the poor—"

"Well, anyway, you do have a tremendous place."

"Would you like a grand tour?"

"Not really."

"O—okay." She remained undaunted. "Upkeep is murder, as you can imagine—"

"Sure."

"And the architecture is quite out of place for this area. It's a fusion, you see, somewhat of an anomaly. Down by the formal reception, outside, I'm sure you noticed the carriage house guest quarters?"

"No."

"That's our version of the dacha, courtesy of Mica Ertegün."

"What's a dacha?"

"Oh, it's just a silly Russian name for villa; it has an exquisite outdoor exedra, too. Mica was a true darling to help us with it, ages ago. And as for the main house, the pre-Arts-and-Crafts style of the East Wing is based on my husband's ancestral home in Bexleyheath, Kent, which was designed by *the* Philip Webb. The West Wing, mind you, is Greenwich style—"

"I'm sorry, but I really don't know the first thing about architecture or interior design."

"Thank Christ! What a bore it is to talk about! In fact, I can think of a few things I'd rather be doing with my mouth right now—"

"Uhhh…?"

"Would you mind showing me to the washroom?"

"But this is your place."

"Yes." Against the slab of the sink, Stella lifted the hem of her gown over the thin smooth of her lisle stockings. She wasn't wearing any underwear, but she *was* sporting a "Brazilian." She took off her wedding ring in the process of getting ready and placed it on the edge of the nearby bidet. "Don't tear this dress, it's vintage Dior."

"Okay, I'll try."

"Don't *try*, do as I ask."

"Fine." So much for romance, folks.

"Hey, wait a second, is that a cat?"

Stella nonchalantly looked over as Jack worked hard to pull down his pants. "Yes, it's a cat. How observant of you."

"Should we let it out?"

"Why, are you bashful?"

"No."

"Then leave it. Believe me, Roger Taney has seen his fair share of swordplay."

"Roger Taney, what's that?"

"The cat. He's named after a former Chief Justice. My husband is fascinated by American history, particularly Civil War and Reconstruction Era things."

"Huh. Was this Taney guy a good judge?"

"Depends. He was the ruling juror on the Dred Scott Case. You know the one that gave the thumbs-up to slavery? Look, do we really have to talk about this now? I thought you were hot to trot—"

"I—I was, I am. It's just…" Jack's groin was still bulging, but his numb fingers were giving him trouble with the belt buckle. Damn the Adderall!

"What's the matter? Are you all right?"

"Sure, fine."

"What's wrong?"

"Nothing! My coordination's a bit off, that's all. Might have something to do with the line I snorted in here earlier."

"You've got coke?"

"No."

"Boy, I haven't done cocaine in eons. Not since the early eighties. Is it organic?"

"What?"

"That could be just the ticket to save me from the tedium of this bash. My God, Jack, I suffer from such terrible ennui. You sure you don't have any?"

"Yes, I'm sure."

"Don't snap at me—"

"Sorry. All I've got is Nembutal and Adderall, that's it."

"Bah, that's kid stuff. I got a walk-in closet full of that pharmaceutical jazz upstairs. What I'm talking about is a real buzz, not some sissy-shit high meant to—"

"Fuck! Shit!"

"What? What is it?"

"Roger!"

"Who?"

"Your cat, your cat! He just swallowed your ring."

"Aw, Christ, not again!"

"Again?"

"There's something in the hand cream I use that he seems to like, I don't know." The cat stood purring, rubbing himself against the faucet of the bidet. "Quick, he probably hasn't swallowed it yet. I'll hold him down and you put your finger in his ass!"

"What?"

"Trust me, it works. I've seen the house staff do it dozens of times. You just pop your index up there and boom, he'll cough that baby up!"

"I'm not doing that."

"You better, buster, or else I'll have to tell my husband what I was doing when Roger happened to swallow my wedding ring—"

"Why d'you even have to take the thing off in the first place?"

"Because cheating's against the sanctity of marriage, that's why! Now are you going to take care of business or am I going to have to tell Dewar what happened?"

"You wouldn't—"

"Try me."

"And here I thought you were going to be the one taking it hard." Stella grabbed the cat by the neck scruff, holding it down. Jack exhaled slowly, calming himself, before ramming his finger in fast.

"Hhhhhhhaaarrrrrgggnnnnnnnaaaaaa!!!!" was the thing's infernal screech, resounding through the walls. Roger jumped 5ft. in the air as the 24 carats were dutifully returned. After that, whatever romantic mood there was dissipated. The entire incident, in retrospect, was the first in a series of unfortunate events to follow.

The Alchemist's Opus

When Stella and Jack spilled out from the bathroom, a tall man in tails was in the midst of tearing a strip off one of the catering staff kids. His finger wagged vigorously, thin lips curled in a snarl: "You are summarily dismissed, you no-good Turk! You're a complete disgrace to your race," he screamed.

"My race?" The previously penitent boy answered, shocked.

"Yes. The Ottomans used to be such a proud people."

Before the kid threw down his catering tunic and stormed off, he snapped: "I'm from Bensonhurst, you stupid English faggot!"

"Shut your face, half-breed mongrel!"

"What was that all about," Stella asked, as Jack followed.

"Oh, Stella, you're finished in the loo?"

"What's with the boy?"

"Nothing. I just caught the dirty little wretch stealing, that's all."

"What did he take?"

"Time, darling. Time. Imagine, sitting in one of my Regency chairs and eating a crab puff while on the clock! I refuse to employ mannerless thieves! And they say *I* am of intemperate, preternatural disposition! Who do these people think they are? I blame social media!"

"Calm down, dear." Stella's husband was a dainty dude, tailored tightly in his trim tux. Jack could tell that starch wasn't the only thing holding him up.

"And who's your little plaything, darling?"

"Mmn, this is Jack. Jack Mitford. He worked on Clint's book. Jack, this is my husband, Dewar Beardsley."

"It's a pleasure to meet you," Jack said, shaking the quasi-cuckold's hand.

"I at least hope you had the decency to cum inside my wife. I absolutely despise when the hand towels get soiled with suspicious semen!"

"Darling, really! We never even got to the good stuff, as it happens. Roger T tried to eat my ring again, can you imagine? Jack here was gentleman enough to get it out. He deserves your Cuban admiration—"

"Admiration? For what?"

"For being a man of action!"

"Don't be ridiculous, no man ever got anywhere in this world by doing things for himself! No, I'll tell you what this bloody blackguard deserves—"

"Jack, there you are!" Jack had never before been so happy to see Clint. The old man immediately sensed trouble. "C'mon, son, Edwards wants me to get this road on the show…"

"Richter, we're in the middle of something rather delicate, if you don't mind!"

"Yeah, and what's that?"

"I'm attempting to decide whether or not I should be giving your wanton crony here a right thrashing—"

"Why did he wet his wick with Stella's panties?"

"You shameless degenerate!"

"What? It's not like it would be the first time, Dewie! Most of the denizens of South Fork have had a go up there at some point or another. Face it, Stella's Brazilian can't be beat. You know it's true, even if ya are a pillow-biter—"

"You're a despicable bastard, Richter! I knew I should never have let myself be talked into compering this thing."

"Well, if you'll remember (my good fellow), you agreed to host this because *I* agreed to overlook your company's Apartheid dealings with the likes of Verwoerd and the Botha boys back in the day, as well as your spearhead of eco-assassination initiatives through the Wise Use Federation Front—Wuff!"

"Mere speculation—"

"Not to mention the fact that I kept my mouth shut about your Nordic tra-la-la buttparties with Billy Pierce, National Alliance leaders, and the rest of The Order faeries, shoving silicone Armanen runes up each other's blanched sphincters! But believe me, I still have plenty more volumes of memoirs to write, so why not do us all a favor and shut your bigoted mouth, Dewie! Now, if you'll excuse us, we have a book to go schlep."

Clint tugged at Jack's arm, who let himself be dragged away from the speechless couple. He was in a daze. He needed more Adderall to set things in perspective. But when Jack reached into his pocket for the vial, Clint snatched the bottle and hurled it into the woods.

"Hey! I needed that!"

"No, you didn't. I'm pissed at Ernesto for getting you hooked while you were up there in the sticks. That shit'll turn you into a babbling fucking train wreck. Save your brain cells, stick to booze." Instead of medicine, Jack lit a cigarette. A poor substitute, but at least he still had his Nembutal stashed in the other pocket.

"Well, anyway, thanks for saving my hide back there."

"Don't mention it. Stella Beardsley, huh? Jeez, kid, you don't fuck around do ya? Straight for the top."

"Look, she was the one who propositioned *me*. Next thing I know I have my finger up some cat's ass—"

"Jesus, she sure has become kinkier in her old age."

Out back, Florian was up on a dais, in the midst of introducing Clint's book. Everyone stood calmly in a frozen mass. An atrium with retractable glass panels had been erected as focal point for the reading, in case of bad weather, and it refracted light as an enormous prism would; its clear podium, trellised in white roses and made entirely of diamonds, scintillated in the late November light.

"Free, signed copies of the two-volume set will later be given out as parting party favors," Florian was saying, adding then: "And here he is, ladies and gentlemen, the one and only Clint Richter!"

Jack left Clint by the stage, receding to one of the bars by the edge of the stone pool. He ordered a triple Glenmorangie 1976 and swallowed a cocktail of Nembutals to settle down—such ferocious ferment wasn't good for the nerves, or the stomach.

He surveyed the crowd, meanwhile, examining the stretched faces listening to Clint's ad-libbed intro banter. Jack's gaze met Jude Lippincott's, who returned his wave in such a dismissive manner that he wondered if she even remembered who he was. What was the proper etiquette for past orgiastic partners? Divining the intricacies of this socialite set was an art form all its own.

Clint read several earmarked passages, largely a collection of comedic anecdotes. The recounted events were surprisingly innocuous—given many of the well-known people involved, and many of the famous settings—but the banality of the book was lost on the audience. This memoir may have been Clint's, but it was about them. The mirror was wide, therefore, and the scope important. Ordinary rules faded, inconsequential in the face of celebrity.

Jack was on his third triple Scotch when Clint finally finished. It was during the applause round, before the orchestra began again, that Jack got the tap on the shoulder. He tried to contain the look of disappointment on his face as he turned around:

"Merrick! W... what a surprise."

"Don't look so disappointed, Jack."

"I'm not." He sipped, as a temporary respite. "I'm surprised, that's all."

"Don't worry, I don't have a mini-caliber Derringer pointed directly at your nutsack. I'll have what he's having," she told the barman, before settling her elbow on the side of the smooth bar top. "So, this is where you've been hiding yourself? Didn't know you had a thing for high-society shindigs."

"What are you even doing here, Mer?"

"Gee, it's good to see you too, Jack." Merrick's drink arrived and she paused to try it. "Mmm, yumm. You always did have good taste in whiskey. Too bad you were also a bottomless pit whenever the word 'booze' was mentioned. How's that crutch coming along, by the way?"

"You didn't answer my question, what are

you—?"

"I'm friends with Stella Beardsley, if you must know. From the Von Furstenberg Collective. She invited me." The Great—capital "G"—Maestro began conducting the bandstand orchestra in a polonaise, prompting further mingling amongst the (now relieved) guests. "Ugh! Can you believe that old East German biddy up there?"

"Who?"

"Masur! The fucker's emeritus, or at least he was until he died—metaphorically-ish. For gosh sakes, these po-mo, method impersonators are charging twice the price for half the delivery. When are these pricks gonna learn?"

"Guy seems fine to me."

"What d'you care? You don't know the first thing about music."

"Have I ever said otherwise?"

"Actually, Stella told me they tried to get that mental retard conductor phenom from Montreal, Nézoot-Sanguiné—or however the hell you say his name—but get this: he was too busy with some other private gig for blubber eaters up in the North Pole. Can you believe the nerve of that little Canadian prick? Too busy! When did those pissant yokels start thinking they were better than us, huh? We say jump, they say how high!"

"I really have no idea what you're talking about." Jack took a generous guzzle from his drink and began feeling the pharmacological tingle he'd come to know so well. His barbital tolerance was on the rise, but when the babies kicked, they still kicked. "So how well do you know Stella? I don't remember you ever mentioning her before."

"I told you already, Jack, pay attention. Von Furstenberg. Plus, we're on the Board of Trustees at the Whitney together. Except for the occasional sordid affair, art's her life. Helps to have a husband who's usually too busy gobbling knobs to care. She spends half that dickwad's fortune on art, which isn't a bad way to live."

"Art. Is that what you'd call the monstrosity over there?" Jack pointed to a long, rusting fence that looked like it belonged in a shipyard. "Looks familiar for some reason, why is that?"

"That's because it was part of 'Tilted Arc,' remember that joke? The thing's by Dickie 'Site-Specific' Serra. That asswipe alone is responsible for a whole slew of installation a-holes like David Mach, Olafur Eliasson, and Rose Finn-Kelcey. I can't stand those kinds of sculptors and performance art bullshitters."

"Serra?... Serra? Ow, right, that's the thing that used to be in front of the Federal Building. I remember now. I thought they tore that blot down and sold it for scrap."

"They did, but Stella also used to be on the Art-in-Architecture Board of Directors—which commissioned that ugly-ass thing in the first place—and she saved part of it to bring here. Pretty clever, actually, she made the taxpayers foot the bill on that one! But let's face it: Her taste in art is awful, reprehensible even. Have you been inside the house yet?"

"Yeah."

"And have you seen the number of David Hockney, Claes Oldenburg, Allen Jones, Haim Steinbach, Damien Hirst, and Ed Paschke she's got on display in the house?"

"No, my mind was on other things."

"These so-called important conceptual art pieces are just Veblen goods, if you ask me."

"Veblen goods?"

"Things that increase in popularity simply because they're expensive or because they're popular. It's kind of an economic Catch-22. Pop Art is the exemplification of that in our day and age—cliché, right? But absolutely true."

"When did you become an art expert?"

"I've reinvented myself, baby."

"Gee, that didn't take long—"

"That's what being independently wealthy is all about. Besides, who's got the balls to say anything to someone like Stella Beardsley, am I right? Art phonies are so completely phony that—at the end of the line—they manage to become authentic, know what I mean? Poetic somehow."

"I guess."

"Speaking of authenticity, how was your

trip?"

"I'm sorry, what?"

"Florida, Texas, Arizona, California, and Washington State, am I right?"

"How the hell do you know anything about that?"

"Didn't Clint tell you about the Great Richter Runaround?"

"Tell me what?"

"I put you up to it."

"Up to what?"

"The whole shebang, darling."

"You're so full of shit."

"Oh yeah? How d'you like the embedded message then? One last post-marital FUCK U from me to you, just to express how much our time together meant." As the plausibility of Merrick's story dawned, Jack's features contorted in a sort of repulsed sneer. Bitterness bloomed. He'd been fooled by the oldest fury in history.

"You bitch!"

"You dope."

"Why?"

"You've always been gullible, that's why. I was just hoping to have a bit of fun, but you made things way too easy. What else are ex-wives for?"

Jack threw his drink in her face, which caught her off guard. The move actually caught him a little off guard, too. They both stood, staring at each other for the longest seconds of their lives. Then, Merrick lunged forward in a soaked effort to kick Jack squarely in the testicles. When he moved, however, things quickly fell apart:

As Jack swung around to avoid the lethal blow, his arms sailed through the air in concentric arcs. Stumbling backwards in a drunken wobble, his hand violently made contact with the soft of human skin. He'd hit a poor, innocent little boy in the face. Tears raged on the pre-teen child, who yelped for his mommy. Merrick, meanwhile, had tripped on the edge of Jack's shoe and plummeted to the ground, splitting her lip in the process. Witnesses stood by in awe, panged by a slight guilt at having thoroughly enjoyed the unfolding of circumstance. This was the vitriolic spice of the post-game show.

Jack apologized profusely to the boy at first, and then to his mother, who let the piacular confusion wash over her before a flood of obscenities poured forth. Suddenly, Clint appeared out of nowhere and took control of the situation-cum-disaster.

While Jack stood slumped, pharmaceutically incoherent, miracles of propriety were being worked on his behalf. The mother and child were quelled to a semblance of reason somehow, but not before she screamed: "Take that child-beating drunkard outta my sight!" Clint continued to appease the maternal maniac while lashing out at the ego-bruised Merrick, whose chin was streaked in blood.

"You told him," Clint yelled. "That wasn't our deal! I said I'd do it! But you couldn't wait, could you?"

"No, fuck him."

"No, Merrick, fuck you!" Clint swooped down on Jack and led him up to the main house. Weaving through the crowds of congratulators, who'd missed the momentary spectacle of abuse. Both men did their best to appear happy, cordial, obliging. Christ, what a mess.

In a mahogany room with a river-rock fireplace, map memorabilia, and a stag-horn chandelier, Clint finally let go of Jack's arm. He pushed him into an oversized leather chair, simultaneously soft and hard.

"Now, let's be calm, Jack—"

"Calm! You used me, man!"

"Used you? How d'you figure?"

"First, by sending me up to Canada as your errand boy for a goddamned fox pelt—"

"It was wolf—"

"Whatever! And then I find out that you had me drive around like some clueless, asshole putz all because my ex-wife put you up to it!"

"That's not, strictly speaking, what happened."

"Oh, no?" Jack stood up, walking over to a caddy of bottles by the bookshelf. "Well, why don't you tell me just what the fuck did happen then, you're so good at spinning bullshit—"

Clint's arms were crossed as he eyed Jack's

movements carefully. "Don't you think you've had enough?"

"No, I don't."

"You're right. Make me one too, then."

"Argh, all he's got here is vermouth—fifteen different kinds of vermouth!"

"Fine." Jack picked a Portuguese vermouth and poured it out straight into two large Brandy snifters. Clint pulled out a thick stogie from his breast pocket, and a box of matches. "Do you mind? This might help me get through—"

"Go ahead." Jack brought the glasses over and lit a cigarette of his own. Clint puffed on the end of his Montecristo until a great cloud billowed. One of the uniformed waiters walking by the open doorway suddenly stopped and entered the room with a servile swagger. He carried a large, silver hors-d'oeuvres platter:

"Aahrem! I'm sorry, sirs. But Mr. and Mrs. Beardsley gave specific orders that there was to be no smoking in this—"

"Shut up, shithead! Can't you see that we're in the middle of something very important here? Now beat it!"

"No need to be rude, sir!"

"Rude? This is my natural tone of voice, moron!"

"I'll have to inform the Beardsleys at once—"

"You go do whatever in the hell you need to do, maggot. But leave that tray!"

"Up yours!" The waiter did as he was told, however, and left. On the platter was duck pâté carved into the massive shape of a duck. A pond of crackers surrounded the meat-paste beast.

"First of all, Jack, don't take any of this so personally. It started out as a kind of joke or social experiment but—"

"*Social experiment*, what the fuck are you talking about? Stop equivocating—"

"Don't you dare use fancy language on me now! I'm trying to come clean."

"Go ahead!"

"You remember when you were first up in this neck for the Lippencott thing—"

"Yes." Jack sat, pulled on his cigarette, and reconsidered. "No, not really."

"Anyway, sometime after our first talk outside on the porch you went and got looped—as was the whole point of the thing—and I lost track of you. Later on that night, I ran into Stella in the upstairs Orgy Room—"

"That's convenient—"

"We did our best to get into the groove, but her hoohah's never tickled my fancy—maybe we've known each other too long, who can say for sure? Anyway, we eventually decided to make our way back here. The Love-In was a younger scene, and we're both older models. Neither of us could handle the kind of abuse those types of psychedelic sex shenanigans provide, at least not like we used to—"

"Oh, boo-hoo, old man!"

"Would you just hear me out? I'm trying to explain here…"

"Like I said, go… a… head."

"So, things were pretty quiet when we got back. Dewar was at some summit in Abu Dhabi, and Stella said she was feeling lonely. She let me crash out in the dacha, but roped me into a dinner party the following night. That's when I met Merrick. She and Stella are friends, you see—?"

"Yep, I know."

"Well for your information, I had no idea who this woman was, I just liked her legs. These Hampton dinner parties are just the civilized way our older set mixes things up—"

"Wait, what are you saying?"

"I fucked Merrick."

"What!"

"Hey, are you really gonna start pointing fingers now? You've had it off with my stepdaughter *and* my niece, buddy! At least I had an excuse, Merrick calls herself Merrick Morgan."

"That's her maiden name—"

"How the hell was I supposed to know?"

"True."

"And besides, I'd only just met you a few nights earlier and you'd been a bit of a smug literary prick, too."

"Smug?"

"Oh, yeah." Clint took a pensive puff of his

cigar, and then a long sip of his vermouth. It wasn't as revolting as he'd anticipated. "So, long story short, one thing led to another and your ex-wife landed in my bed. Later on, I told her that I'd met this great writer turned ghostwriter at the Love-In and it didn't take long for us to put the pieces together. I told her about the memoir and about my other idea for a covert ops exposé. Meantime, she convinced me that you'd been a terrible husband, that you used to beat her, that you were a pervert—into kiddie porn and bestiality—hung like a fruit bat, with a tiny speck of a micro-pecker, you know, the usual gag."

"None of that's true—"

"I know. I know. Hindsight, kid."

"And so what? She came up with this stupid scheme to send me around on that pointless goose chase—?"

"It wasn't pointless—"

"Was any of the shit you sent me off with true?"

"Yeah."

"All that covert crap?"

"Yeah, all of it. And it wasn't crap. Every bit of intel on every single one of those bases came to me from reliable sources—my men on the inside. Genuine articles."

"Burger Kings, my ass!"

"Don't try to understand government defense strategy, *that's* pointless. Anyway, we're getting off track here. I had a map up on the wall in my study, you see, with pins placed in each of the locations. When she saw it, she flipped. She was the one who noticed the message, not me. Merrick thought that she'd come up with a brilliant plan to give you the finger, and I didn't correct her. It's best to let a woman get full pleasure from her jollies, especially when she has absolutely no clue what's going on—"

"Why d'you even help her?"

"Because I initially said I would, and I'm a man of principle. A deal's a deal. But you're missing the whole point about the map message, Jack, that's what I'm trying to tell yaw. I tried explaining that when you were on Orcas, but y'bit my head off!"

"I might have been more inclined to listen if you'd told me about the stiff one my ex was sending me—"

"That's just it: in actual fact, that missive was America's Dear John to Russia and the rest of the world's Commies during the Cold One. Those strategic points were chosen to spell out the F-U-C-K to them, and if your trip hadn't been cut short for this literary bash you'd have seen that the message continues through with the Midwestern States and some of the Prairie Provinces—you're only halfway there."

"So that's it?"

"Settle down, Jack. I don't know what you're acting so pissed at me for. I mean, I let your ex-wife think that she was pulling one over on you to get her off your back, that's all. Women always love to feel like they have the upper hand, when in reality they don't control shit. Believe me, just because the Old Boys' Network plays dead doesn't mean it is—in fact, that's the true subterfuge of the modern day era. You're a part of that now, which means we have a whole lot more to talk about—"

"You did me a favor then, that's what you're saying?"

"We did each other a favor. Look, I thought I'd send you on a set of roguish adventures, let you booze and whore to your heart's content, get you out of your head for a while. Why not? I got the money to burn, and it was entertaining… so sue me! No harm done."

"Talk to my liver about that—"

"Besides, we figured it might even get you back into the writing game. The real writing game, that is, not this mass-market memoir malarkey."

"*We*, who's we? Merrick couldn't care less about my writing career."

"That's right, she doesn't. No, I'm talkin' about my old pal Tom McGuane. He insisted that I send you, even when I was having doubts, which is why it took me so long to get in touch after Jude dropped you off to recover at my place. Remember? McGuane's a writer, too, up in Montana, but you probably knew that. He was sure you'd get a kick out of the trip and come out of it with enough material for a—a whatsitcalled, 'Picturesque Novel'...?"

"Picaresque."

"Yep, that's the one. Like Tommy says: You done been bushwhacked, son! He's around here—somewhere—if you'd like to meet 'im—"

"You really are a fucking asshole, you know that?"

"I've been called worse."

"I trusted you—"

"Why? Haven't you ever heard: Don't trust anyone over 30?"

"Oh, I'm also naïve, too? Great."

"Don't forget prematurely old. *But at my back I always hear/Time's wingèd chariot hurrying near...*"

"Now you're quoting Marvell at me?"

"Look, all I'm saying is don't get carried away with the inequities of life, Jack. That sort of thinking will rot your brain and numb you to the world. 40 is still young, you should be out having fun, getting into trouble, partaking in all sorts of madcap misadventures."

"What? What are you talking about?"

"Ahh, talking's overrated, don't you think? I defer to Joseph Campbell on that. *The Hero with a Thousand Faces*, you read it? It's all in there."

"Yes, I have read that book, and it has nothing whatsoever to do with what you just said—"

"Hmn, maybe I was thinking about something else…"

"You are so full of shit, man." Jack threw his cigarette butt in the fireplace, which immediately lit the kindling. Within minutes, a raging fire began to crackle. Jack finished the vermouth in his glass and poured himself another. He began pacing in front of the fire, fuming, using the vigorous movements to wriggle a few more Nembutals out of the vial in his pocket without alerting Clint. There were no plates, so he scooped up a tremendous glob of pâté with a faded draw cloth hanging on the wall, adding a handful of crackers to the red satin. On his third or fourth bite, he popped a couple of lose pills.

"Anyway, what you being so uptight about, Jack? You've got a fortune in the bank and I've given you a fresh start. Did you see all the dickwads out there scrabbling to get your card? You've packed a lifetime of networking into a few short hours. Show a little bit of gratitude! Where would you be otherwise, huh? Drunk on some cheap cans of beer in what used to be an empty apartment, right? That's all your ex wanted, by the way, was to get rid of you for enough time to clear the rest of your stuff out of there, to leave you with absolutely nothing. Zero. Zilch. Of course she helped us both, in the end, by making the redecoration process a snap."

"Yeah, and thanks for that too, while we're on the subject. It looks like a goddamn

Architectural Digest magazine shat designer *turista* all over my place!"

"You got real problems seeing the big picture sometimes, don'tcha kid?"

"I—!" Jack's scoff sounded like a slammed door. "You're a real piece of work, you know that?"

"Thanks."

"I'm serious, Clint, you're one in a million." Jack could feel his heart racing, which shattered his nerves. Despite grumbles from his stomach, he kept stuffing pâté into his mouth. Beaded sweat began to form on his forehead. "And what about this agoraphobia business, was that just a bunch of hooey, too?"

"Not totally. I do have a form of imposed agoraphobia, it's called house arrest. The shitsacks down at the IRS nabbed me a few years back for tax evasion, and when I was indicted, this was the best punishment money could buy. I even had Milken and Sununu giving me pointers! I'm limited to within a ten-mile radius of my house, for another few months, which isn't bad. But I'll tell you, money sure don't buy what it used to in this country, certainly not where the Feds are concerned."

"Is it getting hot in here?"

"You are standing by the fire—"

"I know, but…" Jack felt his knees weaken, and his tongue swell. Had he taken too many pills, was it the booze? He leant against the desk, finishing the rest of his pâté, and wiped his mouth with the red satin in his hand.

"Get your stinking mouth off that," Dewar shouted, as he burst into the room. "Jesus H. Christ, do you know what this is? That's the sash Stonewall Jackson wore when he was killed by friendly fire at the battle of Chancellorsville. It's worth an absolute fortune! Give me that, you idiot!" He snatched the Civil War sash away from Jack and turned to Clint. "And you! Put that disgusting contraband Cuban out immediately!"

"You Pharisee! You hypocrite!" Clint stood, puffing one more great cloud of smoke out at the room before throwing the stub in the fire. "You used to have a three-pack-a-day habit, for fuck sakes!"

"Times change, evidently. I don't want you in this room any more, Richter, and I don't want you in my house."

"You're kicking me out? You can't kick me out, this is my stinkin' launch party!"

"I don't care, I want the both of you gone!" Dewar nudged Jack, who wobbled as he began heading for the door. "Is he all right?"

"He'll be fine," Clint said. "No thanks to you!" The hallway was teeming with activity. Guests had flooded the confines of the house in search of food, backstabbing anecdotes, and lip-loosening libations. "Come on, Jack, let's get you some fresh air. You don't look so hot."

They tried zigzagging through the crowd,

with Dewar pushing intently behind, but the front hall and reception room had morphed into an immovable schmooze. Arms grabbed at Clint, petting him in pleas for attention. The goods were just getting started. Gossip and gripes multiplied as the affluent attendees dug in their heels. They were speeding through cocktail hour, undaunted: Drink, drink, drink, and drink some more! Pure possibility came into focus as decibel levels were amped into the stratosphere.

Jack seemed to be turning green. He needed fresh air, space, and quiet. The sound of the reception rang through his head as he tried keeping up with Clint. The front doors, only barely visible, were like a bountiful beacon of light in a vast darkness of night.

"Clint, dahhhling, you were absolutely divine earlier! Just like these petit fours and dacquoise delights. You absolutely must try some, they're absolutely divine, too!" Jack was swaying uncontrollably by the time they were stopped by Alva Astor-Vanderbilt-Kellogg-Fish-McAllister-Gould, a veritable heiress from the pedestrian First-Four-Hundred roots of Old(e) New York.

Even Dewar, in this case, couldn't rush the mountain. The fat of Alva's Upper Crust sides pushed at the flensing seams of her dress in a roly-poly pressure pop. She was—arguably—*the* very essence of Gothamite Society, the pulsing heart towards which ran all the shoddies, climbers, parvenus, leeches, and social blackmailers of the gilded group. Alva was real deal blueblood, exclusively bred-in.

"Alva, hello."

"Have you heard?"

"No. What's that?"

"Steven's thinking of remaking that Jaws picture, right here in Georgica!"

"How wonderful!"

"Wonderful? It's dreadful. Think of all those plebian Tinhorns clogging up our roads from here to Montauk!"

"I'm sorry, Alva, I just need to get my friend Jack here out of—"

"It's set to be another one of those blockbusters—if that's the right word—and from what I hear he's going to set it during whatsit—*Amistad*?—so he can kill two sequel birds at once. Honestly, I don't know why the public bothers with that revisionist little Zionist—" At that moment, Jack could no longer hold it in. The event was foreordained. He opened his mouth and a great roar of regurgitated pâté, vermouth, whiskey, and Nembutals exploded over her face and chest, garnishing the House of Givenchy she wore; the vomited sequent drenched the front of its sequin diamond design. There she stood, the most important woman of New York society, covered in bile.

"AAAaaaaaaaaaaaaaaaaaaaaaaaahhhhh!" Alva was a mute, beached whale in the dunes.

Those loud, ear-piercing screams were not hers, but those of her equally engorged entourage retinue.

Now that his body had rejected the trail of poisons he'd poured into it, Jack could at least vaguely comprehend what was happening. He was being clubbed from behind by a relentless coterie of crazed sycophants and asslickers, avenging their queen. And if the hateful herd wasn't going to kill him before he yelled out "Watch it, you fuckin' pack of prissy bitches," they sure as shit weren't going to spare him afterwards.

Like a wall, they plowed towards Jack, a disoriented, disheveled, drugged-out, drunken weakling in the lurch. His hands rose up in self-defense, his feet inching backwards at an uneven pace. The events were rushed, clumsy, and interminable, unfolding disjointedly in that dialectic space of time.

There was a gasp, some shocked expressions, and a few outstretched hands before Jack toppled backwards into the Champagne fountain of the central foyer. His tuxedo was soaked, flecked in vomitus splatter, and he felt altogether defeated. His body mustered its entire force of will to pick itself up and trudge out to the front lawn, where it finally allowed itself complete collapse.

There, broken, his limbs and bodily functions let go. Later, the last image he remembered, before his blackout to the Sheriff's station and beyond, was Merrick's face. He remembered the crocodile tears on her cheeks, as she nodded to the officer: "That's right, yes, he assaulted me and that 12-year-old boy over there. No, I'm sorry to say this isn't the first time…"

Doublends Jined

The following day, Jack was quietly released from lock-up. Inexplicably, all charges in the matter had been dropped. He'd been dressed in a matching pair of Sesame Street hospital scrubs, presumably because he'd completely ruined the tux with excreta. As the cell door opened, Jack nodded apologetically to the deputy who'd taken him in, vaguely recalling something about calling the officer a hairy fascist asshole. The young policeman then politely proceeded to return Jack's personal effects: a lighter, a pack of Marlboros, and seventeen cents.

"What about my pills?"

"Sorry, Mister Mitford, we disposed of those before we realized they were prescription and not just for pleasure. Our apologies." Tit for tat. Seemed fair, considering the grief he'd cause the poor pig, who was just doing his job after all.

Jack signed for his property and hobbled out of the Suffolk County station. His bones ached from the police brutality he'd endured (textbook tactics), as well as from the inordinate mess of booze, barbiturates, and psychostimulants he'd ingested since this whole Richter trip began courtesy of the Lippincott Love-In.

Outside, the sun shone bright above a cool November breeze. He wondered how he'd get home, back to the City from here, but that could wait. First, he lit his last cigarette and sat down on a public bench. The smoke filled his lungs with pangs.

His keys, identification, and credit cards were back at Clint's, in his travel bag. He'd have to hitch down there first, make the walk of shame, and try to hold on to as much dignity as humanly possible. He took another drag. Joy crackled through his skull. He crumpled the soft pack of paper, foil, and plastic, tossed the ball, but missed the rim of the garbage can.

"Hey, pick that up, you filthy bastard!" Jack was too tired to look behind him, or to move. He flipped the voice a bird instead. "Hey, you disgusting degenerate! Yo, punk, I'm talking to you!"

"All right, all right! Would you give me a break? I'll do it in a second, relax!"

"Don't use that tone of voice with me, Mitford!" When he turned, Jack saw Clint standing on the sidewalk across the street.

"What are you doing here?"

"We came to pick you up." He pointed to Pappy waiting down the road by a bright orange Meyers Manx dune buggy. "You're gonna have to come to me, though. That cop shop is 10.01 miles from my house, and if I step across the street, this leg bracelet I'm wearing will blow my foot off."

Jack took another drag of his cigarette

before he stood up. He then tossed the butt at an overflowing outdoor ashtray, put the crumpled pack into the trash, and walked towards Clint.

"Thanks for coming," Jack said, as they shook hands. Clint had a black eye. "What—?"

"Don't ask," Clint answered, motioning to the car. "We both look like hell."

"What happened?"

"The fat cow didn't want any society press on the incident, so she convinced that little brat's mother to let things $lide—and I took one for the team, both ways. Chalk one up to the social climb. One way or another, I s'ppose we've all got to 'Dree one's weird,' as they used to say."

"To what?"

"To suffer our fate."

"Huh."

"That's what I've always said."

"And Merrick?"

"Guess she just had a change of heart."

"So that's it?"

"That's it."

"What now?"

"Well, who knows? For starters, got any plans for Thanksgiving?"

"Staying out of jail."

"Great. Come over to the house, we've still got a pretty decent after-party happening."

"Yeah?"

"Yeah. Besides, I've got a completely

new idea for a book I really think you'll totally dig—I've even got the perfect title, it's from an old Dylan song, just wait 'til you hear it. C'mon, hop in!" Jack grabbed hold of the silver headache rack, easing himself painfully into the back of the rolling thunder machine. "Home, Pappy, on the double!"

The buggy's tires squealed as they pealed down the road in a skid. Clint cracked two beer cans from under his seat, passed one to Pappy, the other to Jack, and then opened his own. The three road pops came together in a collective cheer as the fiberglass car blew past the first of many stop signs.

The tarmac trench tore a straight shot towards the ocean. Jack leaned back, grinning uncontrollably as the wind ruffled his hair at high speed. Clint handed him a pair of aviator shades, which blocked the glare of the sunlight surround. Soon, they would be on the beach, with sand gritting their teeth. From here on in, chaos reigned. Freedom clogged their pores as the past faded fast behind.

www.ingramcontent.com/pod-product-compliance
Lightning Source LLC
Chambersburg PA
CBHW032122160426
43197CB00008B/487